Savvy ME...(Not)

JUDI K

ISBN
978-1-963254-12-9 (Paperback)
978-1-963254-13-6 (eBook)

TABLE OF CONTENTS

FORWARD

"To make mistakes is human; to stumble is commonplace;
to be able to laugh at yourself is maturity."

—William Arthur Ward.

******

Many of our fans, who knew us well asked if I would write a book
about how Jim and I met. After thinking about it for some years,
I couldn't start from when we met; I had to go back and recall
the turning points in my life that finally brought us together.

Whatever comes out of these pages, I ask readers not to assume,
not to judge but to realize that my experiences are how I saw
them at the age they were happening. I can't change that.
Several events in my life sent me on unchartered roads and
I felt I had no choices. So enjoy, relate and laugh, too!

The last Christmas before my Mom died, I
had a quiet moment with her. She was sitting on the steps
to the recreation room,
watching the family party below,
I sat on the step next to her feet.
I leaned my head on her knee and her hand rested on my head.
She said, "My lost lamb. You are my little lost lamb."
I was 60 years old.

CHAPTER 1

The Shape of Life As I Remember It

The homes we lived in were always full of music, drama, acting and performances. Everyone could sing to some degree, and Mom loved it when any one of us performed in any capacity. Although my two older sisters and I took piano lessons, my sister Jane was the only one of us who stayed with it long enough to read music proficiently and play some difficult classical pieces. There was a lot of pantomiming and lip synching, too. No one was exempt; we mimicked commercials, comedians, singers, actors and each other. Dad and Mom both came from families that had good singing voices, and many other artistic talents. It seemed we all could draw or paint to some degree, and some of the cousins took that talent into their adult lives. I enjoyed drawing.

Our family moved fairly often when I was a child. This was life as we saw it, and everything was an adventure. I felt no insecurities then. I was a middle child, the third and last of three girls (four brothers would come later). I would like to say that I looked at each move as an adventure...I felt safe enough, flanked by loving sisters with dad and mom as our umbrella. I would *like* to say that, but I am not sure that I realized the significance of each relocation until now. I was able to fit into each move which I believe, is a tribute to my parents. In each new home, they were able to settle us in comfortably, and did not sound any alarms, so we would never be apprehensive about new friends and schools. Moving often made me

1

adaptable, independent and wanting to face new things. Much later, I was able to infuse that attitude in my own children.

Mom was a beautiful, ambitious lady, short on height but long on talents, abilities, and ambition. She wasn't afraid of hard work and took each new challenge on with determination. Dad came from a handsome, well-educated family that owned and lived on a farm. Both Mom and Dad came from Arcadia, Wisconsin. Arcadia is my birth town, whose slogan was "Home of the Arcadia Fryers."

The Arcadia Fryers were not a baseball team, and they weren't a religious order—they were real live chickens, whose "feet never touched the ground". At that time the idea was new and thought of as healthier and cleaner. The chickens were grown for their fine, tender meat. Now, of course the big deal is "free range chickens". I prefer chickens that lived in their own condos. The thought of chickens prancing around in their poop turned me off. My Mom's brother, uncle Lloyd (Fernholz), had co-founded the Arcadia Hatchery and helped it grow into a large industry. It was his initiative that persuaded A& G Co-op to expand into producing broiler chickens. Arcadia Broilers/Arcadia Fryers would become the company known as "Gold n Plump" chickens years later. My uncle Lloyd got the nickname "the Chicken King" within our family.

The Fernholz side *and* the Erickson sides of my family were all achievers. Talents abounded and none of them were afraid of hard work. Mom's mom could sew, crochet and embroider, and would can fruits and vegetables and all the while, take care of the house inside and the gardening outside. My own Mom did all that, plus was one of those people who could take a plain or run-down house and primp it into clean, new living quarters. She could sew beautifully, was good with numbers and volunteered for every possible occasion. Later in life, when my four brothers were in school, she would be instrumental in getting the school band into competitions and made their uniforms and banners by herself. With every move, she and Dad did a little better, while encouraging his growth in the business world. They had stayed on the farm with Dad's family when they were first married. Dad had 5 brothers and 2 sisters. As I understand it, there came a time when the oldest brother, Ervin, agreed to buy his siblings out of their share of the farm. That was fine with Mom, who wanted to move on, and she encouraged Dad into going after a management position with Central Lumber Yard. Dad was good with numbers, as was mom. They both could take measurements quickly and accurately and give estimates with ease. Mom had a habit of reciting the times-tables when ever she needed the result of a measurement. She could rattle off those tables faster than I could think of them.

It was the first of our many moves, but. I was about two or three when we made a move and, although I have some pictures of us in New Richmond, I don't remember any of it. I do, however, remember summers at the Erickson Farm. I also remember toddling around in our first house and yard. It was in the town of Arcadia.

At that house, Mom would sew our detailed matching dresses for my two older sisters and me. We always matched somehow, either with fabrics, style, trim or simply the color. We were like triplets born three and four years apart from each other. Mom would crochet and embroider embellishments on our clothes. Later, she showed me how to crochet little flowery circles that, after enough were done, she would crochet together into a lovely bedspread. I remember that from pictures from our house in Menomonie. Mom was able to do anything, and therefore, I thought I could too. Our imaginations were vivid, and we could find plenty to do using what we had, and this gives me fond memories.

There are a few things I remember about living in that house, and one of them was when my sister Jane and I were six and three years of age, give or take a few months. Jane and I would 'sail' Popsicle sticks through the rain pipe that ran in the gutter under the driveway, imagining it to be a long deep river. Oh, how I wished I could make a sail for my tiny raft—and a rudder! We would draw little stick sailors on the Popsicle stick rafts. Put them in the flowing water, they would sail through the pipe, and we would meet it at the other side of the driveway. When that got boring, we walked around the block, just chatting. And at the house on the corner of our block, Janie caught sight of a little yellow rubber duck on someone's porch steps. She told me to get it so we could sail it through the pipe. I made a dash to the steps and got the rubber duck. We ran like the thieves we were and got back to our driveway and put it in the stream. Although it had gotten very shallow, the duck still moved awkwardly into the pipe. I waited on the other end of the pipe for it.

It didn't come out. We bent over and looked in each end of the pipe and got our hair wet. We laughed when we saw each other through the length of the pipe. Janie would challenge me: "Look Judi, can you see my eye"? We tried to reach into the pipe to get the stuck duck and got our dresses dirty. We couldn't reach it. Then Janie got a long stick and poked into the pipe. I watched from my side, and we giggled each time we saw each other's eye through the pipe. I slipped into the water at my end and got my shoes wet. Suddenly, Mom called us in to the house. She told us to give her our dresses so she could wash them. She put them into a tub to soak and quietly waited for us to wash our hair so she could set it. Setting it meant she would section off our long hair and use her finger and the rattail of a comb to create curls. My hair curled easily, and still has some natural turns and waves, and Janie's natural blond hair was thick and healthy. While mom was setting our hair, we got our 'talking-to'. It wasn't about the clothes she had taken such care to sew for us. It wasn't about our dirty arms and knees and wet shoes, but it was about that we took something that wasn't ours: the rubber duck. That night, Janie and I sat on the front steps hoping that duck would finally work its way out of the pipe and show itself. Janie whispered, "Mom must have eyes in the back of her head." We didn't dare leave the steps in our clean PJs. The rubber duck would have had to have legs because the gutter had gone dry. The next day we saw that a twig had lodged itself in front of the duck, jamming it, and it looked like it was dead center of the driveway. No arm or stick could reach it. We talked about how we would make restitution without being found out. Jane went into the house and came out with a nickel. Then she gave me the nickel to give to our theft victim who was missing a rubber duck. I think she took the nickel out of mom's purse. I gingerly walked across the lawn to that house and laid the nickel where the duck had been when we absconded with it. It was our self-assigned penance. Now mom was out a nickel, and we didn't have a duck. It was a hard lesson.

Mom had a lot of 'slogans' as she called them. One for every happening such as "Sweep before your own door," and "It will all come out in the wash", "People who live in glass houses shouldn't throw stones", and "Practice what you preach," and she would use them often. The most used one was "Where there is a will, there is a way," and she lived up to that one fully. There were slogans for rocking chairs, open doors, cracks in the sidewalk, old people, children, money, itchy palms, itchy feet and anything else you might think of. If it rained while the sun was out, it was a "Devil's Wedding Day."

She would say, "Never criticize anyone unless you can do it better." That one covered her own personal criticizing ways—because she *really could* do everything better. How it would work with me, I wasn't sure, but I was my mother's daughter, and later I would have an ego- (or irrational)- that forgave all my criticizing. But that would change, too.

Mom was also a beautician, and during the Second World War she worked to "keep us going" while Dad was in the army. One day, while Joan and Jane were in school, I got 'plunked' down on a big stuffed easy chair at a neighbor's house while Mom went to work at the beauty shop just a couple of blocks away. I had my bottle of milk in one hand and my blanket in the other. I was afraid to move in that strange house for some reason. I didn't move for the whole time mom was at work. It was probably for only 2 or 3 hours, but I remember the scratchy nylon upholstery attacking my bare legs. Once in a while the lady would peek around the door opening to see if I was ok. I remember being afraid. Funny how some things stay in the memory bank.

Once in a while, I went with mom to the beauty shop where she worked and I marveled at the outer-space type of machines the ladies would sit under to agonize themselves. Each curler had an electric wire attached to it, and I wondered how the Medusas could sit so still for so long. Mom would say, "You have to suffer to be beautiful." I wondered where she got that one—probably from the beauty shop. My two older sisters didn't hesitate to use it often, whether in jest or not. Try sleeping in prickly hair rollers or pin curls and not use *that* slogan. By the time we moved to St. Joseph, Minnesota, and just before we moved to Fargo, mom hassled dad into converting to Catholicism and gave him a middle name: Joel. Her own name was Johanna Theresa. She proceeded to name each of her 7 newborns with 'J' names. My sisters were Joan and Jane. I'm Judy. Mom gave me the middle name of Theresa, the same as her middle name. Later, my brothers would be named Joel, Jon, Jim and Jeff. She kept me involved with the naming process by asking me what 'J' name I would choose. When she suggested one, I would agree with it. When it came to Jeff, she 'wondered' which way to spell it: J-e-f-f-e-r-y, or J e-f-f-r-e-y. "We" decided on Jeffrey. She was good at inclusion.

Seems in the families of my parent's time, babies were always named after someone else in the family; someone who was from a previous generation, or someone famous who they admired. We have several Jims in my heritage, some Jons too. I think Mom enjoyed Judy Garland's antics, and so I got the name Judy, a popular moniker during Garland's reign. That name, for people my age is 'a dime-a-dozen'.

Dad's side of the family was Norwegian Lutheran. Mom's side was German Catholic. The Catholic side won, so Dad had to go to church and make up confessions just like the rest of us. I think Dad decided to convert just to please Mom. And it did. Later, in Fargo, he even joined the Knights of Columbus and would tease her by not letting her in on their big "secret." She knew she wasn't supposed to know or even ask, and I would hear him tease her and say he didn't want to go to hell and that's why he couldn't tell her the big manly secret. I knew he didn't believe a word of that. He would laugh with a wheeze, a kind of a "gotcha" laugh. She would whisper, "I suppose you're right, Harold." Then there would be silence. They were totally in love. It was a beautiful thing to feel a part of. I was safe. I'm not so sure my younger brothers ever felt that kind of security. But that would be their story. I know I never felt it again after dad died.

Although the Knights of Columbus are too cultish for my taste, it felt good when Dad joined a club of any sort. It felt like we were really settling in to a town we would stay in. He also liked to golf. One day he took me along, and my younger brother Joel came too. Dad talked the manager into giving me a 'job'. Dottie showed me how to make hamburgers, and malts. She even let me count out the change for one of the customers. I was probably around nine or ten years old at that time.

For her own lunch, Dottie showed me how to grill a special sandwich.... A buttered, grilled bun bottom, a layer of fried salami, a layer of fried baloney, a thin fried hamburger patty, a layer of cheese and fried bacon, topped with a fried bun top. She gave me a part of it, and the delicious juices dripped on the counter as I bit into it. I said, "Mom would call this a 'Dagwood Sandwich'". Dottie said, "Let's call this a 'Sloppy Dottie'". I laughed with her. For a long time after that, when I stayed home to babysit my brothers, I would make a sloppy Dottie for Joel and myself. Joel became a big fan of "Sloppy Dottie" sandwiches. I think he would remember those days with fondness. He was 4 years younger than I was, and somehow we got along just fine, watching the same shows on TV, saying "Shmock, Shmock", just as Steve Allen did, and we'd mimic Don Knott's quivering nervousness, along with the other comedians that played in the skit "Man on the Street".

And we both competed with the cousins when we played baseball on the farm.

"Our" farm was my second home, and I found myself there during the summers of my youth, bonding with my cousins and loving my grandparents and my cousins and many aunts and uncles. No matter what town we moved to, or how far away, I would get to have my summers on the Erickson farm in Newcomb Valley, near Arcadia Wisconsin.

Every morning there, the smell of freshly baked bread would permeate the house. Immediately, my mouth would water and I would hear footsteps on the creaky, worn staircase. I would hop out of bed and race to the kitchen barefooted to be sure I would get the crisp, warm 'heel' of the loaf. Grandma would make sure I got it. Freshly churned butter would melt on the hot bread and we would drizzle sugar on it. "Just a 'pinch' of sugar between our fingers would be enough". Janie would pinch the sugar and squeal, "ouch, ouch, don't pinch me" and I would laugh and copy her. One day Aunt Merle gently put sugar on the warm bread with a spoon. She would hold the spoon carefully over the buttered bread and tap the handle lightly. The sugar would fall softly and evenly, like a feathery snowfall. I copied her. Then my cousin Freddie and I would practice, so just the right amount of grains would sprinkle the bread. We could do away with more than a half- loaf of that delicious bread just at breakfast time. Luckily, there were almost always a couple more loaves rising in the big beige pottery bowl, covered with a damp flour-bag cloth to keep the dough from getting dried out while its slow rise held us impatient for it to ready for baking.

Grandpa, the ruler of his farm kingdom, was always present at breakfast. Sometimes he would pour his coffee into his saucer and sip from that. He said it would cool the coffee for drinking. Freddie and I would copy him. We all drank coffee: we were Norwegian. Behind him, the old radio on the shelf that hung on a stark wall, looked like a big, fat loaf of dark rye bread with a huge dial on it. It would be asking, "Who was that Masked Man?" Then Tonto would answer dramatically, "*That* was the Lone Ranger" and the William Tell Overture would fill the kitchen. Grandpa would reach for the knob to hear the next Burma Shave commercial. We sat quietly waiting and when the punch line came, we would laugh, believing it was very clever. Then we would repeat the line and everyone would laugh again.

At times, we would wake up to the sweet smell of either fresh cut grass or hay wafting through the big old farmhouse bedroom windows with the welcoming breeze coaxing the lace curtains into waving 'good morning.' Looking at them, Janie would say that the curtains would make good wedding veils, and we should play 'wedding'. Janie and I asked Grandma if we could take the curtains down to use them to play wedding. Grandma said she had a couple of extra panels we could use. She went to a big chest in the loft at the head of the steps; where, across the 8 or so feet of floor were the doors to the bedrooms, and removed neatly folded lace panels, and my sister Jane and I would take them with us and play wedding in the yard. We would make communion hosts out of soft bread that we cut into circles and flattened with our palms. To make the large circle for the 'priest,' we would use a water glass and press the opening of it onto the bread to perforate a round. For the little hosts, we used a shot glass or even a bottle cap. 'Receiving' them from each other, we were careful not to chew the bread. Everyone *knew* you couldn't bite the body of Christ. "I wonder if it would hurt Him," we would say, as I lightly rested my teeth on the host, tempted to just leave slight marks in the bread, then expecting to hear Jesus' booming voice: "Don't you *dare* bite down". These days, communion takers are allowed to chew all they want, but there was a time, long ago, that that dry host would cling to the roof of our mouth, waiting for saliva to disintegrate it. There wasn't much saliva, either, because we weren't even allowed to drink water after midnight until after we had received the host.

For our make believe weddings, I would sometimes be the bride, sometimes the groom and sometimes the priest... whichever character we agreed on, we played to the hilt. When Jane was the groom, she would put a little twig over her upper lip for a mustache and talk in a commanding voice. When she was the priest, she was so solemn I imagined a halo over her head. Sometimes we would sputter out some of the Latin we learned: "Dominus Vo Biscum". We would take tendrils of the *Spirea* flowers and make tiaras. I figured the nickname for that bush wasn't "Bridal Wreath" for nothin', and with lace curtains on our head, holding a branch of wilting Spirea in our sweaty little hands, we would do the 'hesitation' walk down the make-believe aisle while singing to the tune of "Here Comes the Bride": "Dum, Dum daDum"…"Big fat and wide"…. "See how she wobbles from side to side"…. Then laughing, we would roll down the hill and land in a cocoon of lace curtains at the base of the back porch.

That porch was as wide as the house, just as the more formal front porch was. The front porch door opened to the front room that sported an upright player piano. Janie and I would play a duet on the keys and turn the switch/handle under the keyboard to get a 'rinky-dink" sound. We weren't allowed to use the rollers unless someone was there to supervise us. The front porch had stately white balusters with matching 'gingerbread' corners and large, blooming hydrangea bushes on both sides of the steps. We called them "Snow-ball bushes", the expanding yard was well manicured, and lined with a row of pines, a second row of apple and plum trees. The aforementioned **back** porch led into the kitchen and had a chair on it that Grandma would sit in to peel apples for the next fresh pie. This porch was well used, and it had no railing, which allowed my cousin Freddie, who was the same age as I, and me to jump off from anywhere except for one end. Because, at that end was a small space just before the "tin roof shanty" began. The roof of the shanty almost met the roof of the porch, so when it rained, a thin veil of raindrops curtained the doorway, and had to be passed through. We would get a few drops on our heads as we jumped across the abyss between the two structures. In that 'shanty,' grandma's wringer washing machine would whirr away while we watched the uncles strain the milk they had just gotten from the day's milking. I always wondered how there would be whole blades of grass stuck in the filter from the milk passing through. My uncles would laugh and say the cow didn't chew it enough. Then some of that milk would be kept in the icebox, and the rest was taken to town, in cans with handles and covers on them. Nowadays, you might be able to find those cans in antique stores and used as decorative planters and even umbrella stands in some homes with country decor.

The "shanty," as we called it, was an all-purpose utility room. The corrugated tin roof made wondrous music whenever it rained. As soon as rain started to fall, we would head for the shanty to listen to the sound it made against the metal roof.

My uncles would use the shanty to leave their outdoor clothes, and dirty shoes from the barn and the pastures, and wear house clothes and house shoes. Sometimes they would go out there to play cards, and the ladies and kids couldn't join them because they wanted to 'cuss and smoke.' When they told me that, they laughed, but I took it seriously. I think we called it a shanty because of the tin roof. Mom would sing "It's Only a Shanty in Old Shanty Town" and I instinctively knew those shanties in old shanty town weren't anything as nice as *our* shanty. At the opening on the far side of it was a huge weeping willow tree. It had branches that swept the ground. Often Jane and I, and Cousins Janet and Freddy would sit under it and have a picnic or a tea party. It was a massive umbrella that kept the air under it cool. When an adult was pushing the lawn mower to go under the willow, I would dash to hold the branches up so the branches wouldn't get accidentally cut by the spinning blades. I liked the privacy that the long, soft branches afforded us. There were times, however, that they must have trimmed them 'when I wasn't looking'; I could see the tips of the branches just hovering evenly over the grass. Luckily, in a few days the weeping willow's tendrils would be dragging again.

My cousins and my sister Jane and I would play "Annie-eye-Over" the shanty with objects we would hope to catch from one side to the other. I am not sure how many knotted up socks and other objects would get caught on that roof, never to reach the other side. My arms were barely strong enough to throw anything far enough to reach the peak of the roof, but when I did, Freddy and Janie would make a big deal out of it patting me on the back and exclaiming how 'strong' I was. Life was good.

As my sister Janie got older, I became the only sibling spending the summer at the farm, at least for a couple-three years. My uncles would allow cousin Freddy and I to ride along on the hay wagon to pick up hay bales. Those summers I developed a good tan and strong arms from trying to pick up the bales and move them into position on the wagon as the men tossed them onto the flatbed by hand. Of course, I could only move one bale, a little at a time, but my uncles were patient. There were other farmers there, too. Neighboring farmers helped each other during threshing time.

I was probably seven or eight years old when my uncle Ray gave me a job while he would operate the tractor on the Windmill Hill. The Windmill Hill was an expansive hill in view of the back porch where, years before, they dug a well and erected a windmill at the top to pump the water. I think at this time my uncle Ray was courting my aunt Florence, and I could tell that my other uncles heartily approved of Ray Urbick. This day, Ray was cultivating the windmill hill with the tractor, and he told me he would give me a nickel to run down to the house and get a jar full of icy cold water from the kitchen pump. I loved how the pump worked. It was a small pump attached to the counter on the side of the sink. You didn't have to start it by pouring a jar of water into it like the big pump outside. It just took a few extra vigorous pumps of the handle to get the water to start coming out. I had to stand on a chair to get leverage. Being Uncle Ray's runner made me feel important. One afternoon I made four nickels *and* got a ride on the tractor. It was a banner day.

Ray Urbick had become a part of our farm family after Aunt Florence's husband Alfred died. The story goes that Florence was pregnant with my cousin Freddie when it happened. Freddie's older sister Janet was two or three years old. I had never known anything about it at the time I was spending summers on the farms. But when the tragedy struck, my Grandpa got in his car and went directly over to the Toloken farm to get his pregnant daughter and his granddaughter, bringing back only the things that Florence owned. Then Florence lived at the farm until Uncle Ray came around sometime later. I shouldn't try to tell the story, because as the rules to this book go, I have to keep my line of writing to my own memories, my own discoveries of the period. Now, I'll get back to my day of working for my soon-to-be-uncle Ray as he plowed the Windmill Hill.

The big John Deere tractor tilted as it circled the hill in rows and I was perched next to Ray. I liked the smell of his pipe with the stem clenched between his teeth, but I didn't like the feeling of being on the big tilted tractor. I was on the lower side of the slant, and it was scaring me, so I asked him to let me off. So he stopped and the loud motor churned in neutral as I jumped down from the lowest part of the tractor and started running away downhill. I imagined the tractor was behind me, rolling over to squash me. The mammoth back tires were taller than I was, and I imagined giant tread marks across my body, leaving herringbone dents across my middle. I got to the fence at the bottom of the hill and climbed over it so fast I don't think I even touched it. Safely in the yard, I turned to venture a look. And there was Uncle Ray, riding the tractor quite upright and just fine in the afternoon sun. I waited for another signal that he wanted water, but I didn't get one. "Oh, well, tomorrow is another day" thought Judy O'Hara. And there *would* be many tomorrows where I would spend summers with my cousins shuttling between Ray and Florence's farm, and the Erickson farm. Wonderful, endless days of playing in cornfields, taunting the pigs, finding stray calves, and wading in the creek…oh, and chasing the cows only to get yelled at for doing so. "It will ruin the milk," Uncle Ray would say with his pipe held in a grin. In the late afternoon we would come home with the cows, and the majestic day would be crowned by walking across the yard to the house to have a hot meal, with fresh raw milk and fresh baked bread waiting for us. After dinner, and after we bathed and ready for bed, we would sit quietly in the yard and count the stars against the navy-pitch sky.

Back on the Erickson farm, the threshing days would start early in the dawn, when farmers would eat an early, hearty breakfast for strength to hold on until noon while working the fields. Grandma would always serve a full dinner around noon and a smaller supper in the late afternoon. Sometimes my uncles would come in for a break to have a piece of fresh apple pie and a cup of coffee, depending on how close to the house they were. Or sometimes we would bring the pie and coffee out to them. We sometimes found ourselves gathered in the church basement, for a funeral or whatever reason, surrounded with fresh baked pies. I remember my first taste of lemon meringue pie. It was so pretty, it took a while for me to put it in my mouth, where it melted deliciously. (Later, in my skinny days, when I worked for Cook County in my early 20s, my coworkers and I would go across the street to the Bismarck Inn and have a beer….and a piece of their lemon meringue pie. Can you imagine that combination?)

Sometimes, in the evenings, my Uncle Eddie and Aunt Merle would have us all sit at the big, round oak kitchen table with the big carved claw-and-ball feet, and we would tell stories and play simple card games. It was dark outside the windows, except for one lonely yard light perched at the top of a telephone pole just outside the yard. On the other side of the screen door, crickets sang their choruses. Uncle Eddie taught me how to make Kool-Aid, using real sugar, and he would pop corn in a crank–type popper. I stood on a chair and got the glasses all lined up and started to pour the Kool-Aid into the tumblers just as the popper got so full that the lid popped open. I was so surprised that I kept staring at the kernels that no longer fit in the popper and were climbing on top of each other to escape over the sides of the kettle. Without realizing it, I was pouring Kool-Aid full-up-over the edge of the colored aluminum tumblers, onto the counter where it ran onto the floor! The stove and floor held just as much popcorn as Kool-Aid. The adults all laughed at the sight, and I laughed then, too. No one in that family ever got angry at anything. They just accepted what came and found humor wherever they looked. It was a wonderful life. I'm not saying we didn't get disciplined; the discipline was never harsh but was enough to make us think about what we had done and wish we had never done it and *never* do it again! Sometimes it only took a 'look'.

Grandpa Erickson was also the Sheriff of Trempealeau County in Wisconsin. Before he would leave in the morning for Whitehall, which is the county seat where the jail house is, or when he went fishing, he would admonish Jane and I and our cousins Freddy and Janet not to climb in the apple trees and pick all the apples. I don't remember ever saying, "OK, we won't, Grandpa;" after all, that would be lying. We would wait until he left in his car with the rumble seat. We would watch until we could see the dust from it on the dirt road just past the next farm. Then Freddie, Janet, Jane and I would each take to an apple tree, scramble up as far as we dared, and wedge ourselves between some branches. We knew enough to get down if one of us spotted a new dust cloud over the road into Newcomb Valley and coming our way.

The lookout was the one who climbed highest, and that person would shout a running update on the movement of the dust cloud as it got nearer. Sometimes it would wind up being just the mailman in his jalopy truck.

We would eat apples till we were green. I'll never forget the crisp bite into the fruit that sent the juice flying out the sides of our mouths, and the juice on our cheeks would be evident as the day wore on because the dust and dirt from playing would stick to it. Between talking to the mailman and seeing our sticky faces, I am sure Grandpa knew what we were up to, even though he never said so.

The Erickson farm was nestled in beautiful Newcomb Valley. It was the 'first' to get electricity, and to get the roads to it paved with shale. Those perks were evidence that being in politics paid off even in those days. To this day, our farm is listed as an official "Century Farm," having remained in the family for well over a hundred and fifty years. Even though the barn, the chicken coop and shed have fallen to old age, the stately old brick house that my great, great grandfather had built and homesteaded is still standing on the rise at the foot of the Windmill Hill. It is surrounded by more hills that are *now* much less thick with trees far beyond, but the road into that valley is still a beautiful experience. The remains of the shed are still on the property. One big, wooden beam still lies in the rectangle of foundation where the shed housed the car with the rumble seat. That wooden beam once had a twin and the two beams had been placed the exact distance apart to fit the wheels of Grandpa's car, to keep the car out of the soft, wet earth.

Grandpa didn't like us playing in the shed. 'We could get hurt'. High above was a loft floor, and there were two-man saws and scythes hanging from the rafters in the loft that covered half the vaulted ceiling. He was probably afraid we would make our way up there, after all, we were often found climbing the ladder into the hay barn where we also weren't supposed to go. But, as soon as Grandpa was gone for the day, Freddy and I decided to play Cowboys and Indians in that shed. We would be very careful not to get hurt so Grandpa wouldn't find out. The shed was down an incline, and rainwater tended to gather on the ground that made up the floor of the shed. Erosion was evident from the rain that had recently created a trickle that carved its way like a road map through the dirt to the beams. We pretended the two wooden beams were the banks of a river. Being chased by imaginary Indians, Freddy yelled, "Jump!" and we did. Freddy's longer legs made it across the 'river' and I didn't. My short legs stopped me just as short of the other side. I fell against a gas can and knocked myself dizzy. Freddy ran to get Grandma. She came and got me, walked me back to the house, and washed the gash over my eye. She asked if I wanted to go to the hospital and get stitches and I said no. I had never heard of anyone going to hospital to fix a cut. Saying 'no' made me feel important as I thought, "no tough cowboy would want to see a doctor anyway"? Geez, we were built to take bullets-without-bawling (a new slogan?). At least I could say I refused to go to the hospital. Grandma made a butterfly bandage and applied it to my wound and then I took a nap. When I woke up, the pillowcase was stuck to the dried blood on my forehead. The next morning I would have to face Grandpa.

At breakfast time, Freddy and I were sitting at the big round table watching the toaster heat up. Grandma had just hung up the phone. She had been listening in on the party line. She knew who got a call from whom because she knew the number of rings for each of her neighbors. They all did the same thing, and sometimes would inadvertently get in on each other's conversations. No one seemed to mind. It worked better than a corporate conference phone-in. While we were waiting for Grandpa to come to breakfast to serve up our punishment along with the toast, Grandma told me to get Jenny Gilbertson on the phone.

"How many rings, Grandma?"

"Two short and one long," she said.

I picked up the spool-shaped earpiece attached by its cord to the brown wooden box on the wall. and turned the crank on the side of the box. Ring, Ring, Riiinnngg! We could hear the ring at our end, too. Actually, every house in the valley that had a telephone could hear the ring and tell who was getting the call. I held the earpiece out to Grandma. "Ye-n-ny?" I heard grandma say, and she would continue in Norwegian as usual.

This morning, though, we were somber. I hadn't faced Grandpa yet. I heard the stairway to the kitchen creak with the weight of Grandpa's step. I knew I was in for something not good after the accident in his shed, especially since he had told us not to go in there. Grandpa stopped on the bottom step and looked at me. I must have been pitiful with the swollen noggin and bloody bandage because he only said, "Poor Judith." It sounded more like "Pore Yudit" in his Norwegian English. Grandma had gotten to him. He wasn't angry. I was still uncomfortable, though. The toast sprang from the toaster with an extra loud clack.

Around that time, my dad's older brother, my uncle Basil, would be elected Sheriff, following in grandpa's footsteps. I remember going to visit my cousins Roger and Clark, who were Uncle Basil and Aunt Stella's children. They all lived in a huge house in Whitehall which also served as the county jail.

Aunt Stella would cook for the prisoners at the same time she cooked for the family. Next to the kitchen table, where we ate, there was a small opening...if I remember right, it was like a bank-teller's caged opening, iron bars behind the wood door that slid up into the wall, and with a slot at the bottom deep enough to slide a plate of food through, and later, receive the used dishes from it. When I was visiting one time, she used her regular dishes to serve the jailbird, because she knew him, but they usually used a tin plate and tin cup to serve the person behind the bars. I vaguely remember someone showing me the tin cup and plate and letting me hold the cup. Ever since, when I pass a hunting equipment/camping department in a store, I look at the tin cups and plate sets and remember Uncle Basil and Aunt Stella's Jailhouse kitchen.

Clark, who was the closest to my age, and his older brother Roger would arrange for me to sit next to that opening and try to scare me, saying "Be careful now, Judy, the big bad man's hand is going to come out and grab you." We would laugh, and I was a little leery, but knew whoever was behind the wall wasn't a dangerous sort. And although Aunt Stella's kitchen was big and warm, like her heart, I rarely went in there without keeping an eye on the caged opening in the wall at the end of the long table.

Many years later, after Mom died, I went back to Whitehall (County Seat) to look around. I went to the records department and the only thing left of that house/jail in Whitehall is an aerial photograph. The man who was helping me did find a few old campaign ads, though, that were of my granddad.

There is a huge book of the history of Trempealeau County available that tells much of the story of Grandpa's father settling down in Newcomb Valley, building a stalwart house and becoming one of the county's most respected citizens. It tells how he had to take a wagon pulled by oxen, all the way to Winona MN to get supplies, having to walk along side. He would be gone for days at a time to carry out that task. His son, my grandpa Edward grew up to continue the farming, and he became the Sheriff of the county and raised 8 children; making sure they were educated and well read. Aunt Florence taught at the one room schoolhouse just outside our valley. Today, she is approaching her 102nd birthday, and is still as bright and chipper as ever. She still lives in her own apartment and takes care of herself. She also communicates using her computer/tablet.

******

Norwegian words would spot our conversations, and one of them was "Drekkadar"…a word meaning Paradise according to Mom. For Florence's 94th birthday, she treated herself to a laptop computer and learned to use it quickly. It is such a pleasure to be able to communicate with her by email when I can't get to Arcadia. Recently, I asked Aunt Florence about the word *Drekkadar* and she said that *Drekka* actually means "water" and that *Dar* means "valley." There is a glitch in the spelling…with all the dialects and the fact that a word can change an entire meaning with the substitution of one letter…I've been looking for 'Drekkadar' in the Norwegian dictionary on the internet, and for the life of me cannot find it, using every spelling I can think of, so, well, you'll just have to take our word for the description. It was our description. And whatever it really meant was never revealed to us.

When mom and dad married, Mom found a secluded area of the farmland, wooded and full of blackberries and wildflowers, and she dreamed about having her very own "Drrrekkadar." It really was pretty. She would plant her wishes in my imagination, and I 'saw' her yellow dream house with a big, white porch, tucked deep into the lot flanked by steep hills, lush with greenery. But it was not to be. The lot Mom showed me is still empty, still wooded with brush and wildflowers. She did get a yellow house though.

It was in Menomonie Wisconsin. Dad bought a lot on a small hill, with a bigger hill behind it. We lived in an apartment over a neighbor's garage while waiting for the house to be built. Janie and I would search the framed house after the workers were gone and collect 'slugs' punched from the pipes. The iron slugs were perfect for playing "store." There were nickel sized ones and quarter sized ones. Some were designated as pennies, and some were dimes. We were "rich." "Ka-Ching" Jane would say as she 'rang up' a sale on our imaginary cash register.

Mom could watch the house from the window over the apartment's kitchen sink. I knew she was anxious for her first ownership of her yellow Cape Cod house. The hills and the trees completed the setting for her: *a Drekadar in Menomonie.*

One day, after the carpenters were gone, Janie and I sneaked into the partially built house to see where our rooms would be. We were told not to walk anywhere in the unfinished upstairs. In the 'front room', we spotted a wooden sawhorse that the carpenters were using to support boards they had to cut. We made a seesaw out of it, but it didn't work very well. The raw board scratched our legs and was hard to hold on to. So we decided to take a look upstairs. We went up the forbidden stairs. They were temporary stairs that more resembled a slanted ladder with flat steps and it was scary to be able to see through the backs of them all the way to the first level. I know we were told not to walk on the 'floor' that was simply the first layer for the ceiling downstairs. There was no real flooring yet, but it was so tempting to balance on the two-by-fours that would support the future floor. Janie said, "Look, Judy, it will hold me." "Janie, ", I squawked, "You're not supposed to walk on that!!"

The next thing I saw was Jane disappearing through the drywall ceiling and landing flat on the end of the 'seesaw' below the hole she had made. I straddled the rafters upstairs and screamed. Mom had been eyeing us from the kitchen window above the sink in the temporary apartment, and she came running across the lawns, saying "Oh, oh, oh, oh." She had seen Jane disappear though the ceiling and drop past the window opening of the front room below. When she reached Janie, she stopped and took a huge sigh. Of course, Mom slapped Jane's butt and yelled at her before she hugged her in relief. It turned out Janie was only bruised, and we made fun of the possibility of there might have been a big nail sticking out of the board that was our 'seesaw'. We took it a bit farther through our laughter when we claimed that if she had landed on the nail, she would have shot right back up through the ceiling. We were cartoon characters.

The steep hill behind that house was full of trees and brush, forming a sort of private wall to our back yard for us. Janie and I would climb the hill a short distance, till we found a spot to build a grotto. Grottos are big in small towns. We fashioned a brush cave big enough for a statue of the 'Blessed Virgin Mary' to stand in, and we decorated it with dandelions and wildflowers in front of it. Jane went down to the house to get the statue. It looked beautiful to us; we put it in our makeshift grotto and would kneel in front of it and try to pray. Of course, it was the Hail Mary monologue, and the next day Mom asked us where her statue was. It had been a gift. So, we removed Holy Mary from our grotto and replaced her with a doll that had no arms.

It was post World War Two, and sugar was scarce for some reason. So was celluloid, so film was precious. As far as the sugar went, I would climb onto the counter and reach into the top shelf of the cabinet to get a coveted sugar cube that mom was saving for company. We also would take the heavy cream from the top of the milk in bottles and put it in a jar. Then we would take turns shaking the jar until we had soft whitish butter. In the winter, the milkman would bring our milk early in the morning, and it would sometimes freeze, heaving the expanding cream straight up creating a cream stump. Then we could simply cut the cream stump off with a knife and drop the chunk into a jar, ready to shake when it melted.

Because of the film shortage, I was somehow the only child lucky enough to have a formal 'baby' picture taken at a studio, sitting on mother's lap. Dad had entered the war late, because he had three children. The military took fathers with small children last. He was on a battleship nearing Kobe Japan when the radios announced the war was over. But he was picked to stay behind in Japan to help rebuild some of the buildings that were destroyed. He was given a young non-military Japanese gentleman to translate and help where ever needed. The man was sort of a personal valet to Dad. Dad's wartime scrapbook has some postcards that were sent to him once dad left Japan. The young man complimented my dad on his kindness and ability to teach. They always started with "Master Harold" and "Harold-san" It's just great to see those notes, and the saved letters that dad wrote to mom and to his parents.

CHAPTER 2

Summers on the Farm

Some summer mornings back at the farm, I would go with Grandma or Aunt Merle to 'pick' eggs. We would enter the hen house amid the squawking chickens and rustle some fresh eggs for breakfast. I *felt* like a rustler, sneaking in and searching for an unguarded nest. We were "rustling-up some breakfast," I thought. I needed some chaps and a mustache- and a gun to hold those hens hostage. I remember gingerly reaching into a nest and picking up two eggs. They were still warm and I would say, "Ugh" at the thought of holding those eggs that had just dropped out of a chicken's behind. Each egg that I picked up got an "ick" or "ugh" from me. And, I was afraid the mother hen would get mad at me, too, and try to get even, but I stuck close to grandma, and holding on to her apron, and made it safely out of the coop.

Sometimes we would clean eggs to sell in town. I first did that at Aunt Hattie's and Uncle George's farm. In Wisconsin, most everyone seemed to own farms. In our little valley alone, there were the Gilbertsons, the Arnesons, the Axness', the Hansons and the Ericksons (us). Our own family had more than one farm, as those siblings and cousins got older and went into that way of life for themselves. Aunt Hattie was my great aunt on my Mom's side, but *everyone* called her Aunt Hattie, regardless of the relationship. Aunt Hattie was an antique collector— way back when items that would **now** be called antiques were antique. I would refer to her many collections as antique- antiques. Her crowded house was always interesting; and a little spooky to me at the time. I liked looking at the giant grand piano though, with the many detailed carvings in the legs, sides and music holder. I can only imagine how valuable her things were when she died many years later and the estate was auctioned. I didn't get to the auction, but I heard it was wildly successful.

Aunt Hattie's farm had an electrified barbed wire fence around the barnyard, and we were told not to touch it for obvious reasons. That didn't stop me, I just had to see what they were talking about and experience it firsthand. I didn't hear that expected "zzzttt", but I sure felt it. No wonder the cows and calves were so well behaved.

Aunt Hattie's daughter, Rachel, was near my age. As little girls, Rachel and I would swing on two swings that hung from one of the big old trees, and with each swoop we would sing a singsong slogan for a popular soap ad: "Weeee… that Oxydol Sparkle." Her big sister Georgine had recently broken her leg, and was sitting in the screened-in porch cleaning eggs. She showed me how they cleaned eggs for sale. She handed me a piece of waxed paper to use to gently rub any debris from the fresh eggs. "Why not just wash them?" I asked her, and she explained, "because then Mother Nature's special invisible cover would go away and the eggs wouldn't stay as fresh inside." So we used waxed paper so as not to hurt Mother's Nature's seal of protection, and each egg got treated very gently by hand, and then carefully put in big wooden boxes with little wooden squares to keep the eggs from rolling during transportation to town.

Sometimes, when Grandma needed a break, I would visit our cousins in town. My mother's brother, Uncle Lloyd and Aunt Delores had as many kids in their family as we did in ours. (however, after my dad died, Lloyd and Delores were able to top us by having one more). Sandy was my age, and we had much in common, along with two other cousins our age, using any pencil we could find, we often drew and fashioned antique paper outfits for our paper dolls. We designed a variety of outfits and included little fold-over tabs so we could dress and re-dress our paper dolls. Outlandish paper hats had a little slit in the center to accommodate the head of the paper doll. We were pretty good at dreaming up big bows and decorations to drip from the crown of the paper hats.

The Fernholz side of the family were in-town folks, and seemed to find plenty of creative things to do indoors. It must be where I got the feel for charades, pantomiming and lip-synching, as well as artwork with pastels, pencils and crayons. Aunt Delores also baked fresh bread a couple times a week, and my Uncle Lloyd was always busy, usually at the Arcadia Hatchery or out hunting raccoons.

Sometimes I would see a lot of raccoon skins curing outside of the shed in the back yard. Aunt Delores would say, "Oh, you don't want to go in there, it really stinks." She was right. I could smell the stench of carcasses as I neared the shed, and only once did I follow Sandy inside.

I didn't pay much attention to the older or younger cousins in the family either; Sandy was my buddy; she was my age. We fit. My siblings could match themselves up with the others who were their ages. First borns with first borns, second with second, etc. Uncle Lloyd's huge front lawn sported rows of raspberries. We would spend hours chatting away eating the fresh fuzzy berries till we had to move to a group of bushes with more to choose from. "Don't eat all the raspberries, I need them for dessert!" came Aunt Delores's voice from the open window.

It is the Erickson farm, though, that I am most connected to. It was a safe haven that I knew was always available even though we moved every few years. It's still there, and I continue to find it the only place that has still have the same feeling throughout my life. After Mom died about eight years ago, fifty-some years after *Drekkadar*, I drove there with my adult daughter Johanna, to show her where I'd had so many happy childhood years. The wide wooden gate that Freddy and I would ride on when someone swung it open so long ago was wrapped with a chain and locked, so Johanna and I parked on the side of the road and sat and looked at the old house. Suddenly, from the car, as clear as day, I saw my sister Jane, my cousins Freddy and Janet, Grandma and myself. Grandma was standing at the side door, hands on hips with her perennial apron protecting her housedress, chuckling at us while we played. Janie's spirit had a big bow in her thick blonde hair and was yelling my name as plain and audible as it could ever be. We were all dressed in our Sunday best. The voices I heard included even my own. I almost yelled back "I'm here!"

It was so startling I burst into tears. My daughter was baffled and said, "Mom, these are supposed to be happy memories." I said yes they were. Then I explained what had just happened. For a couple of seconds, I had just experienced another dimension. It was so sincere that I knew she believed me. It was so real, so wondrous and sweet. I wish I could do it again.

****

I was in the second grade when we moved to St. Joseph, Minnesota. Before that, we were living in Menomonie, Wisconsin, where Dad gave *that* new lumber yard a jump start. Later, while we were living in St. 'Joe', Dad would be asked to manage a new Central Lumber Yard in Fargo, North Dakota. Obviously, he had gotten the lumber yard in St. Joe going well enough. "Lickity-split," Mom would say with a big smile. "Your Daddy got it going Lickity-Split."

The lumber business owners knew they could count on Dad to give each new lumberyard a solid start. Soon, we had found ourselves temporarily in the little burg of St. Joseph, Minnesota, where there were hard-hitting nuns during the school year and outdoor movies in the school yard on summer weekends. I remember my second grade teacher, Sister Jolunda. She was not meant to be a teacher and didn't hesitate to slap a face or belittle a child. I felt sorry for the kids who were yelled at for the smallest infraction, including me. But when the little girl behind me got so scared she wet her pants, I placed myself in another dimension: just staring at the nun and watching her lips move while removing myself to a paradise somewhere...until she turned her wrath on me. She pointed her bony finger at me and started yelling.... "and YOU".... and went into her diatribe of infractions she perceived I was committing, while my imaginary self went swinging on the moon's crescent. Not too many years later, after yet another move, my brothers and I would be returning to St. Joe in a whole different setting and circumstance. My dad will have been killed.

The first time we lived in St. Joe, Mom talked the bank owner into making a deal that would let us live in his big house, where he would occupy only his own master bedroom and bathroom. It was a small, stately mansion with elegant features. Sometimes he would come to the kitchen to eat, but most of the time I rarely saw him. In exchange, she would do his laundry and keep up the house and pay a small rent in return for us living in the rest of the house. It was a grand house for a small town; Daddy could walk to the lumber yard and we could walk to school. Mr. Crever was hardly ever seen coming and going. Many years later when I saw *It's a Wonderful Life* with Jimmy Stewart, I looked at the banker in the movie and was reminded of kind old Mr. Crever.

Sometimes, when we knew he was gone for the day, my sister Jane and I would sneak into his big bedroom, with its massive furniture, and open the chest at the foot of his bed. We would be in awe when we picked up the small sized high-button shoes that had belonged to his deceased wife. We would carefully unfold a silk blouse with a high lace neck and make up romantic stories about Mr. Crever and his wife. We would try to place the things the same way that we found them, but one day, Mom gave us a 'talking to' for going in there. She said Mr. Crever had asked her to talk to us. He was a gentle man, and he probably found that his things were disturbed…and who else would have done it?

The house had two stairways to the upstairs. The formal one at the front of the house had a carpet runner in the middle of the dark wood steps. A big mahogany pillar stood guard at its base. The stairway had a lovely, leaded glass window over the landing where the stairs curved to continue the climb. The back stairway was plain and functional, leading to and from the kitchen to the upstairs. How we loved chasing up, over and down those staircases. At the main entrance to the house, there was a spacious, heavily pillared front porch and Mom made it feel like an added living room—except for the big, black, hairy spiders that would make their homes temporarily in the corners of the ceiling.

Spiders in Minnesota have to be pretty hardy to make it through winter. One day, knowing those furry visitors with the crooked legs were holed up in their thick, cone-shaped webs, I refused to go through the porch to go outside. I knew from experience that when those little eight-legged creeps decided to run, they were too fast and too sneaky for me. Mom took me by the hand and, said, "They're more afraid of you than you are of them," and she daintily picked one of the spiders up by one of its crook'd legs, dropped it on the floor and squashed it under her foot. I heard the round body pop—Spider Juice. "Now you try it," she said. "Don't worry, they won't bite you." I thought that if one bit me, I would at least know where it was. I shuddered but I did want to face my fear. I picked up a big book, crawled up on the wicker couch and slammed the book on the web. I'm glad the slam of the book was louder than the pop of the spider. "There," Mom said, "That wasn't so hard, was it"—it was more of a statement than a question. There wasn't much left of the spider on the book cover, the legs were flattened out in all directions and they weren't even attached to the pulp. I never touched that book again. I wasn't cured.

From then on, when I saw a spider on the floor, I would drop a big book on it, and leave it there; safe in knowing the creature surely wasn't strong enough to get out from under the epic, just in case I hadn't killed it. Let someone else pick it up. Sometimes I wasn't so confident, so I would stand on the book and jump on it.

To feed my fear of crawly things, I saw a movie, the original *Blue Lagoon*, an unrealistic black and white film that as it played, you could hear the reels turning, making a kind of crackle. In it, the two young, angelic looking children were alone in the wooded area of a tropical island, catching pretty butterflies. The young boy spotted an unusually beautiful one caught in a spider web far bigger than he was. That scene alone gave me the willies. He wanted to free the butterfly. He began tearing gently at the web to loosen the colorful wings, and the vibrations awakened an immense spider that started crawling down the web. The boy didn't notice at first, but I sure did. I have no idea what happened then, because I squeezed my eyes closed for the rest of the movie. "Is it gone? Is it gone yet?" I would coarsely whisper to Janie. She would say," no it's still coming after him", and I believed her for the rest of the movie and kept my eyes shut hoping she would soon say it was gone. But she never did.

"Drats, foiled again," we would often say when we got fooled. We had taken it from a Dastardly Dick cartoon and made it our very own slogan.

Mom kept a razor strop hanging from the closet door in the front foyer of the house. We were afraid of it. When she did use it, it was only as a prop, held threateningly in her hand. Once, while lecturing, she slapped it against the doorframe, and my feet left the ground, shoving my heart into my throat when I landed. I never felt the strop physically, of course, and I am sure my sisters never did either, although we all liked to say we did when we wanted to scare our younger brothers into doing something for us.

By then, we had a brother Joel, and a couple of years later, Jon and then Jim. (It wasn't until a few years later, in Fargo, that we had the youngest brother, Jeffrey). Mom and Dad said they were practicing 'rhythm', the Catholic word for birth control, but it only worked for two or three years in between kids. Years before, in Arcadia, and before Dad went into the service in World War II, Mom and he only had us three girls. After Dad got back, she started having boys. Mom would say, "The Army made a man out of Harold," with a silly grin. They were lovers. It was comforting to be around them together. As a little tyke, when we lived in Arcadia while he was away in the war, we had a small flag hanging in the window with one star on it. I would climb on the couch, pat the flag then jump down and salute, exclaiming, "*My* Daddy is in the Army!" My sisters had taught me to say that. I would stand swayback, with my belly extended, feet together and make a childish salute in order to make that proclamation. The adults enjoyed it. And I wished my Daddy could see me.

****

Back in St. Joseph, behind Mr. Crever's house, I played in the back yard with my little friend, Mary Lou. We pretended to be circus acrobats, and I would try to walk on the wire wash-lines pretending I was one of the tight rope walkers in the Barnum and Bailey Circus we would see every year. I never made it even one step; the wires weren't tight enough, but I was determined to keep trying. Mom would say to stop it because we were stretching out the lines and Dad would have to tighten them again…. "AND, if you fall on the lines," she added, "you'll be sliced into bits." We would laugh and mimic pieces of the body, pre-Monty Python-like, moving around on the ground. Of course Monty Python comedy wasn't around then, but our dippy humor was. Mom would look away smiling. Wash lines had no plastic coatings back then. No matter how much you cleaned the wires before hanging the wash, they left rust imprints on the sheets and pillowcases where the clothespins pinched the fabric. We would have to tear small squares of white cotton remnants to put under the clothes-pins between the wash and the line to keep the rust from marking the wash.

The ends of the wash lines were attached to T-shaped supports made of three inch– I'm guessing- (diameter) iron pipes. I liked to stand on top of one pipe/pole, where I would balance as long as I could and then jump to the ground. I balanced for only a couple of seconds, but it felt a lot longer. Then I would beg Dad to build a trapeze for me. He would say no. I would argue that he had the whole lumber yard to get the supplies from. He still said no. Dad would change the subject by 'hiring' me to dust at the office and sales room of the lumber yard.

Back then, I figured lumber yards did everything from blueprints to basements and roofs— the carpentry, roofing, plumbing and electric stayed 'in-house'; with little outsourcing. Rows of pull out bins of bulk nails and screws and electrical pieces compelled me to examine them. I found a little thing shaped like a little tiny flashlight for my doll. It was actually an electrical wire nut, the piece that holds the ends of two or three electric wires twisted together. They still make them that way, but most are now plastic, with a little copper lining, but old or new, they look like miniature flashlights. After my dusting job, Dad would pay me a dollar. Janie got two dollars, because she was older and smart enough to 'help' with the bookkeeping. She was good with numbers, too. She always talked me into buying the two of us a malted milk at the drugstore with my dollar. In those days each malted milk was twenty five cents. She liked Chocolate, I liked Vanilla. She always drank two at one sitting. Then she and I would run to the main yard of the lumberyard, just across the drive-through that was used by the big trucks that came along to unload. We would climb way up on the neatly stacked planks of all sizes, the heights of the stacks differing as we made our way over them. The entire lumber supply was roofed with corrugated steel to protect the lumber from the elements, sort of what you see at a Menards or Home Depot. Jane and I would sit on top of the lumber near the roof and sing "It's Only a Shanty in Old Shanty Town."

I still love the smell of fresh cut lumber. When we got tired, we would climb down and stand on the big wooden scale where the trucks carrying their load of lumber would get weighed. We would pretend that we could actually make the weights change, and would call out, "Under Two Tons– you are free to go!!" Or, "Over Two Tons– unload!!" Then we would kiss Daddy goodbye and run the couple of short blocks back home to the Crever house with my quarter stuck in my socks, and Jane's two dollars in her fist.

****

It was in the Crever house's back yard where I was hanging from the pipes that served as railings for the cement steps to the back door. Since the drop from the railing was about four steps down, I had room to dangle upside-down with my bent knees wrapped over the railing, the back of my head against the side of the stoop. I resented that I couldn't swing back and forth. I could only move forth, like an abs-crunch, and risk hitting my head when I swung back to hang straight down. "Now if I had a trapeze, I wouldn't have to worry about it", I thought.

One day, I was climbing on the railing, facing out, and lost my balance. Just at the time Mom was sticking her head out the window above me to tell me something, I went sailing face first against the cement steps. I chipped a front tooth. Mom hung out of the window yelling, "Oh, oh, oh"–which she often did when witnessing a tragedy, then, "Judy, Judy, your teeth, your teeth!!!" She was probably thinking I couldn't be a toothless movie star. I hung there, by my knees, upside down, crying with blood trickling from my nose and mouth until she got downstairs to help me down and clean me up. I looked in the mirror and cried, "Oh, NO, I look like a witch!" and sobbed some more. I hadn't really knocked out the whole tooth. It was just a sizable chip that, if the materials had been invented at the time, could have been filled in with porcelain bonding. But at that time, the dentist decided he had to destroy the entire tooth to make a cap for it. So, the dentist knocked it out. I don't know which was worse: smashing my face against the cement stoop or enduring the tool that that dentist used.

St. Joe didn't have a dentist, and Mom had taken me to St. Cloud, a more sizable town nearby, and she trusted the dentist. He used a big metal wheel attached to the drill that looked like a lumber yard's buzz saw, doll-size, and he rammed its spinning points against my tooth until the rest of the chipped tooth broke off. I can still hear the buzz saw noise clanging against my then near- normal tooth. The trauma to my gums would later warrant a root canal because of an abscess from abusing the tooth. That tooth has cost me big bucks over the years but has also provided a few good laughs.

One time, years later, during a date with my future (first) husband, we were in a fine restaurant in Chicago and I laughed at something that was said. The "HAH" catapulted the cap out of my mouth, over the table and under the next table full of diners. I kept my upper lip pulled down over my teeth to cover the gap and spoke as if I had left my teeth at home. I got down on the floor, wearing my black lace cocktail dress, (size 6 at the time) high heels and nylons with seams, and with beautifully coiffed hair, crawled on the floor to the next table to find the cap. I saw it resting against a man's shoe. "Don't move," I said as I grabbed his ankle. I couldn't tell them what I was looking for, but at least I got a hearty laugh from the onlookers. Because of the ill-fitting crown, I carried around a small tube of Polident 'just in case'. And forty-some years later, I would name one of my musical groups "Polly Dent and the Flossers" as a salute to the memory of that early dental work.

After about a year in J.C. Crever's house, we moved into a tight Georgian style house on the highway. In those days, towns were literally built on the highways. The house wasn't my Mom's type, but she needed to have some privacy for her family. Looking back, I think it was Mr. Crever who needed the privacy.

The siding on the house was clapboard and there were no trees. Mom didn't like the fact there were no trees—and no hills. It was flat as a pancake all around that town. We missed our Wisconsin terrain. Behind that house was a huge meadow and at the far end of that meadow were train tracks.

Joanie and I shared a bedroom, and I would watch her put on lipstick at a mirror that was surrounded by pictures of movie stars. Pages from magazines with photos of Marlene Dietrich, Ava Gardner, Jean Harlow and Janet Leigh overlapped each other like a huge collage...My favorite was Susan Hayward. I loved her movies. As Jane Froman, Susan would toss her head slightly, allowing her chin to jut upward, and as she looked into the face of David Wayne; her little pug nose and shapely lips endeared her profile. She had a deliciously smoky voice that made her more attractive. When she was defiant, she would toss her head back with a slight jerk.

There were two windows in that bedroom that faced the railroad tracks. Did I say that the tracks were about 2 blocks from our house? Late at night, maybe ten o'clock or so, Joan, Jane and I would lie on our stomachs across the bed and try to count the train cars by the groups of lights that separated each of the passenger cars.

When the train was past, we would compare notes. I rarely had the same total, but they would tell me I'd got it right anyway. After a while, I would be counting alone, and then they'd say they got the same total, or lie with a one number difference. That way I would be kept busy while they read movie magazines. At daybreak we would go to the track to look for and find a flattened out penny and bring it home. I think Joanie and her boyfriends were the ones who put the pennies on the track. Mom said to never try putting anything on a train track because it could derail the train.

I wouldn't consider putting even a gum wrapper on a railroad track, but I was fascinated by the warm, flat, smooth, lopsided penny that resulted when someone *else* broke the rules.

One day, alone in the meadow, I was running back from the tracks and there was a parting movement in the long weeds. I stopped to look. Maybe it was just the wind. It wasn't.

The snake cut a path leaving a wake beside it in the long grass, and it got too close for me to keep watching. I turned and ran as fast as I could, (positive it was on my heels making its sneaky way into my anklets), to tell Mom about my close encounter of the worst kind. Mom said it was just a garter snake and that it eats bugs and spiders. Was I supposed to like it because of that? It was just trading one nightmare for another and that was the end of the discussion.

Our neighbor had stalks and stalks of hollyhocks, in all colors, and she would let us take some of the flowers and shuck seeds from them. We would get as many seeds as we could and bring them to Mom. Soon we had our own hollyhocks. It's still my favorite garden flower. Colorful hollyhocks lined the sides of other homes, too. Some of those hollyhocks also flanked my friend's house.

Across the highway from "the old Meyers house," as we called it, lived my friend Eileen Dullinger. It was a real adventure to cross the highway to visit her. Trucks with wheels as big as me would go by, giving a little honk for a hello. I would wave. When it was safe to run across, I would scoot quickly across and jump the grassy gutter that separated Eileen's lawn from the highway. It was just a two lane highway, as most were then, but for my small frame it was a wide span to cross.

Mom would call us for dinner when Dad got home (later, she got a big bell), and I would head home. One day, I ran across too soon. As a semi truck got closer to the lane that I hadn't even reached yet, the driver started honking, and an 'Audie Murphy'-type urge flashed inside my brain. I didn't know what was coming on the side I just about crossed and I couldn't take the time to look, so I couldn't change my mind. I dove down and rolled into the gravel on the other side of the highway, just as the huge semi rushed by. I could feel the heat of the truck; the hot wind from the massive wheels as I lay there. "I made it!" I thought while my heart beat hard and fast. Pleased with myself, I strutted home to enjoy dinner, sporting bloody elbows and skinned hands and knees. Daddy was standing at the door; his face was pale, and he said quietly, "Don't you ever do anything like that again". He had seen the feat and he wasn't happy about it. He was probably wishing we were back safely on the farm.

When I was in the fourth grade, in St. Joseph, Minnesota, I found out we would be moving to Fargo, North Dakota. I don't think we had occupied the Old Meyers house very long before this directive was given to Dad, and I think that Mom was relieved. My parents, my two sisters, three younger brothers and I rode with Mom and Dad to our new location. Dad had been given a very nice job with yet another branch of the Central Lumber Yard. Mom liked Fargo, and so did I. She and Dad talked about this being their last move. And it was.

Fargo was a big city to me. It still remains in my heart as the best place for a pre-teen and teenager to grow up. It is quite safe, an "All American Town", and it's not so big that it is intimidating. It was the first place we lived where there was a variety of ethnic cultures and religions. Everyone was impressed with our Jewish Mayor, Herschel Laskowitz, who drove a beautiful, lilac colored Lincoln Continental. He would always wave and say hello to people. His corner house on 8th Street South was beautifully landscaped, as were all the others in our neighborhood. We eventually lived in a nice house on 7th Street and 15th Avenue South, a few blocks from the Mayor's house, in St. Anthony of Padua Parish on the South Side of Fargo.

But when we *first* moved to Fargo, Mom had found us an ample house in St. Mary's Parish on the North Side. It had a renter using one bedroom. I knew this house would be temporary because it was not Mom's style. Before the physical move, she had made one of her deals that would include housekeeping the renter's room when needed and bringing him soup on a tray. Mr. Aasen was ailing, and he had the first bedroom at the top of the stairs. He might have been the owner of the house. I really didn't know. The house was old, but Mom did some of her sewing tricks for drapes and curtains, and she reupholstered our old furniture. She was the Martha Stewart of the 1930s and 40s, and on.

This first house in Fargo was stucco, with dark areas where moisture had lifted the stucco layer away from the structure. The detached garage was set back from the house and it had a fair sized back yard that needed some TLC. There were patches of dirt where grass had worn away from neglect. Mom tried to ignore it. "Now, if this were *my* house," she would say, "I would paint it butter- yellow." We were from the Dairy State, after all. I know she would have torn away and repaired the damaged stucco, and would have planted beautiful flowers and bushes if she could have. But she had more aspirations.

I was in a strange new world. I started the fifth grade immediately, because the school year had begun a few weeks before we got there. I sat down at my assigned desk amid unfamiliar surroundings and tried to take the spelling test—the very first thing offered on my first day in my new grade. The nun spurted out the words and I could tell the students were used to her odd way of pronouncing words. One of the words was 'film'. But she pronounced it "Fil-Um." I thought that was how teachers in Fargo talked, and I attempted to spell the word. I wrote, "Phil-um," wondering what it meant. I was embarrassed when I got my graded paper back; until a classmate started calling the nun "Sister Mary Phil-um" after we left the schoolyard that day and we giggled. Sharon Cullen's apparent understanding bonded us immediately. She lived only two doors away from us. Sharon was pretty and she was kind, and so was her mother. I met her dad once, when he came home from work the same time as everyone else's did in those days, 'just in time for supper'. The screen door to the porch of their house didn't quite fit, maybe it was warped, and letting it swing shut wasn't enough to close it solidly, so we were always told to pull the door shut by the dangling hook. The inside of the door didn't have a handle, so the hook-and-eye screw served to close it tight. I spent many after-school hours in the comfort of Sharon and her mother's presence.

When Mom wasn't cleaning our house, waiting on the renter, or working as a cashier down the block at a small grocery store, she would be busy in our basement, washing and ironing clothes. She had figured out a way to "chounce" my dad's suit in a cleaning solution, too. After all, they were living in a big city now, and Dad had to look the business man's part.

She would put her cleaning solution in a clean tub, and she would use a designated plunger to 'chounce' the clothing, creating a manual agitator like a washing machine. She had coined the word 'chounce' for that action, and I still use it. I haven't found it yet in any dictionary. Mom had created her own little 'dry' cleaners. Sometimes she would let me take over the chouncing, watching me to make sure I wasn't too rough with it. When she deemed the suit clean, she would rinse it and hang it to dry on hangers, then later, she would press it perfectly for Dad to look good at his job, and for going to conventions. One would never guess it hadn't been done professionally.

Mom had an electric iron, unlike her mother, Grandma Liz, who had to put her heavy flat iron on a stove top to heat it up every few minutes while ironing. Gram's curling iron worked the same way. The skinny rod would have to lie on the stove to get heated up enough to singe her hair into little curls. For ironing, pressing cloths or cheese cloths would be dampened. They were then used to lay over the wrinkles and the hot iron coming down on them created steam. I still use cheesecloth to get the wrinkles out of fabrics that might get shiny from the hot iron if no cloth were between the iron and the fabric. Sometimes, when time didn't allow for ironing, the things that needed ironing would be dampened, then rolled up and refrigerated (to prevent mildew). When we could get to the ironing, the clothes were evenly damp from being stored together in that roll.

Soon, we moved to the South Side of Fargo, where things seemed nicer and newer. All the yards were manicured, and the houses were clean and fresh. The yards were all grass and had no worn patches. Mom and Dad were moving up in the world. Mom, as you can see, was creatively frugal. I got that from her, too. Years, later my daughter would start calling me "MacGyver Mom." She still does.

My life was heaven for a few years. I loved that house, that town, that school and my neighbors and friends. It was that house that I later wrote about, and the story was published twice, the second time ten years after the first. The second time it was published with an added story to close the circle. But I want to tell you about that later.

It was at this house, at 702 15th Avenue South, that I learned to do some gardening. Gardening was another one of Mom's talents. She knew what flowers grew best together, what greenery would nourish the soil, and how big the various flowers would grow. She would plan what she wanted to plant, and where to plant it, by the sizes and colors of the blooms; and the expected time of bloom. There were blooming colors all summer long, the heights complimenting each other. When one species faded, another would be freshly blooming, and so on. Separating the plots, she liked to use periwinkle, a hearty ground cover with blue flowers. Dad and Mom would bring saplings and bulbs and "Bishop's Collar" home from each trip to Wisconsin. They brought ferns from the woods, and iris and sedum from our farm, where plants, trees and flowers were so lush that the few pieces they took to transplant would not be missed. (Years later, mom would bring plants to my home in Northbrook, where I had a big yard and my own impressive gardens. We started naming the plants in honor of my Erickson uncles and aunts. Sedum was Basil and Stella, and Aunt Sadie had given mom some Hen-and-Chick plants to bring me, so we named them Orlen and Sadie, and so on).

On trips to Wisconsin, Mom would have Dad stop the car on any road that had lush ferns and sumac growing, and they would dig a few roots out and bring them home to Fargo. Mom showed me how to plant various plants and flowers, and I helped her and Dad plant a tree in the side yard. They put a handful of nails in the hole so that when the nails rusted, the soil around the roots would get aerated. I think it worked. Although I can't find any nails that will rust, to this day I am a fairly good gardener—except for disliking bugs, a fetish I can't shake.

One day, when I was following Mom's directions of where to dig, my spade dug up a big green grub worm. I let out a shriek, and Mom went to the house and got a Mason jar and had me put the worm in it, then she put a lid on the jar. "Now, watch him, Judy, he's a tricky little guy, he thinks he can get out of the jar," she said with a wry smile.

I was terrified that it actually *would* escape the jar, so I kept guard. "You will have to make some air holes in the lid so it can breathe," Mom instructed. (Did I care if it could breathe?) I couldn't say that out loud, but I wished it *would* stop breathing. But even so, I probably would have kept an eye on it, to make sure it wasn't playing dead. I didn't want a worm to foil me. But Mom's intentions held my interest. She got a nail and a hammer and showed me how to puncture small holes in the lid. The fat, green worm made its way up the side of the jar by spitting a sticky substance on the glass, and then used it to fasten its feet to. It moved up its sticky, zigzag ladder, and when it reached the middle of the jar, it stopped and looked at me with a big grin on its pompous face, and then it continued till it got to the lid, and then sat there confused. "HA!" I said to it. Mom said to give it a little bit of grass. I wouldn't open the lid to do that, but I did manage to slide a couple of blades and drip a little water through the air holes. I lined up all my equipment on our picnic table that Dad had built for us, and stood there gaping at the worm, wishing we had worn gloves to dig in the dirt.

Fifty-some years later, Mom would still weed her gardens with bare hands, preferring to weed right after a good rainfall, and sometimes during the rain, so the roots would pull out easily. Her last garden, in St. Paul, Minnesota, was as beautiful, rich and full as any *Good Housekeeping* magazine photo. And with all her physical labors, she always managed to be primly dressed and have a clean manicure. Saturdays were her day to do her nails and set her hair. In those days people dressed keenly for church meetings and doings.

But back on the South side of Fargo, we had a fairly expansive lawn for our corner house, and on the opposite side of the garage, a huge garden. Dad had erected a clean, white wooden fence shaped with wide white boards that looked like the border fence of a ritzy horse ranch. More than ever, I still wanted him to build a trapeze for me right in the middle of the garden because in that sized space, there would be room enough for the trapeze to swing forever outward on long ropes. "I promise I will land between the rows," referring to possibly ruining the carrots and the tomatoes when I jumped off the trapeze. I figured I would have to shinny up the poles to get to the height of the trapeze—uh, no, I would have a ladder on the side of the posts. There. I had it all figured out, but Dad still said no.

I gave up on my glamorous circus act dreams and decided I could jump off the roof of the garage instead. Our detached garage was built to hold one car. It stood a good distance from the house. My friends Claudia and Linda and I would climb up to the roof of the far side of the garage so Mom couldn't spot us. We would then sit on the slanted roof, (away from the house), hunching over with bent knees, thinking that then we would be invisible to her, while mustering up the courage to jump. It didn't take a long deliberation until we half sprang, half dropped into the air. We did it a few times, making it safely to the ground without injury. We decided to do it again in the fall, agreeing that we could rake up enough leaves to cushion our landings: Corporate Improvements 101.

One day, as Mom was sewing upstairs near the tiny balcony at the rear of the house, I had a strong urge to tie a small sheet at the corners and leap from the balcony, holding the sheet like a parachute. The balcony was higher than the garage, so I would have more air-time for the way down. She guffawed and said I would fall fast and straight down. I was convinced that the sheet would slow the fall. She said, "go ahead, but if you hurt yourself, I'll give you such a licking that you won't be able to sit for a year." I decided not to jump.

Mom had been sewing some doll clothes for my "Effie" doll, a copy of a Ginny Doll. Dad had made a three-storey doll house for my Effie, and Mom was sewing a miniature fur coat with a matching hat and muff out of white rabbit fur. It looked a lot like the coat and muff she made for my sisters in New Richmond before I grew into their clothes.

Everything I saw became usable for Effie. When I saw an empty Band-Aid box with a hinged lid, it became a clothes hamper for her. I painted it yellow and added a little decal of red flowers. Then I saw that a little tin aspirin box could be painted, too, and used for her miniature flatware. I found another 'flashlight' in the electrical section of the lumberyard... "MacGyver Mom: the Early Years."

One year, when Dad returned from a convention, he brought each of us kids a bag full of give-aways. Note pads and pens with advertising on them, can openers and key chains, erasers and plastic coin purses with company names on them were in bags for each of us. Then he came back to me. He had stopped to buy a little rose-colored and white print dress for Effie, with a matching bonnet. It had a pinafore attached, and I squealed with delight. It was a great gift, and so very special. I still have Effie and the dress, and the clothes Mom made for her and, although the rubber bands that hold the doll's arms and legs onto the torso are somewhat dry, the little rose dress and matching straw hat that Dad brought home for me are still in near-perfect condition. Dad had nicknamed me "Heart" when I was born and I could feel the warmth of his love. He always called me "Heart," (or "Heart-Heart" as I would repeat it in baby talk). By the same token, my Uncle Jim, one of Dad's brothers, called me "Pumpkin." I liked that, too. I would plod around with my stomach rounded out, living up to my nickname, saying "I'm my daddy's Heart-heart and Uncle Jimmy's Pumpkin."

My classmate, a brilliant student named Carol lived nearby in a lovely English Tudor corner house. Her Dad was my mom's obstetrician, who would deliver my brother Jeff when he was born. Doctor DeCesare enjoyed making things from wood in the neat little space of his workshop. One day, he made a deal with my mom: since all of us girlfriends had Ginny Dolls, he would make a four-poster bed for Carol's doll and one for my Effie. In return for Effie's new bed, Mom would sew a canopy, a matching pillow and bedspread, and little satin sheets for both dolls' new beds. The little yellow taffeta bed spread with pillow shams had shirred yellow netting layered over it, and Mom even made tiny pillows with white satin cases trimmed with tiny lace. Carol DeCesare and Judy Erickson had upper-class, spoiled-rotten Ginny dolls.

A year or so later, my friend Claudia graduated from a Ginny doll to a 'Barbie' doll, and that grossed me out. Why would we take care of a full-grown adult doll? Barbie didn't need a mom; she could make her own dang bed. Claudia, who was a prim and proper young lady, would be the one to fill me in on sex, too. I figured that was why she got Barbie. I really wasn't interested, but I guess we were supposed to ask questions. At first, she said that you have to do 'it' every time you want a baby. I wondered what 'it' was. Later, after I had repeated that to everyone I knew, she told me, "No, you're wrong; when you get married, you only have to do 'it' once, and then you can have as many kids as you want." It sounded like I would be rewarded for getting through 'it' once. I was relieved. I was starting to get the drift of what 'it' was. She explained it in just a few words, and then she went to saying you must do 'it' every time you want a baby. Shocked, I thought, "My Mom and Dad did 'it' *seven* times!!" I left the subject untouched after that—Pollyanna in the making. Years later, I met the love of my life and found out "it" was the best thing ever.

Claudia's family lived on 7th street, a few blocks north from our house. Her Dad owned a heavy equipment company designed to take old roads out and make new ones in one fell swoop. Bill and Marie Collins would become close friends of Mom and Dad, just as Claudia and I were. I picked Claudia's Mom to be my confirmation sponsor, and Claudia picked my mom for hers. My name then became Judith Theresa Marie Erickson. I was happy. Mom and Dad dressed up for the occasion and after the ceremony at church, we all had dinner at the Collins' house. Claudia and I had to wear white as all the prospective confirmation candidates did. I can describe a Confirmation as a Catholic Bat Mitzvah.

Of course, *my* dress had rhinestones on the collar.

****

I was a good athlete, and I was good at my ballet and tap lessons. After seeing my girlfriend Mary Erpelding skate like a ballerina beautifully on an indoor rink, I dreamed of being an ice skater too.

In the winter, our neighborhood had a large ice-skating rink that was kitty-corner from our house on the south side of Fargo. The property was the baseball field of the Clara Barton Elementary School. At the start of winter, the city would come around to flood the entire field and let it freeze. One of the nice things about living in North Dakota was that once a rink was frozen, it didn't melt until winter was over. We practically lived on the rink. I started to dream of being a *great* ice skater. I taught myself to do some small 'waltz' jumps. I pretended to dance on the ice and imagined I was a ballerina, only instead of my point shoes; I had blades on my feet. My 'jumps' were only a couple of inches off the ice, but I felt as though I were airborne for wide spans. Sometimes, Claudia and I would skate full force toward a huge snow bank, then vault and tuck into the air, somersaulting just enough to land on our backs and upside down in the bank of snow. It was exhilarating. We figured if we would keep practicing, we would finally make it all the way around and land on our feet. We never did. One of our classmates, Delores did, though. So, I immediately lost interest in practicing that trick.

North Dakota has a lot of strip mining for coal, leaving a nearly invisible layer of carbon everywhere. I rarely noticed it, but I heard Mom complain that she had to clean the windowsills 'all the time'. She had never experienced soot— dust though, she had conquered and vanquished.

Sometimes, the skating rink would have a slight grittiness to it from the soot, but I didn't care. I had no idea that skate blades were so important, as I would learn later. But then, I had hardware store skates, and we would put them on in our house and walk across the street to skate without the benefit of blade guards. Hassle free sports! I loved skating so much that, even as the snow melted in spring, I would get up early while the puddles were still frozen, find a patch of ice and use it as much as I could. Sometimes it was just a small, frozen spot, where all I could do was 'spin' in my own way. And I do remember my first pair of ice skates.

It was in Menomonie, Wisconsin, at East School. Just a short jaunt from our yellow house. I was in kindergarten. Dad came home from work one night with a box full of used skates. The skates were faded and had limp ankles that folded over. We all tried on the different pairs, and the ones that fit me were figure skates. All the others were hockey skates. It didn't matter to us that the flimsy leather had no support at all, or that the skates were black. At first, on the ice, I kept tripping on the toe picks, falling and falling again. It became a challenge to get to the edge of the rink without tripping, landing on my stomach. The next day, my ribs were sore. Bellyflopping on the ice drove me to best that incompetency, and I kept trying, and soon learned to skate without letting the toe picks rule my strokes. But let's get back to Fargo.

I couldn't wait to get my chores done so I could put my skates on and get across the street. There were times when tumbleweeds would roll and slide across the rink, propelled by the winds off the flat eastern North Dakota plains. A couple of times Mom would have me bring a tumbleweed home, and it if were nice enough, she would spray paint it and sprinkle glitter over it to make a decorative piece for a Christmas corner in the dining room. She would do that with cattails, too, brushing the natural colors of the plant with matching paint. Those cattails lasted in large vases for a very long time, and they always looked fresh and pretty.

Throughout my childhood and even later, mom always had some craft idea to show us, or that she would work on herself.

In Fargo, she bought some thin, colored sheets of foil and put them on the dining room table. Several pastel colors, of shiny colors like aqua, pinks, light greens and golds. She sat me down and said, "Here, I'll show you something". She went out to the porch and brought in an armload of stems with the dangling grains dripping from the ends of each wispy thread-like stem. Then she tore small pieces of the pastel-colored foils into pinky-nail sized pieces, and painstakingly wrapped each little dangling oat grain with a different color. I copied her. Each stem had 15 to 20 of the little dangles to cover, and there were several wispy 'stems' on each larger stem. When each and every grain was wrapped, she stood them all in a vase. The gracefully moving colors shimmied in their metallic pastels, and it was a lovely sight. All it took was to walk past them, and the light weight of them shivered with their glimmer. And then there were the rainy days mom had us kids string puffed oat cereal onto toothpicks, making shapes of stick people and stick dogs to play with.

Mom really liked nice things, and managed to own Franciscan dinnerware (not an easy feat with 7 kids around)… and a few Spode china pieces along with crystal candelabras. A sewing genius, she could copy any fashion design the movie stars were wearing and her creations turned out even more beautiful and, more than likely, better sewn. (30 years later, I toured the Lyric Opera House, and saw the exquisite costumes being made and the intricate French seams and detail reminded me of mom's work.)

By the eighth grade I was in love with ballet, getting one private lesson and two classes every week throughout the eighth grade and part of high school. I don't know how Mom swung it, but I got my own ballet shoes, toe shoes, and she sewed the prettiest tutus with rhinestones attached to puff- sleeved satin tops for me. At first, I inherited my sister's tap shoes which were quite a bit too big for me. I found the length helped me 'flap' nicely, but hindered the 'shuffle' and it was impossible to kick without losing a shoe– soon, kicking off a shoe to hit a target became a game, and mom gave in. I got shoes of my own.

One night after a ballet class at the studio, which was on the second floor of a large building in downtown Fargo, I was the last one out, except for my teacher. I left my tote and coat on a folding chair in the studio and went down the hall to use the bathroom to freshen up to go straight to a basketball game at our high school. I was looking in the mirror and saw a disheveled man standing in the doorway, holding his swollen privates for me to see. I yelled out for Mary Kay (Swanston), my dance instructor. Afraid of being blocked in the small bathroom, I used my shoulder to push the man to the side and ran back to the studio a couple of doors away, where Mary Kay asked what was wrong. She looked up. He was gone. She called the police and my Dad.

Daddy came to get me and we went home to the waiting police. I tried the best I could to tell them what they wanted to know, but I was embarrassed to talk in front of my dad…or to the policemen. I could only get as far as… "He was holding his…his…naked (gulp)…thing…."

I was relieved when the police nodded and didn't pursue my answer any further, saving me from groping for the easier words. After the cops left, Dad drove me to the high school for the rest of the basketball game. There I heard about a 'flasher' in town exposing himself to everyone and anyone. I bragged that I had seen the culprit that very evening. "He was showing me his 'thing' right there in public!" I boasted.

For a time after that, we girls would walk in groups, and look over our shoulders at any sound. If we saw anyone on the sidewalk ahead of us, coming toward us, we would cross the street until that figure was a safe enough distance past. A few years later, I saw a 'tongue-in-cheek' comedy with Paula Prentiss and Richard Benjamin, and her character got flashed while walking in Central Park. Instead of getting scared, she raised her eyebrows, widened her eyes wagged her limp wristed hand like an upside-down fan, and gave a wolf whistle, confusing the flasher. I laughed out loud and wished I had had the nerve to have done that when I had been flashed.

When I was in the seventh and eighth grades at St. Anthony's, my sisters were off for a year or so, to Chicago to satisfy Mom's wishes of having some show business in the family— As if we weren't already drama queens. Joan and Jane were 2/3rds of a trio that won a contest that included a week at the Chez Paris nightclub and a "year's recording contract" with Mercury Records. They recorded a '45' for Mercury, and as the year came to a close, another '45' for a spin-off label called "Tweed"— all four songs were original and fitting the pop scene then. The Fargo part of our family had gotten listed on a Mercury record distributor's list, and so we would get one or two new 'forty-five RPM' records every few days. Mom would let me have them as soon as they arrived, and I wondered which disc jockey was missing his deliveries. I was then in eighth grade, and I would take a bunch of the little records over to Linda Rasmussen's house. Her phonograph was made especially for stacking 45s. We would set it up on the cement of their new driveway and practice dancing. We would try the jitterbug, the "Dirty Bop" (which by later standards wasn't 'dirty' at all) and all the 'in' dances. When we got good enough we would cruise the periphery of the Crystal Ballroom on Friday nights where we could watch the older kids dance up a storm. A few of my classmates were really good at pairs, and those who were 'going steady' had worked up some choreography for the "Dirty Bop." Classmates Charlotte and Mike always drew a crowd of onlookers when they danced together.

Besides dancing on the driveway at Rasmussen's house in Fargo, four of us girls would meet every Saturday after chores and play Canasta for hours. It was a long game, sometimes requiring three decks of cards, and would take as long as three hours to play. And sometimes we would play more than one game in a day, stopping to raid the fridge for lunch. Sometimes Linda's mom would make a stack of sandwiches for us so we wouldn't have to stop playing.

Record albums weren't as common as 45s. Only the big names had enough songs for an entire album. But heck, who needed albums? We could stack as many as 12 or so of '45s' on the phonograph. When the stack was finished, we would simply turn the entire pile over and let them drop and play automatically. High Tech of the early fifties…Hi-Fidelity was 'in'.

After a while, the 45s stopped coming in the mail. Maybe being on that list had really been a mistake and they corrected it. My sisters started to call home for money. They had an ongoing contract with a nightclub in Lyons, Illinois. They had played there 5 nights a week for almost a year and someone was getting tired. During that time, I got to take a train to Chicago to visit them. All three of them were living in a studio apartment on Stone St. near the Gold Coast. I was in awe. There was a little cubbie door in the wall to the hall, next to a little refrigerator, where the milkman would leave fresh milk and pick up the used bottles. We would go to the beach, using the tunnel under the outer drive and come back, where Janie would 'race' me to their floor, by using one of the two elevators. One day my sisters took me to Riverview, where the rollercoaster did not have seat belts, gravity would lift my skinny body as the coaster would start down the giant hills. Then, you could also see the ties of the tracks through the floors. I would hang on so tight at the top of the crest, and still could not stay sitting tight. I didn't like it one bit.

My sister's booking agent had kept them busy for a while, but once the contest's prize had run its course, interest waned–.not from my Mother's point of view, though. She had personal dreams 'for her kids'. The prize had come with booking agents, promoters, chaperones, publicists, and managers. Venues and live music were plentiful. Clubs evinced a full show including a chorus line, singers, comedians…Today, clubs don't come close to doing all that. Thirty years later, the closest I came to that early popular music type of evening was Gary Miller's Celebration Dixieland Band, where they mixed some rehearsed comedy acts in between the regular music performances. No chorus line, though.

But, in the eighth grade, I didn't care what my older sisters were doing, except that I liked telling my friends how they were leading a glamorous life and I could prove it by showing off the gowns Mom sewed for them. Mom could draw her idea on newspaper and make a pattern out of her design. She would go downtown to get fancy fabrics and make three matching dresses for the trio. If the fabric wasn't fancy enough, she would sit for days on end, hand-tying each sequin with a tiny bead on top of it into swirling patterns on their dresses. If she wanted a gown to have stripes, she would sew grosgrain ribbon in long, angular lines in a striped pattern that flattered their figures. I remember one ice-blue satin gown with a sweeping ribbon of beads down the front. It was so beautiful. I loved helping mom with her sewing...and I was glad to have mom and dad all to myself while my sisters were gone. The girls in the trio were very young and had a chaperone the whole time. I remember the chaperone's name was Gretchen Eisenhart. I thought they were on top of the world. On the other hand, I wanted nothing to do with their life. I was the athlete, and babysitter, and mom's helper, and was very happy with it.

When the trio wrote home for money, Mom got their local piano player and the parents of the third singer of the group to chip in with her and Dad and send them three hundred dollars. I just didn't understand that. I thought they were making money. Savvy Me.

That happened a couple of times and then, a few weeks later, Joanie called again. Mom started to cry. Joan had announced she was getting married and the trio would break up. Drama had entered my pre-teenage years big-time. My mother cried and denounced the man for crushing her dreams. The man named Joe had 'ruined her life'. From then on, Mom and Joan would tearfully blame Joe for everything. But, years later, I found out the interest wasn't there: they were too young; especially my sister Jane who was only sixteen to seventeen years old while they were in Chicago for that time. Joanie got wooed by a glamorous man who wore big diamonds on his pinky and talked loudly. He reminded us younger ones of Cesare Romero. My sister's escape came in the form of the man named Joe. I was fascinated.

Immediately, Mom asked if I would start singing. (WHAT? And give up my Effie Doll and my bicycle rides with Claudia?) Dad echoed Mom's statement and added that I was the same age as Janet Lennon of the Lennon sisters. My dad loved Janet Lennon. Geez. Janet Lennon was on TV. How could *that* happen to *me*? I would shake with anxiety when I had to answer the phone or ask a question much less sing in public. I could never do that! I had seen the messy dressing room at the nightclub. I saw the legs of the chorus girls through their torn fish-net stockings and smelled the sweaty laundry left crumpled on the floor in their haste to change and get back on stage. Costumes that looked great from the audience's point of view actually had stained armpits and torn seams. I wanted to be different from my sisters. I liked babies and living in a house. I liked sewing and taking care of my brothers. I would rather be like momma.

But Mom would plunk me down on a chair in front of the radio while she braided my pigtails, and she would have me work at harmonizing with anyone who was singing on the air. If I stopped, Mom would pull my hair very tight. Sometimes it felt like my braids were stretching my eyes into two three-inch-long slits. Two small braids started right at my temples, which then joined the larger braids at the back of my head. When she was done, it took a while before I could close my eyes tight because it felt like the lids were so taut. There was a time when her sister, my Aunt Vera, came to visit. Mom asked her to braid my hair while sitting in front of the radio, too. She must have told her to tighten up on the grip at certain times, so some of my notes became "OW" every few words. "...Or would you like to swing on a- OW! star,...Carry moonbeams OW! home in a jar...."

****

CHAPTER 3

The Reluctant Singer

I remember staring at the radio that was ensconced in the light wood entertainment unit. The blond wood matched our Story and Clark spinet piano. It was a Magnavox 19-inch TV in a console that had a sliding door that hid the adjoining radio and pullout style phonograph turntable—a Hi-Fi. The sliding door had a fake leather cover with a decorative gold squiggle imprinted around the edge of the fake leather. That television brought the black and white world of Hit Parade, Homer and Jethro, Mitch Miller, the Loretta Young Show, Lawrence Welk, Dinah Shore into our living room. And Jack Parr, Homer and Jethro and Dean Martin became familiar weekly entertainment. All those shows were variety shows which were very satisfying, and we looked forward to the next week.

The big tubes in the back of the TV were menacing. A TV repair man would work in the back of the set, while holding a mirror in his other hand over the top of the set to reflect the results of his replacing or adjusting a tube. Sometimes I would hold the mirror for him so he could use both hands. The whole scene fascinated me.

Mom and Dad would sit on the re-re-reupholstered beige couch while the rest of us would lie on our stomachs in front of the screen, propping up our chins with our hands, elbows resting on the shag carpet. I hated that shag carpet. It often stole something I dropped and wouldn't give it back. Once I dropped my jar of pennies and it took a long time to find the ones that had escaped into the vast wilderness of gold wool talons. During the next several vacuum cleanings, you would hear a penny being captured and lost forever into the dust bag.

Mom found a couple of my girlfriends' mothers and talked them into having their daughters sing with me. Libby sang lead, and Roberta and I provided harmony. We would have to wear my sister's old suits, because there were three matching ones that fit us pretty well, and then we would sing from their old three part sheet music. My sisters sang in whatever key the music was printed in. Now it seems weird to hear anyone sing those tunes in a high voice. It just doesn't work, maybe because now those songs are so much a part of the jazz repertoire, where head voices don't seem right. Libby, Roberta and I– as a trio– weren't very good and I didn't care. I would rather be at the pool or riding my bike with Claudia. I didn't want to be like my sisters. You had to spend hours in front of a mirror, acting stupid. Everybody sings. Anybody can sing. I wanted to be everything else, even a nun. Well, to my dismay, Mom arranged for her new trio to perform at a school function.

During practice, Libby, Roberta and I would start to giggle every time Libby took her solo line, "and the sweet silver song of a lark." It was from the song "You'll Never Walk Alone." Even though she did her part as the lead singer beautifully, her mouth would start to quiver when that part came due. We watched for the quiver, and it would turn into a giggle. Even if Libby didn't quiver right away, we would start giggling. It was contagious; Roberta and I would chime in, and we all laughed until we couldn't breathe, involuntarily snorting in mouthfuls of air. And just like those practices, we shamefully did the same thing on stage. We never finished the song. We got to that part of the song, the corners of our mouths would begin to shake and the three of us started laughing until we were finally ushered off the stage. Makes me think of the Gong Show. We sat at a table with heads hanging in humiliation but still breaking out in sporadic giggles if we dared to sneak a look at each other, until one of the staff stepped behind us, put her hand on our shoulders, and gave each of us a lovely pair of white gloves as a gratuity. The gloves had tatted flowers in the corners of the cuff, and Mom said they were very nice gloves because between each finger was a gusset. I felt better and, to my relief, Mom didn't badger me anymore about being in a trio. But she did have my dancing teacher make me sing a song in a dance production.

The recital was held in our High school's auditorium. My sister played the piano accompaniment. The scene was a group of kids at a soda fountain. Mom had sewn a green and white cotton dress for me, with white puff sleeves and a laced-up midriff like a corset attached to a full skirt with lots of white crinoline that puffed the skirt out. The number was choreographed as a jitterbug type of dance. I had to hop up on the soda fountain counter and sing "Saturday Night Rag" while dancing the steps that the gang of dancers mimicked on the floor. It turned out pretty good and I got a big applause. HMMM, Maybe singing wasn't so bad after all…

As I said before, we were all drama queens. Mom was an ace at tearing up, Joan cried consistently. I think it was to get the boyfriends to hug her. Mom had beautiful, light blue eyes, dark hair and fair skin. She was not one to cry in public, but, like a flirt would, she would let her eyes well up, so they would glisten. "Just like Susan Hayward", I would think in my 1950's mentality. I tried it a couple of times, but I only managed to wet my eyes thinking they were glistening…but when it came to really crying, I could spill like Niagara Falls. It wasn't pretty. I tried to follow suit. When Mom cried, I'd cry. When Joan cried, I would cry. Joanie would call Mom from Chicago, tearfully complaining about her marriage. It had been a mistake. Joanie didn't belong in the big city. She should have been home with us, where she was happy. She couldn't handle the lifestyle that her husband was used to and she didn't know how to conform. Coming from Fargo, and thrown into the big wonder-world her husband had was too difficult. The stories grew; we could have been tabloid reporters. Joe was a loud successful businessman. Joanie and Joe had a nice house, sports car and town car, furs and jewelry. She was only 21, and I thought that was how it was supposed to be. You get out of school and get married. *But Dad was killed before I was out of school, and Jane and I never had the chances that other kids would have. The security of having a roof over my head never came. Never.*

CHAPTER 4

Sundown After a Sunny Youth.

After dad died, I was feeling the usual fear of not having a place to live my whole life. I pictured myself sitting on a sidewalk with a tin cup. I hoped I would have a monkey when that time came. One of those days was when I saw the ad in our school that recruited nuns. I started getting serious about looking in on the possibility. I stood there reading the perks about the field, and started daydreaming about living in a convent. At least I would have a roof over my head. Never speaking, which would suit me just fine. Suddenly, behind me, there was one of my new teachers, a nun who had taught my oldest sister seven+ years earlier. The nun looked at me and said, "I hope you aren't as selfish as your sister Joan." It was a mean and thoughtless thing to say. That blunt blurt took me by surprise. I was humiliated. "My sister is *not* selfish." I blubbered, then turned and ran to the Chapel down the hall where you're not allowed to talk. I cried hard, releasing the dam, and let the tears accumulate in the seat of the pew in front of me. As they ran down the back of the pew on their way to the little pond forming on bench area, I hoped I could keep crying until the tears filled the pew, and I focused on that. Somehow when a 'religious' person says something like that nun did, it really burns, and I wanted it to. That way I could stay mad and have an excuse for bawling. I imagined that St. Bernadette must have cried a lot for being humiliated by those around her. I forced myself to keep crying, sometimes the drama brought ideas from watching the movie stars crying delicately on the leading man's shoulder.

A little sniff, a slight head toss, a shudder…shiny spots on the guy's suit coat from your tears and wet nose that you pretend aren't there… "Oh, look, now I've ruined your suit". Then she would take his hanky, and she would blow her nose and hand it back.

The release of tears felt good. As I remember this episode, it dawns on me that maybe I was grieving over my dad's death. I had no sense of maturity, so I lost myself in tears. Maybe when there were enough tears, I would look for a Popsicle stick and float it back and forth in the pew-pond. Maybe I would even call Janie, who would come there and sit at the other end of the pew-pond with *her* Popsicle stick. I walked over to the holy water font and scooped up a palm full and added it to the 'pond'. I didn't want to grow up. Ever. The tears were still coming, a bit slower, but my face was red and swollen. A nun came in and knelt beside me. She didn't say a word about the lake in the pew in front of me. She asked why I was so sad. I didn't tell her. After all, martyrs don't rat on their persecutors. Growing up was not my forte.

****

CHAPTER 5

On to the Early Years in Chicago. 1960- 19-

I stayed at my sister's house in La Grange while earning some money to get my own place. Brother-in-law Joe would sometimes be going downtown at the same time I would leave for work at the Recorders Office. At that time, he had a Lincoln town car, and sometimes he hired his cousin to pose as his driver. When Joe drove me to the LaSalle Street side entrance of the County Building in that big black limo, I imagined that people thought I was connected to the mayor somehow. I would get out of the town car and clip clop through the revolving door in my spikes and go to the typing pool in the Recorder's Office. One night Joe said he could pick me up and give me a ride back to La Grange, too. Usually, I took the Blue Bird Bus.

On the way home he took lower Wacker Drive, and he pulled up to a swarthy looking man and rolled his window down halfway. He started talking to him in a low voice. I was in the passenger seat, watching the exchange, Joe introduced me as 'his sister-in-law' (with no name). I said hello to the man's pock marks. Then we drove away and Joe said, "You know who that was?" I didn't. He looked at me showing his long, nicotine stained front teeth, with the corners of his mouth turned up. "Well, he had better watch his back, he's walking on thin ice." Two slogans in one sentence! I figured he got them from my mother's stash. Then, in my young, slightly addled mentality, I also thought he was full of baloney and that it was just another one of his made-up stories to impress young people. Joe was a genius in a business sense, but he was also full of colorful stories— some made up and some not. Either way, he was the 'dad' in my life for that short time. I loved being around him.

The next day, the paper had a picture of a crime scene. A body had been found in the trunk of a car on lower Wacker drive. I looked at the picture, and it looked just like the man who had come up to the car and talked to us. I convinced myself it was, and the car looked like Joe's, but it wasn't...it just *looked* like his. At least I think it did. The savvy kid from Fargo ND.

Often, when we were eating dinner at my sister's house, Joe would refuse to sit with his back toward the window. Before the incident on Lower Wacker Drive, I didn't believe his hot- shot reasoning; I figured he just got a kick out of seeing our reactions to his statements. But since then, I pretend to understand. (Hey, I saw Goodfellas.) The way Joe told his adventures, though, was always more colorful and lightweight, no matter how loud he hollered, so whoever would listen could choose to believe it or not. At that time, he was the only color in my life. The only.

CHAPTER 6

Back to the Safe World in Fargo...

Before the death of my dad, life was getting to a place where those of us living in Fargo were a real family, living a happy, normal life. Norman Rockwell subjects, if you will. There were picnics in Lindenwood Park, music lessons, and swimming pools, afternoons of tennis with my friends, visiting neighbors and babysitting jobs for teens. Dad would sometimes Bar-B-Q in our side yard for us and for our visitors. His accountant, Harvey Engbretson and his wife Sylvia were often over to help with the barbeque, play charades or to watch TV.

Charades was **the** game. The rules were followed to a tee, with one on each team watching the second hand of their wind-up wristwatch, and the game provided a lot of laughs. We kids were pretty good at it, but Harvey was the funniest player. He was the most uninhibited and we loved it when it was his turn. Mom, Dad, Harvey and Sylvia were great friends. After Dad died, Sylvia and Harvey moved to the town that mom moved to for her second marriage. Then some years later, Sylvia and Harvey moved to International Falls and Sylvia stayed there long after Harvey passed away. After that move, Sylvia never missed sending me a Christmas card and note for the next 12- some years. I recently got in touch with her kids via Face Book and learned that Mary, her daughter looks in on her these days.

In Fargo, two doors away from our corner house, I often would babysit for the Scheel kids. Mr. Scheel owned a hardware store downtown Fargo and drove a beautiful Jaguar. It was black with the long-curved fenders like the Munster's family car that I would notice years later. But it wasn't comical. It was elegant. I loved to ride in it. A body wouldn't even lean when the Jag turned a corner. Mrs. Scheel was a striking lady with strawberry blonde hair, and her children Steve and Becky looked like her. Bobby was the youngest and I couldn't say who he looked like the most. Mrs. Scheel hired me to babysit. The three Scheel kids were well brought up, and easy to take care of, and I wound up sitting in the kitchen most of the time reading or just staring out the window, telling the kids to play nice and having them wash their hands when they came inside. Even though I was told I could take a bottle of pop, I rarely did, and then I would put the empty bottle back just where it came from. Mom always said to leave a room as clean or cleaner than when you came into it. If I took a piece of wrapped candy, you would never know I disturbed the pile. Sometimes if there were a dish of chocolate, I would take one from the middle and rearrange the pieces to look as though none were missing. Once I figured out that was a sneaky move, I brought my own treats from home with me to their house.

When the famed tornado passed over our end of Fargo and then destroyed much of the North side of the city, along with our brand-new high school, Mr. Scheel got his big camera out and shot a picture of the funnel just as soon as it was safe to go outside. I believe one of his pictures was featured in the newspapers and in our yearbook. That tornado had threatened during the afternoon.

Just before the tornado came, my girlfriend Maryanne Murphy was visiting, and we began to walk to her house from mine. The leaves on the trees were eerily still and there wasn't one sound. Not one bird chirped. The air was so still and had a yellow cast. We got spooked and hurried back to my house because it was closer than hers was. Her parents had a lovely ranch style home in a pretty neighborhood a few blocks away.

We just got in the house when Dad pulled up in front of the house, shot out of the car, ran up to the door and said to get down to the basement. My brothers and MaryAnn and I went to the basement, while Mom and Dad ran around the house opening windows. When I asked them why, they said so that the glass wouldn't break from the pressure... an old wives tale, I found out later. We huddled in the basement next to the canned fruit cellar, which was a separate cement closet. My 3 brothers stood wide eyed huddled close, while Mom held Jeffrey. Maryanne and I giggled. Someone suggested we get in the canning cellar. I refused. I had seen a centipede run in there and I would rather face the tornado. I had not only *seen* the centipede, but I *heard* it run over a newspaper with the bionic pitter patting of a jillion tiny feet. The Tornado was over us.

Our house seemed to shudder slightly, and the funnel sounded like a freight train was passing through. It was deafening. Then it was over, and a heavy rain started. Maryanne tried to call her parents to say she was ok. Back then we had 4 digit phone numbers. 6284. A bit later they had to add a 2 in front of that and then later, 'Adams', to include A D. It became 'Adams-2-6284' Big city living. We weren't allowed to use the phone unless it was for necessary calls. It took me 40 years to finally allow myself to use a phone for any lengthy conversations.

After the storm's noise dimmed, we went outside just in time to see the funnel touch down on the north side. It was too far for us to guess that, but we heard it on the news. It had wrecked our beautiful new high school and some nearby neighborhoods. One entire family of children was wiped out along with their home. I think their last name was Munson. The row of small caskets at the funeral was pictured on the front page of the Fargo Forum. It is an indelible boggling memory. It didn't touch the South side of Fargo, and except for having no phones or electricity for a while, we weren't out of anything else that a new teenager would notice.

Dad's route to the Lumberyard had not gotten hampered, and none of us had any idea of the hardships the North side neighborhoods suffered. We weren't allowed to go to the North side to see our friends or the school; because of downed electrical and telephone lines and other rubble.

The National Guard was out in full force to prevent looting in the damaged area of town. Once again, rules would be broken. My girlfriends and I sneaked to the area and tried to avoid getting near any loose lines and we would keep an eye out for any National Guardsman. We had to climb over obstacles of trees and telephone poles for blocks before we got the shock of seeing our school with the huge, gaping hole through the side of what was the new gymnasium on the second floor. The floor, even though it was cement with steel girders supporting it, seemed to feel soft and unsure beneath our feet. It felt as squishy as the lower level where the post tornado downpour flooded the halls and lockers and science rooms. Those science rooms were 'garden' height, so that when you were taking classes in them, we still had the benefit of light from full sized windows at grass level.

That year, I took general science instead of home-Economics because I was more comfortable in a boy's world. I was used to being one of the boys. After all, my two older sisters were referred to as "the girls," and we referred to my 4 younger brothers as "the boys." I was somewhere in between, and I truly enjoyed being the only girl at home for the few years that I had Mom and Dad to myself, having only to look after 'the boys' and the foster babies.

One morning during general science class we heard a lot of yelling and whooping as books, notebooks, portfolios, pens and pencils rained down on the grass at eye level for us.

As quickly as it started, the same roaring crowd charged down the staircases and invaded the mess and picked everything back up. It had been Coach Sid Cichy's class. The entire room had planned it for the minute Sid got a call from the office and I think the entire mess was cleaned up and the kids were back in their desks by the time Mr. Cichy got back to the room minutes later. It was a fast maneuver and I heard it was successful. Another time, during my history class period, Mr. Cichy got an apple from each of a few students. They lined the apples up on his desk and waited for the office to announce that he got a call. When the announcement came over the P.A., he had just gotten out the door when everyone who brought him an apple ran up to his desk and took a big chomp out of it, then set it back on Sid's desk. When he returned, he stood to speak, looked at the apples— now with gaping white and brown-tinged craters, and said, "Indian-givers" and continued his instruction. We all loved him for that. Besides, he had coached our football teams into championships year after year. Later, in the national media, the legendary Roger Marris would applaud his alma mater coach and school, and by the time Sid retired after many years of coaching the 'Deacons', he would have a 231-38-3 record from 1948 to 1977. The Fargo native also notched 11 undefeated seasons and won 15 state titles and will have had 17 straight championships at Shanley. We were proud to be freshmen during those championships at Shanley High and every game was a thrill.

I didn't know that my life would soon unravel. *Everything* would change. The best way I can get through this next part is by inserting a copy of a story I wrote several years after my Dad's sudden, untimely accident. It was an event that changed all of our lives completely. The changes weren't good.

******

> *News: Harold Erickson killed in car accident. September 3, 1957. He was 40 years old. He is survived by his 40 year old wife Johanna Fernholz Erickson, daughters Joan, 21, Jane 18, Judy 14, and 4 sons, Joel, 11, Jon 8, James 5 and Jeffrey, 2.*

It would be many years later that I would write about this huge change in our lives. I will have been in my second marriage, and taking a writing workshop with the venerable Harry Mark Petrakis. I wanted to honor my mother in a way no one else could. This is the finished piece published 8 years after it was written as a college project:

Arcadia news Leader, 1988

> *Usually, trips to my mother's house in Minnesota are planned at least a couple of weeks in advance. This time, a last minute idea making the trip from Chicago to St. Paul came from an Amtrak advertisement in the newspaper.*
>
> *My children had never ridden on a train, and now they were having a short vacation from school with no particular plans. Spontaneously, we decided to surprise my mother by making the trip unannounced.*
>
> *We hired a taxi to get from the train station to her house. The front door was unlocked.*
>
> *"Hi, Mom," I yelled as I walked into the house with my two children in tow.*
>
> *"Judi!" she exclaimed, "Your timing is perfect." She smiled impishly as she continued. "I have to arrange a trip to Canada for my 55+ club and supervise the church dinner this week, so you can take over my column for me this week. My boss wants a human interest story this time, preferably about someone from this area." Mom writes for the town's weekly newspaper, and for her church's newsletter. She usually used the column to write about her senior citizen's club.*

On one hand I was flattered. As a writing student, I was being a given a professional assignment. On the other hand, I was disappointed. This was her greeting after not seeing us for almost five months.

Now, anyone who knows my Mom knows that when she's around things get done; many things— sometimes all at once! If I weren't there to take the assignment for her, she would have found a way to hand one in anyway... church dinner or no church dinner, club trip or no club trip.

My children got busy with my two youngest brothers while I considered Mom's request to do her newspaper assignment. I explained that I had hoped to go north for a day or two, to take a leisurely look around our old hometown.

We compromised. I would go for a day, and take her notebook along.

The next morning, I boarded a North Central airplane and turned to say goodbye to my children, my Mom and her husband.

I was on my way, unwinding a clock, turning the years back to the 1950's. After 20 years absence, I returned to Fargo, North Dakota, a town where I had spent some of the most important and devastating maturing years of my life.

As the plane landed at the small airport, I had the feeling that this trip would mean a lot to me. A rental car was waiting.

As I drove south on 7th Street I saw that very little had changed. Finding the old house that our large family had shared long ago would be an easy task.

I came to the corner of 15th avenue and 7th street. The house was still there. A new coat of paint had changed it from white to beige, and there were new steps to the front door.

I parked the rented car and took a slow walk from one end of the premises to the other.

Turning the corner, my pulse quickened as I realized I was looking for something. Each step in that direction was a step back in time. As I walked along the side of the house, I realized how clearly I could remember the oak tree in the back yard.

It was big enough to hold two or three of us on each half of its forked trunk. The tree was like part of our family. It was where my brothers would go to share their secrets and where I would sit to hoard my dreams.

As I looked back, I thought that the tree's strength and its outstretched branches described my life in this house. The tree's fate was my fate, as well as my brothers'.

One fall day in 1957, (Mom and Dad had gone to visit grandma in Wisconsin, it was my oldest sister's wedding anniversary, and they were coming up from Chicago. I was appointed babysitter for four days. They had taken brother#3 with them because he had a chronic ear infection, and it was inflamed. A few minutes after they left, they came back to the house because they forgot to bring a bottle of water for Jimmy...Mom was holding the ailing Jimmy in her arms and Dad parked right in front of our house, came up to the door and handed me the baby bottle and asked me to fill it. I did and brought it back to him. As I handed it to him, he said "Goodbye, Heart".) For some reason unknown to me, I didn't include this last paragraph in my story...I've told it but didn't put it in print. I don't know why; but I am glad I am re-reading it now.

They were only gone for a couple of days and this day; my younger brothers and I were eating cookies in the kitchen of this house. Through rain splattered windows we watched the big oak tree sway in the increasing breeze.

"How strong our big oak is," Jonny mused as he popped a crumb of cookie into his mouth. The leaves began to shiver and flap against the rising wind and rain.

I got up from the table to get some milk, and poured each of us a fresh glassful. By then, our tree was gyrating in the downpour. We told each other that this tree could defy any threat, win any fight for survival.

Suddenly, there was someone knocking at our front door. Startled, I jumped up and pulled baby Jeff out of the high chair. With him in my arms I went toward the desperate hammering noise and just then a deafening bolt of lightning split the oak tree smack down the middle, and one side cracked off.

My wide-eyed brothers huddled around me; we looked from the window to the front entry when Aunt Vera pushed the door open and came into the house.

Rain had smeared her mascara and her shoes squished with each step she took. Her face was drawn with pain, and she hesitated before she spoke.

Impulsively, she gave me a hug, took a deep breath and said, "Get the boys' clothes changed. You have to go to Wisconsin right away. Your Daddy was in a terrible accident."

I didn't have to ask if he were alive.

I wanted to scream and run out to the back yard and climb my oak tree to be alone. But our tree was for dreaming; there was no more branch to sit on.

My legs wouldn't take me there. My mouth wouldn't open, and most assuredly, I was very alone.

I turned my head to look out the window. I couldn't see the leaves to my tree anymore.

Aunt Vera was waiting for us. We all followed her out into the rain to our uncle's waiting car. As we filed into the back seat, I turned to see the dismembered limb of our oak tree lying in the mud with brutal marks where the lightning had torn it away.

Fargo was a railroad hub that supported nearly every passenger or freight train that was running. Ben and Vera got us all to the station and on the Northern Pacific to head to Winona and be picked up there and taken to Arcadia. My brothers and I sat together in the two bench-seats that faced each other, and Janie rode alone with strangers across the aisle. She was able to strike up a conversation and I could hear her talk about Dad's accident. The boys squirmed and slept, and I could tell they knew something horrible had happened. I don't remember who picked us up in Winona, but mom was there. Little Jimmie was being taken care of by the aunts in Arcadia. The ride to Arcadia was barely tolerable. My brothers slept sporadically. My jaw stayed tight making my throat muscles ache. My eyes stayed dry. A tremendous pounding inside my head increased with every mile of road we overtook. When we finally arrived in Arcadia, trance-like figures took over in slow motion. We were shown where we would eat and where we would sleep. We were at Aunt Delores's house. There were relatives all around us.

They told us to eat. "Get something in her stomach-she needs some strength", a far-off voice said...The town doctor who knew everyone who had ever been born in Arcadia took a look at us. I was caught in a whirlpool, reaching out for my brothers and they for me. We came close to grasping one another, but other forces, people, pulled us apart. It was a living nightmare.

At the funeral, I didn't notice the crowds until Aunt Vera mentioned them. My grandfather had once been sheriff of Trempealeau County. After him, my uncle became sheriff. I supposed the crowds could be attributed to that fact— and of course the deceased's young age drew many people, too. Dad was only 40, he would have been 41 in 3 more months.

Outside the church, I looked around. I ignored the coffin being carried through an archway of swords held by uniformed men. I drifted along with my mother and my brothers into the waiting limousines*. The train of slowly moving cars arrived at Calvary Cemetery. My brothers and I stood in a neat row with our mother, joined by our married sisters.

The small town of Arcadia doesn't really have limousines for this purpose, but my brother in law Joe from Chicago made sure they were there to accommodate the family.

We stood silently with elbows touching, bodies ready to burst. I looked for Aunt Vera and saw her standing close behind my mother. Each of us children were handed a rose, the soldier broke the stem of my mother's rose. They folded up the flag, removed the crucifix from the coffin and handed these two things to my mother. Taps echoed in the surrounding hills. That ordeal was over. Another ordeal was about to start.

The rest of that day is blurred memory. I only know I did not look forward to the trip back home to Fargo.

The ride back to North Dakota was as torturous as the ride to Wisconsin had been. No one knew what to talk about. Everyone was afraid to speak. No matter what was said, the subject always turned to something about our dad and the mention of his name was surreal and painful.

Finally, one of my brothers turned to me and asked, "Do you think we'll ever be able to climb our oak tree again?' "Of course," I answered, trying to appear assured. But in my heart, I knew I could never use our tree again. My dreams were broken along with the tree's fractured trunk. Exhausted, I fell asleep for the rest of the trip.

When we reached home, mother nursed our emotional wounds for a few days and then got the four of us situated at school. I slightly remember Grandma Erickson coming to stay with us for a few days: Daddy's mom. She was always patient, quiet and as helpful as she could be. I remember watching her darn socks. It felt good to sit next to her. Dad was a piece of her. With the new school year starting, there would only be one child left at home. I never really appreciated Mom's spunk until then. She had her own ways of pumping up her taxed emotions and those of her children.

I opened my eyes as the stewardess stopped at my seat with refreshments. I was back in the present, on a plane back to Minnesota. It was dark outside the window. I accepted a 7-Up, then stood to stretch my legs.

I sat down, pulled out the notebook Mom had supplied me with when I left that morning, and began to write the following:

"At first glance, my mother looks like any other petite, fair skinned lady. But give her a chance, and her countenance will fill a room...or a town, for that matter. She can organize whole parishes, put business back in the black, maintain clubs that she creates and contribute hours of weekly charity work. Loved and envied by her peers, this miniature tornado with translucent blue eyes continues to raise a family she started almost 40 years ago. Her abundance of capabilities emerged most significantly over 20 years ago, during a particular episode in her youthful marriage. That story begins with my father's untimely death and the days that followed. How she coped with the predicament and grief formed a memory that will linger clear and unopposed by time in my mind's eye.

At 14, I was the oldest of 5 children left at home at the time of Dad's fatal car accident, and the only daughter at home. I remember the hopeless void we felt at first and forever, and I knew Mom felt it too. I could tell when she would go down to the basement to pack away Dad's golf clubs or some of his clothes. She would come back into the kitchen with red swollen eyes. Mom wouldn't cry in public. I copied her and cried alone.

Then, one day, I saw a difference. Instead of looking defeated, she returned to the kitchen radiating determination. She had realized she needed a diversion that dictated we supply love and time and energy to others.

We had a chance to help ourselves and help others too. I followed suit.

The first foster baby Mom brought home was an American Indian baby. She asked us to take turns at giving each baby a temporary name. I began the trend by naming the first one "Ricky." He had stick-straight black hair and a smile that caught our love and kept it. "Yep," we all agreed with kid's satisfaction, "He looks like a Ricky should look."

During one period that lasted about six weeks, Mom was asked to take care of three foster babies at the same time. Delicate twin girls who we named Mary and Marie occupied two of the bassinets. They were playful and healthy, a delightful pair of cherubs.

Little "Joseph" used the third bassinet. My brothers named him that because they were sure, with Mom's suggestion, that Joseph was a saint. A newborn, Joseph had come from the hospital where he had just undergone major surgery. His little body was born with a 'disconnected esophagus'. The doctors didn't give him much hope for living, but Mom had other ideas. She attended to his surgery lesion with the dexterity of a nurse, and soon he as well enough to be put up for adoption.

I looked forward to getting home from school every day to see what antics my little brothers were performing, what new things the babies had learned, and I wanted my turn at cuddling them.

Taking care of the orphans helped our days become meaningful and valuable again. But we had our sad moments, too.

Each time a baby was adopted I would cry with grief over the loss. Perhaps this was an outlet for the tears I had held back when daddy died, unshed tears that had been replaced by love for these little strangers who had no parents of their own.

Ours was the busiest family on the block. Neighbors would come to visit and console us, then leave impressed by Mom's successfully run house. Our neighbors, the Scheels, whose children I had babysat, supplied us with new strollers from their store, and Claudia's parents who owned Collins Road construction provided us with a new washing machine. One day, my classmate Carole DeCesare came over with a beautiful orange angel food tube cake, trimmed with beautiful, yellow, real roses, and I wondered if she still had her Ginny doll with the canopy bed that matched my Effie doll's.

It was Mom, who filled our days with the importance of concern for others. Without her guidance, those days would have contained dreadful hours of self-pity and emptiness.

Although she had a limited formal education, her intuition, common sense, and selflessness surpassed that of any professional psychologist. That's how I see it. She had an idea that first seemed illogical because we had our own large family to give our attention to, but it turned out to be realistically creative, sensitive, and fulfilling for me. Today I know we loved those babies because of who they were, and because they provided an escape from the horror of our Father's death. I am just as sure that Mom intuitively knew what she was doing for us those days she brought Ricky, Mary, Marie, Danny and Joseph, David and Linda into our lives. Each of those children was far more deprived than any of us."

I put my pen into my purse, and after the plane landed in ST. Paul, and the other passengers were slowly leaving, I looked over my essay and decided it would be the human-interest story to submit for Mom's column.

Looking up, I found I was the only person left on the plane. The stewardess smiled as she patiently stood near the exit.

I closed my notebook and minutes later, I was walking down the ramp to Gate 3. Mom was waiting. I grinned. She said the kids were at home, my daughter Johanna was asleep and Bill was playing Monopoly with his uncles.

Then she asked, "Did you think of something to write about, Judi?"

I leaned against her as I had so often before. Then putting my arm around her shoulders, I answered quietly, "I sure did, Mom, I sure did."

****

It was a good story, and one that would not only get published nearly 28 years after Dad's death, but again after Mom's death another 30+ years later than that. There is a whole lot more to those months after Dad died, and I would like to put a few interesting facts to paper.

I still managed to be involved in school activities, even though I had to come home after school most of the time. The boys and the foster babies needed someone to look after them when mom left for her evening job. I am not sure how Mom did it, but she sewed a beautiful wardrobe for me for school using the finest fabrics from the store I went to work in. I had gotten a job from my boyfriend's mother who owned the Necchi-Elna Sewing Machine distributorship and fabric store. Before that I worked as a switchboard operator at Sears, serving as a receptionist, and an order taker. It was one of those switchboards that operated by plugs on long Bungee-type cords, just like the switchboard in the Lilly Tomlin sketches. Only I didn't say "Ny-en" for "9" like she did. I did, however, mis-say my boss's name. His name was Mr. Bisch. Like 'Bish'. Of course, I got so nervous when I had to hook his line up while he was standing and watching over my shoulder; I answered him with "Yes, Mr. Bitch" and immediately shrunk down into a tiny pulsing bone hoping to disappear entirely.

At the Necci-Elna Store I learned how to sell, measure, give sewing advice, to demonstrate and sell sewing machines, and some other jobs. The owner was Wilma Blow and she had her own TV show on WDAY in Fargo. Wilma was a fabulous sewer; of course...it was her business. She showed me how to monogram, too, for customers who ordered it. She let me decorate the show room windows. She even let me try my hand at bookkeeping when her regular bookkeeper was away. I liked trimming the windows better. She tried to get me to take a job at WDAY, where they were looking for a children's show 'teacher' with a magic mirror..."I see Johnny, I see Mary, I see Bobby...etc.", in a lady-like singsong voice. I was sure I would have giggled throughout, and I chickened-out of the interview. I felt pretty safe at the sewing machine and fabric store. Every week I would take a couple of dollars from my paycheck over to the shoe store to pay on some ballet shoes I had put on lay away. *Lay-away: the predecessor to charge accounts.* My paycheck from the Sewing Machine maven was not hard earned. I had fun working at that store.

Now, Mom…*no one* could handle a sewing machine like she did. Her machine was pedal energy…not electric, and she had the fastest feet in town. She helped me sew soft woolen slacks for myself and showed me how to cut the fabric so plaids would match at the seams. She showed me how easy it is to line slacks. She would ask me what I'd like, then she'd make a pattern for it out of newspaper and put together the most beautiful gowns for proms and homecoming. For my high school homecoming coronation dress, (I was runner up) she took the lead from my favorite character, Cinderella, and drew it first, then explained what she would do. The bodice was white brocade, as was the apron-like skirt that gathered into a bustle with a big, beautiful bow over a cascade of chiffon tiers peeking from under the part of the apron-front that was drawn back. The bust had matching chiffon gathered and narrowed over the shoulder with a flat square knot. It was beautiful. When we had first moved to Fargo, Mom treated me for my birthday by taking me to see the movie Cinderella." It was a wondrous afternoon of quality time alone with Mom. We then walked over to the Ben Franklin, and she said I could pick out a toy I wanted. I saw a wind up plastic duplicate of the Prince waltzing with Cinderella (wearing my look-alike dress)…. And I have that little keepsake now standing next to a picture of me sitting on Mom's lap when I was a baby.

At the end of my senior year she sewed a fabulous formal for me to wear to a special dance: our senior prom. She took me with her when she bought the material and insisted on using slipper satin for a matching coat and the sash of the dress. She didn't see the fabric she wanted at Necci-Elna, so we went to a couple of other fine fabric stores, De Lendrecies and then Moody's where she drew a breath when she saw what she wanted. It was rich dark emerald, green satin brocade with the top layer of brocade in a slightly lighter shade of emerald green. The Slipper satin matched the brocade, and she lined the matching coat in a white furry lining. The gown had enough yardages in the skirt to create a full circle nearly twice! How she sewed the gathering on that dress so perfectly is a mystery to me. The scoop neck is timeless and to this day when I look at the outfit,

I long to have that little 23-inch waist again, just to put that formal on one more time. If I could wear it now, I would want to sweep out onto a big stage singing Dinah Shore's theme song, " SEE the <u>U</u> <u>S</u> <u>A</u>...In your **CHEV-**ro- let.... America is asking you to call"...Then take a big twirl to show off the dress. I guess I'll have to wait for my next life to do that...I still have that gown.

CHAPTER 7

Lost In a Fog

I started my sophomore year a week after Daddy died. I couldn't focus much and as I said, I liked to get home as soon as school was out. I had to take jobs to help pay for my tuition at our Catholic High School, and for my class ring and other things. But I would rather be at home with my brothers and the babies.

Every day my oldest sister would call mom and complain about her marriage. She was only in her early twenties, and she didn't have to pay a bill or worry about a mortgage or food or clothes. She had a house, and we were trying to keep ours. She had cars and we had to buy an old one that wound up burning up in our driveway! Spontaneous combustion, the fire department said. My sister had no idea of what kind of insecurity the rest of us felt letting everyone know how Dad's death affected *her*…not how it affected us younger ones, or me as a teenager—I was so frightened of not having a house to live in. I heard all of Mom's woes and knew all her problems. She didn't need any of us telling her ours, so I resented those phone calls.

Soon after Dad's funeral, I was sitting in 'the girls' bedroom upstairs of our house and distinctly 'heard' Daddy's car door close. It was six PM; and he always came home from work at that hour when we would have supper. You could set the clock and the table by it. I distinctly 'heard' his footsteps walking across the lawn, and 'he' would pause at the front steps, probably to put his cigarette out. It was so real that I ran from upstairs window to window to 'see' him. Of course, he wasn't there, and I sat alone in the bedroom and cried long and hard and alone. My sunny childhood had eclipsed.

During my Senior Year at Shanley, I had a boyfriend, Dave, who belonged to a car club. I liked being with the man-boys and helped with refurbishing an old pickup truck that I would later try racing in the powder puff derby. I learned how to drive using that truck with a straight shift. I remember having to stop at a light on an incline and I would sweat with fear that I might roll backward when my foot came off the brake. It was a chance that I would let go of the clutch too early and the engine would die or lurch. Lurch *and* die. I didn't like hills while driving "Dumbo", the name Dave gave his truck. Not that our end of North Dakota had any serious inclines. Otherwise, I could lay rubber with the best of them. That truck had no power steering, no power anything, except for the touchy engine, which had been bored out to 352 cubic inches. After a while, I was able to let the clutch ease up while my right foot gently worked the accelerator. 'Dumbo' was deep purple with white pin-striping on it. Dumbo's owner David had a white naugahyde tarp made to fit the bed of the truck. It made the Rod and Custom magazine when a photographer snapped a picture of it at a car show. Dumbo never won any prizes in the car shows, but I always enjoy telling the story about how, when we sunk a new '56 Packard engine into his '54 Ford pickup truck, and removed the rocker arm covers, we found a new wrench laying inside, where we think it had been left from the assembly line that it came from, as though it were a gift. The "Swanks" car club was a fun experience; I still have the green translucent plastic calling card. It says: You have just been assisted by a member of the Swanks of Fargo and Moorhead. At any given time, the members of the clubs would stop and help anyone with road or car trouble of any kind, and then leave the card with the recipient of that help. It was sort of a 'contest' between the car clubs to see how many people they could help out. Some of the members of both clubs had beautifully customized cars. Some could afford to have theirs chopped or channeled or both. I remember Jerry Quam's hotrod; after the customizing of the metal work, he took it all the way out to California on a trailer just to have it painted 'Candy Apple Red' by none other than the creator of the color, George Barris. (Funny how I remember that detail) The shiny cinnamon red with mirror-deep layers of that special red was a sight to behold as it crept slowly down Broadway while 'cruising' downtown Fargo. Hollywood glass pack duals on the cars created muffler music to us. When we went to Detroit

Lakes in the summer, where many of my classmate's parents had summer homes, my friends that were boys and I would sit on the fence in the dark and listen for cars. When one was coming, we would guess the type of muffler it had. I could always pick out the Hollywood dual glass-packs coming toward us out of the dark. I doubt anyone would consider that an accomplishment now.

The remnants of my life in Fargo were about to be swept away. By my senior year at Shanley, a gentleman from St. Joseph Minnesota was calling on Mom, and she liked him. He really was a good man, and my brothers 'needed a father'. Years before, Dad and Mom and Al and his wife were friends in St. Joseph, MN. Alloys Staller had lost his wife a year before my dad died. When Mom told me that Al gave her a 'tingle' when he kissed her, it made me uncomfortable, and I didn't know what to say. I went into denial; I just wanted my own Dad back. Mom stayed in Fargo 'so that I could finish high school and graduate from Shanley', and she then married Al Staller and then we all moved back to St. Joseph, Minnesota.

CHAPTER 8

Growing Up Is Hard to Do

In St. Joe, at Al's house, Mom asked me if I wanted to go to college. The government would have paid for it because Dad was a WW2 veteran. When he died he left 5 of us 7 children under the age of 18, which allowed us Social Security as long as we remained in school. I knew I would have had to have a job anyway, so I took office machines 101 and secretarial training at St. Ben's College in St. Joseph. I got a job right away at Fingerhut Manufacturing in St. Cloud. At that time, Fingerhut manufactured solely car and truck seat covers. Now they have an entire mail order catalog. Even then, though, it was a very large company. I was hired as the Personnel secretary. Mr. Cramer, the Personnel Manager was a very nice boss, and he had me learn how to interview and train, and eventually how to fire employees. He had me learn what the security guards were supposed to do, and how to check up on their rounds by checking the check points. He was a short, jolly man, and pronounced the word 'desk' as 'dest'. He was gently chided by his peers for that lisp, and we all got a friendly kick out of it. The first time I was asked to make an announcement over the PA, my voice came over so loud I saw him jump straight up from the chair at his dest.

It was after about a year of being a secretary that I took a vacation and went to Chicago to visit my oldest sister. There I met a handsome young man. Mom would have said I was 'ga-ga' over him. He was tall and slender; an athlete with athletic awards in swimming and gymnastics, and he worked for his Dad who owned the Speed Queen company that manufactured the first fiberglass speedboat. My brother-in-law Joe had his own tool and die company and collaborated with William Horvath Sr. on building an amphibious boat for recreation, using Will's fiberglass and speedboat building knowledge. It was while I was dating his handsome son, Bill Horvath that I became infatuated with Chicago, and with Bill. After working a while longer at Fingerhut, I decided to return to Chicago to live.

I stayed at my sister's and her husband's house in La Grange Illinois, and when my nephew arrived into the world, I was asked to stay to help my sister with babysitting. I was happy with that, it was a house, it was family, and it was a roof over my head, and holding my baby nephew reminded me of all the foster babies from a few years before. It felt good.

I continued dating Bill and we soon decided to get married. Actually, I think my Mom had some say in that. But I needed a home life. Since Dad died, I had no home. I mistakenly thought that by getting married I would automatically have one. We were too young, and I was too small-town for Bill. By the time we discerned that, I was pregnant with our son. I figured, well this is what I am meant to be, a mom, and I know how to do that. It was the one thing I knew was real. Bill and I rented the upstairs of an old farmhouse in Cold Spring Minnesota…a house that literally sat in the middle of a cornfield. Bill would have some of his Chicago friends come to visit, and we would joke about the sounds the field mice were making by scurrying back and forth between the walls. One of his friends brought a kitchen table for us, which we needed. It wouldn't fit up the narrow staircase, so they hoisted it up on the first floor roof and expected me to open the window to our kitchen of our second floor apartment. I went to the window and noticed that a Minnesota spider had nested between the screen and the window. Bill yelled to me, "Open the window!" while balancing the table on the pitched roof. I stared at the spider and shook my head no, terrified. He yelled again. I shook my head, watching to see if the spider would move. I said, "I can't open the window. It might come in!" He said, "then step on it." I had been prancing around in my ballet shoes, and there was no way I would get spider juice on them. Finally, I heard Bill tell his friend to hold the table while he came in. Now I was afraid of him *and* the spider. He impatiently opened the window and I squeaked. He pushed the spider out the window and looked at me and smiled. They somehow managed to finagle that table through the opening. I was happy. I had a handsome husband and a beautiful baby boy and my own kitchen table. Mom managed to furnish us with other necessary pieces of furniture. I had friends and my own life to build. I was 20 years old. I named my son after his father, and gave him my dad's middle name which was also the name of my first brother, Joel, William *Joel* Horvath. Somehow, I thought that as we got older, we would magically buy a nice house, then a nicer one and so on, and I would have more children, and have my own flower gardens and wear a pinafore apron, and welcome my husband home to a warm dinner and clean house every night, just like my mom, or just like in the movies.

Instead, our marriage folded. No white picket fence for us! Some years later, when I took writing courses in college, I would write a play about a broken picket in the (fence of the American Dream). The play was good and got good reviews from the teachers and students. It's tucked away in a file cabinet with some other things I wrote but never published.

My son Billy was and is my whole life. I just wish I had been able to give him everything he deserved. I was young, and with empty pockets, and didn't know how to plan for his life. In spite of everything, today he is a successful, self-sufficient, hardworking man with a wonderful wife and two children who are just like him.

At the age of 14, Billy had gotten himself a job at a Camera shop in Northbrook. He was about to become a freshman in High School. He continued that job every day after school and on weekends for the entire 4 years. Dave Beneventi, the owner of the camera shop took him under his wing and gave him beautiful lifelong experience. Years later, Bill and his wife Glenda brought my grandson into my life: a huge and continuous blessing along with the birth of my granddaughter 4 years later. My grandson Zach recently graduated from Texas A& M, a half year early, with a Magna Cum Laude in Applied Mathematics. He had, from the eighth grade on, been designing roller coasters. Then in College, discovered he was a master at mathematics. Zach's little sister Natalie is following in his footsteps as a student, and a gentle human being, and I am so grateful that she has such great role models. Bill has always been fastidious about his job; he has his own team at Fidelity Investments, where he has been a trusted employee in the computer technical/disaster recovery area for nearly 20 years. What more could I have asked for? Well, I got a bonus: my daughter.

My daughter Johanna is equally my whole life. I named her after my Mom and I live vicariously through her. She takes after my mom in many good ways. Her adventurous spirit has taken her on exotic trips that last sometimes as long as several months, to unusual parts of the world. As I write this, she is in Iceland with her fiancé, Mark. She attended UW Madison, studied in England and fell in love with living there. She went back there after her graduation and worked for the BBC, and took advantage of seeing more of the world. She returned to the States and went into Corporate and soon made it with honors through business school, studying at night, and she got a Masters in Business. Corporate didn't move fast enough for her, so she got out and went to live in South America, teaching English, and decided to get a Masters in Education. The only help she got was that she lived with me until she could buy her own place. I was a real estate agent then, and we found a perfect condo for her on Waveland and Lake Shore Drive. She now mentors teachers at 4 schools, after the new teachers have achieved their credentials in a program for residency that she helps oversee. Her goal is to make the Chicago Public School system a better experience in learning. She believes that "everyone can learn." Note: at this review, Johanna's success with the CPS is taking her to England, where she will live and demonstrate the values of the program that brought her high school in Chicago to a number one standing in the entire state of Illinois, in expected scores.

I don't know what would have happened to me or to my brothers if Dad hadn't died so early in our lives. I can only believe that my roots would have been stronger and I would be able to be more settled and trustful. But, in spite of myself, I am quite satisfied, and so are my kids. To this day, I am still looking to move, looking for more to do, and resisting any urge to plant any roots.

****

CHAPTER 9

Star Gazing in the Real World, circa 1960-65

Fairly fresh out of high school, and with some experience as a secretary at Fingerhut Manufacturing, I moved to Chicago. My sister's husband had gotten me a job at the Cook County recorder's office. It was a political machine position, trading the honor of having a job for working for candidates. I was only 19 years old, and didn't even know I was a Democrat until they asked me to vote. I went up to my sponsor's office to get my role straight. Tom Matousek, then the Recorder of Deeds, half laughed and said, "First of all, you are a Democrat." (After all, he was my sponsor) I haven't changed since; a sense of loyalty is my strongest ally... and sometimes my strongest enemy.

So, as campaigns came and went, we young secretaries lined up to vote, even though I had never voted before. We had to use other people's names, later finding out they had moved or were more than likely deceased. I voted twice in one day! Our office manager at that time provided us with other people's coats to wear for each vote, as if the people in charge wouldn't figure it out. Of course we thought it was great fun; trading coats and hats with other multi-time voters. Both parties were playing the same game, and we thought we were so clever to wink at each other, not realizing our involvement was a serious and crooked one…or that we were cancelling each other out! The spectacle must have been very transparent!

It was the couple of years at the County building, in the secretary pool that I met some of the best friends I have had since high school. Republicans or Democrats, our jobs were to type land titles for the Torrens System, and the titles in turn would get put in huge books after they were proof read and then OK'd by the attorneys, then stored in the basement of the County Building. At that time the political parties weren't so full of hate; we just accepted each other for what we were, sans plotting and backbiting. (Where has the idea come from that the political parties in our country should be enemies?) We're all Americans.

It would be difficult get fired from a political job in the Daley Sr. era, and maybe now, too, but I always felt I was invincible, so I didn't give it much thought. Rita, another typist took me under her wing. She was a very pretty, street-smart older woman, probably in her fifties then, and I loved her and another lady, Margaret, who was Rita's age, who worked in the same pool. A few years later, I would give my daughter the middle name of Rita in honor of my dear friend Rita Klecka.

Rita knew all the fun people. She would take me along with her, and even though she had a bad hip, and had to use a cane, I could hardly keep up with her. She introduced me to a drink called a Golden Cadillac when we went into Fritzels, which I relished like a dessert; I had never been to fine restaurant or a nightclub downtown Chicago before, without my brother in law Joe or sponsor Tom Matousek leading the way. Rita's good friend Bill DeVry, of DeVry Institute would come in and wave at her, and she would disappear from her desk for the rest of the afternoon. One day, I went with them, and we spent the afternoon on his 95-foot-long yacht out on Lake Michigan. It was glorious. It was how the 'other half' lived.

We had to remove our high heels so as not to scratch the teak wood deck, but once we stepped down into the living room, it was carpeted. The boat had a crew of 3 full time stewards, 3 lovely looking bedrooms- each with a bathroom, and a dining room and kitchen. Mr. DeVry would call someone to bring us drinks, using a phone in the living room, which was also equipped with short wave radios and other necessary paraphernalia. It was awesome to this little farm girl from Fargo North Dakota! I was just a splinter in my youth, with a small waistline and bony frame. We would sail a few hours, or just sit in the harbor, having cocktails, then he would take us out for a casual dinner at a German restaurant and we would all go home. Now, nearly 50 years later, when I drive on Irving Park road, I believe I pass that very restaurant with the old-world German façade.

We continued our afternoon getaways a few times, and one day I asked Rita how she met these moguls. She told me her story. She said she and her late husband traveled a lot, and after he died, she took her money and opened a store. It failed, but she then she took what was left and she and a girl friend went to Europe and enjoyed spending—to the point where they needed to go to the US Embassy to see how they could get back to the states without any money. They had one paid night left at their hotel.

That night there happened to be a party going on in the hotel they were staying, and the racket prompted Rita to check it out. And so Rita and her friend went up to the next floor, and knocked on the door, and said to the person who answered, "As long as you're all keeping us awake, the least you could do is invite us to the party." It was Bill DeVry's party. He made sure she got home safe and sound and they were friends for the rest of her life. Knowing Rita, I don't doubt the story. I loved her impulsiveness, her free spirit, and her stories.

****

CHAPTER 10

Trying to Grow Up

I was quite young when I worked at Cook County's Recorders office, and living in Chicago was an adventure. My young marriage had tried to survive in Minnesota, but my husband was a big city guy and came back to Chicago. When he didn't pay child support, I didn't want to fight it, partly because I didn't want to give my son up every other weekend anyway. I was bound to be a martyr either way. In an attempt to be an adult, I went to my ex-father in-law and told him I wanted to be a Court Reporter, as it paid better than the job I had, 'and I had his grandson to raise alone'. He paid my tuition to LaSalle Extension vocational school. I lived with my steno machine day and night, practicing speed by taking down people's conversations on the El, on the radio, and on the train to Milwaukee that I took to visit my Aunt Vera and Uncle Ben when I just couldn't make it to Minnesota. I worked full time and studied on weekends. The classes were three nights a week. As cousins, Vera's daughter Kay and I were very close, in life experiences and in age. I stayed the weekend with my aunt and uncle even though Kay was away at school in France. Kay and I were very close to two other cousins our ages and the four of us girls stayed very close for nearly the rest of our lives. Fate would have it that three of us would share the closely dated deaths of our mothers.

I carried my Court Reporting machine everywhere; so much so that my relatives joked that one of my arms was getting longer than the other. I would practice every day, on all sounds. Once we students reached 180 WPM, we could get tested and certified. Of course no one talks that fast, but court reporters need to be ready to take conversations where more than one person is talking or arguing at the same time. Pretty soon, a stenographer is taking down the sounds so fast, it is second nature. We had T-shirts made that read (expletive deleted) in Court reporting shorthand, and only a court reporter could read it. If I remember enough of it, it looked like GPTUKYRS. I still have the instruction books, but gave the machine up many years ago.

I used the steno machine for depositions, and freelancing around traffic court. I used it when a temporary secretarial job came up for me as private secretary to the CEO of Stone Container Corporation, Jerome Stone. It was better than taking shorthand by hand, besides the Gregory system wasn't as neat or reliable. I would be assigned to take a vacationing secretary's place for a couple of weeks, and then another secretary's place for another executive in the same company. The Stone Container building is on the corner of Wacker and Michigan, and the first floor was "The London House" a nice bar/restaurant that featured great jazz artists of the day, including Ramsey Lewis and Eddie Higgins. I mention those two because I actually 'know' them now, and had the honor of singing a couple of times with Eddie Higgins. I was too timid to go into the lounge, and I think I was still underage anyway, and besides I would never enter a bar alone. In the early to mid-sixties ladies young and old, were still wearing high heels, dresses and nylons to work, sometimes even sporting white cotton gloves, and ladies did not go into bars alone. I would look in the window and I could hear the music that enraptured so many people.

Having my son live with me as a single Mom was not fair to him. I wanted it, and I tried to make it work, but I lived in East Rogers Park, and had to be at work in the loop by 9, and that had me putting him in day care so early he was the first one there. He never complained, but I could see Billy wasn't happy. He would look at me with his big round eyes that seemed to say, "Why are you leaving me here?" I wouldn't get home until 6 PM or so. My roommate, Del Glass was a gem. Without her there to watch over Billy I would not have been able to have him with me as long as I did. Del's father was Paul Glass, and he had a recording company/distributorship that serviced the Motown talent when they came to town. Del and her then boyfriend–, later husband– Les Reich, both cared for Billy when I was at school or working overtime. Les had an apartment just below ours, so we were all in and out of each other's place freely.

Just before I moved into Del's apartment, I had been living in a studio apartment in the Sovereign Hotel. The top floor had a swimming pool that was managed by the world famous diving champion, Billy McGuire. Billy McGuire taught my Billy how to swim. We had the pool much to ourselves, as my studio was the first apartment that had been converted from a hotel room, I was on the top floor, and it was all mine.

I finally talked to Mom about my son Billy's hours and my hours; I hardly had any time to be with him, and Mom suggested that until I was out of court reporting school, he should live with her. The two youngest of my four brothers weren't all that much older than my son and I was relieved that I had the option, and that Billy would be in a household with normal hours, and big yard, and with my brothers who loved him.

I worked every day and many evenings at the county building, trying to save enough money to have my son back to live with me. Overtime was good pay, (seven or eight whopping dollars an hour) and there were a lot of hours available because the Torrens System was always behind. My sister had me try amphetamines to help give me energy. She had been taking them for weight loss. It was common practice in the 60s. I was already thin, about 112 pounds, and in those days no one knew that these pills were dangerous. All I knew is that with them I could type 3 times as many land titles without mistakes and had energy left over. I was a bionic typist! It was empowering! I continued the typing into hours of overtime, and always remained sharp and alert…under the influence.

The ladies in the typing pool would let me alter their clothes for them so I could earn extra money, and some would let me freshen up their hair style. I was good at both jobs. They would meet me at breaks, downstairs in the huge ladies lounge where I would mark the clothes for alterations so I could take the items home to work on, or I would 'comb out' their hair dos, freshening their look between beauty shop visits, for two bucks a style.

On the way downstairs for one of those sessions, I blacked out. The next thing I knew was that the paramedics had me on a gurney on the first floor and my co workers were crowded around me. The amphetamines had taken their toll. I was put in a hospital in Hinsdale and slept for 3 days, and then slept some more. I didn't even know it. The fifth day, a phone call came. Maybe it was my sister, I don't know, but that person said my son had been hit by a car and he was in the hospital in St. Cloud,

Minnesota. I leapt out of the hospital bed and left the hospital. I got into my car… by then I had a Ford Fairlane… and drove straight through to St. Cloud from Hinsdale… (I sure could have used the amphetamines *then*). At the hospital in St. Cloud, my little boy was sitting in a crib, wearing his tie-moccasins I bought him and he looked up at me, too weak to cry. I couldn't get enough of him, and having to go back to work a couple of days later was very difficult. The saving grace was that Mom treated him like one of her own.

I had grown so accustom to driving that same route weekend after weekend that I could do it in my sleep, which I often did! But 'Somebody up there' likes me, and I had my second out-of-body experience on one of those trips,

****

CHAPTER 11

An Out of Body Experience

I was somewhere between the Twin Cities and St. Cloud, it was the middle of the night and it was densely foggy. I was going too fast for safe control; but for a short time, or maybe a long time, I was in another dimension; I believe my car was being held safely off the highway by some higher force. Maybe it was my guardian angel. Maybe it was Dad. I 'woke' up to see a swamp below my car, but the tires weren't touching it. I honestly felt a very strong higher force. Sometime later, my car was safely on dry highway and I was near St. Cloud.

I have had a few of those ethereal experiences. One of them came a few weeks after Dad's accident. I had just had a none existent 15th birthday, (Dad had died just 6 weeks prior) and I was crossing 2nd avenue on Broadway in Fargo, and a light green Chevrolet came slowly around the corner and stopped in front of me, blocking me from crossing the street. It was Dad. It was our car. The car had no broken windows, or mangled door. He was wearing his suede sport coat, and brimmed fedora with the little crease in the center of the crown, and he leaned over and said, "Get in, Heart." No one else knew my nickname outside my family. I actually got in, and he talked to me while he drove. We went about 4 blocks, and were only about a block or two from the Lumber Yard where he had been working before the accident, and he said, "Well, Heart, I am almost there." I thought he meant he was going to work. As though it were any other day, I automatically got out of the car and we said goodbye. I walked back to the corner where he had picked me up just a while before. Of course, in this reality, our car had been totaled. I know because just after the accident, my oldest sister took us to the junkyard near Arcadia to see the remains of our family car. I sat in the driver's seat and saw blood and hair on the shattered window. It was real. I kept telling myself that I was strong.

CHAPTER 12

A Matchmaker

Some years later, back in Chicago, I was in my routine of working at the County Building and going to school. Senator Ben Palmer, who came into the County building often, always said hello, and one day out of the blue, he said, "com'on, I want to buy your son a toy." We went to a store on Wells Street, and he actually picked out a tractor....a red tractor that Billy could sit in and pedal like a trike. He helped me put it in my car and I took it back home for Billy. When I got back, Senator Palmer then said he would like me to meet someone. I was 23 or 24 years old and as naïve as a 16 year old. I was bought.

The person he wanted me to meet was a lawyer, a title examiner at the county building. He had never been married, and he lived at home with his mother. At 34 years old, he was the baby of the family. Senator Palmer told me that (the lawyer) was interested in me, and he thought he would be a good 'catch' for me. I think that generation talked that way. Actually, this time it was the man doing the 'fishing'. We dated a few times, and it was ok. He would take me to his mother's apartment, where he lived. There were no curtains on the windows, and the back porch had a cot where *everyone* sat to watch TV.

On my 25 birthday, he treated me to a date downtown, and he took me to see the Treniers on Rush Street. It was a group that I fell in love with. They were energetic and entertaining.

Then we went across the alley and saw Francis Fay. She was sort of a Sophie Tucker type, and the whole evening was good. Fred enjoyed Scotch and Sodas, and those were the days when drinking and smoking was 'harmless' and the thing to do. I never really smoked, but I would hold a cigarette, lit, thinking it made me look 'sophisticated'. The few times I actually tried to inhale, I got physically sick; I was never a fan of the effects of liquor, either, but I tried to be.

One date had us in a shabby corner bar where his friend Joey Borcellino was bartender/owner. Joey was a stocky, strong Italian who liked to fight. If a customer looked at him sideways, Joey would literally leap over the bar and 'beat the crap' out of the guy. Then he went back to bartending like nothing happened. My date and his brothers just sat and watched, and laughed. I went to use the lady's room. Two young hooker-looking girls gave me the up and down lookover. I knew I had nothing in common with anyone in the bar, but I was still intrigued by the dark, new corner I had turned. Had the times been different we probably would have lasted for only a couple of dates. But I wanted my son home with me. I had been dating off and on, and was still 'seeing' a young man who was a Chicago firefighter. He was good to my son when he saw him, and took him to kiddy land with me a couple of times. I broke it off with him, choosing an alley instead of a street. Savvy me.

His proposal was less than romantic. I didn't analyze it then, I felt that whatever happened would be my Karma; that I either had it coming or I could handle it. He and I were sitting in his car outside my apartment, and he said he was ready to get married, and he wanted me to answer then and there. 'I had better make up my mind because he was ready, and if I said 'no', he would find someone else to marry'. He said he was told to find a nice girl to marry and then his boss would consider appointing him a judgeship. He wanted that judgeship. He was straight forward with that line. I considered it.

For a girl who liked pretty things, and romance, and love, I truly had my eyes shut! What had I become? I had been working and paying for my own apartment; I knew how to budget to the penny! I was so organized that taking the bus from Union Station to the County Building could only happen if I didn't buy the daily paper that morning. It was one or the other. If I could find an unattended newspaper left on the train, I knew I would be able to ride the bus with the extra fifteen cents, and I was proud to be able to execute this budget. I had self-discipline.

I told him I would marry him and I would like him to adopt my son. Somehow I needed to put a pie-crust condition on the commitment. I wanted my boy to have the same last name as I would have. He was back at my Mom's for the second time, having spent some months there. I think that was what convinced me to get married. I thought being married to an attorney might bring my son back to me and give us some needed time together, and some security.

CHAPTER 13

Sherwin Avenue

We got married by a judge in an apartment that would be ours to live in. It was about a 3 minute ceremony. A lot longer than a round of "love making" in that marriage. The next day, 'the lawyer' told me I couldn't quit my job because I had to pay off my own bills. I was $400 in debt. I would be working 6 more months before I could bring my son home. I worked for 3 more months, and still Billy was at Moms. My new mother in law would introduce me as "her son's burden." The entire family would talk in third person, like, "does she want something to eat?", as though I weren't there and as though they were asking the lawyer to speak for me. He did and he continued to live the life of a bachelor, playing cards and going to the race track often. My husband gave me an allowance of $50 a week even though he continued to treat himself to $400 suits from upscale men's stores several times a year, and he continued to gamble at the 'card room' near Ashkenaz Deli in Rogers Park. My $50 was for food and necessities; I didn't dare buy myself anything unless I got permission from him. Billy finally was back with me when he was nearly 6 years old. My husband was obvious about not liking kids. When I asked him (again) to adopt Billy, he snapped, "Alright, I'll adopt your damn kid." It struck me like a bullet. He had not an ounce of sensitivity or romance; not even pretend. The only time he could muster up any niceness was when he was needed sex. "Just a poke and then we'll be done". Little by little I lost my identity, I was struck by the feeling I had no strength for any reason except to live for my son, and later, my daughter.

Within two years of marriage, I got pregnant with my beautiful little girl. I was thrilled to know I would have a girl. My husband wasn't happy about having to deal with another child. Of course, he loves her as much as he is able to love anyone. But, I know he never put any of us first or even second. His brothers and his nephews and even cousins came first.

By my 7th month carrying Johanna, I started hemorrhaging. I called my husband to get a ride to the doctor. He was taking his Mom to the race track, so he told me to take the 'El', and so I did. What could I do? I didn't have money for a cab, and I didn't even consider it. Doctor Harold Brill told me I might lose my daughter. I thought that if I did, I just might want to kill my husband. Dr. Brill gave me some hormone pills and told me to stay off my feet for the rest of the pregnancy. My dear friend, Anna Levine lived across the hall from us, and she thoughtfully brought something for me to eat while I was laid up on the sofa during the day. She made a great noodle Kugel, and some fresh chicken soup, which I was grateful for, and she made sure my son would eat, too. At night, if Fred came home, he would send a cab to the Black Angus to bring back his favorite meal. I liked it too, but in those days, I wasn't into eating full meals.

My 7 year old son was better at changing Johanna's diapers than her father was. Billy was very protective of his baby sister. I can smile when I remember that when I interviewed babysitters, I would pick student nurses to talk to, and then Billy would have them sit down and answer some questions. He would ask them if they smoked, and if they did, they couldn't smoke near his baby sister! I honestly never told him to do that or say that. I will always have the memory of that little boy who sat so straight on the chair and instructed the much older than him baby sitter!

Bill's brightness continued to shine throughout the years. Even now, when I reconnect with some old neighbors, Andree Eckert will talk about how impressed she was when she met little Billy. Her story is that she was coming home with her groceries to the apartment building we lived in on Sherwin in East Rogers Park. Billy didn't know her, but offered to help Andree. He picked up some of her groceries to put in the elevator and then asked what floor she lived on. She smiles when she explains how he stretched to reach the elevator button. When I think of it, that sure was Bill; he has the same values now, too. He goes out of his way to help someone—anyone. His sister is the same way. ☺

One day I hired a cleaning woman. I told my husband I needed to get out an afternoon a week, and so, Anna and I signed up for a bowling league. I had called a cleaning agency and they sent an angel. Her name was Jimmie Nixon. She was smart and kind and dependable. She would come every week for the next three years and I knew I could go away for a couple of hours knowing my children were safely taken care of. She stayed with us until we moved to Northbrook, coming every Wednesday, taking on motherly jobs and seemed to know just what was needed. One day she seemed to be short tempered, and I asked her what was wrong. All she muttered was "you should get yourself a better man." It was ominous. She did not go any further. I didn't ask, either. I think I would rather be uninformed than put someone on the spot. Years later, her loyalty would have her take the long ride from the south side of the city out to our house in Northbrook to attend "Billy's" engagement party. I stayed in touch with her until she died. I wish I could tell her story. Later, we also got in touch with a wonderful woman named Minnie Bobrick. Her son Sammy wrote for Allen King and several other famous people and programs. Minnie was the most trustworthy babysitter, next to Jimmie, but Jimmie could only babysit the one day she came to work. Minnie was available in the evenings.

Talented families can also be creative. I will never forget Minnie's grand daughter's Bat Mitzvah. Formal and in a lovely hotel, we were all enjoying the delicious dinner, and a song their daughter sang to her dad. Then it was time for dessert, and a big fanfare segued the event. Out came a beautiful huge cake on a rolling table, and just behind it, a Samurai along with a giant curved sword. Suddenly the Samurai, jumped with a loud "Hiieeee" he speedily took to hacking the cake so harshly, cake was flying all over the room, and it was hilarious. It took us totally by surprise. It's the part I will not forget! Of course, the real dessert arrived shortly after.

CHAPTER 14

Lost Again

I enjoyed teaching guitar, and had classes from after school until 7 PM, and on Saturdays. My husband said he didn't like that I wasn't home when he came home for dinner. He had to wait an hour before I got home. "You don't make enough money to make that worth it," he said.

I was damned if I did and damned if I didn't. I couldn't make enough money.

In Rogers Park, after Johanna was born, I got pregnant again. When I told my husband, he said, "I don't want another damn kid. Get rid of it, and I never want to hear about it again!". Those were his exact words. I was reeling. I was living a strange life, and felt I had no control over my own body or my emotions. I was in that programmed scheme of women acquiescing to their husbands. My daughter was only a few months old. My husband wouldn't go with me, so I went alone to see the Doctor. I told him the situation.

What had I done? I had fallen to the bottom of the pit. Any self-esteem got obliterated. My heart broke and I hated myself. It was a nightmare. There was nothing left for me but to live the life I had fallen to. If I were any more cut off from the people I cared about, living meant very little. As a young child, people around me were loving. I felt secure and peaceful. I thought it just happened! I never had had the responsibility of creating and keeping the peace then, it wasn't necessary, it was simply the norm. We trusted each other and loved each other. That was before dad died. But now, real life confused me. Now I was terrified and I realized I wasn't in charge. My only life experiences were taught to me through religious training: look the other way; do not judge, pretend it didn't happen. I felt everyone was right but me, and I accepted that. I felt I should let others tell me what to do. They were smarter. I was caught in a quagmire with no future. But my kids would have a future. I was lucky to have my two children. They reminded me that life could be beautiful. But simply for me, I was isolated from a family life. I let my own life come and go without plans. I had had dreams, but no real plans. I didn't think I was capable of putting any dreams into action. That was for other people. Too many things had to be taken care of first. Had my Dad's death created my own living death? There was no one I could depend on.

****

CHAPTER 15

Some Fun and Funny Times

Our neighbors in Northbrook were Norwegian. I think they were glad to have me next door. There were no other Norwegians in our neighborhood that we knew of. One day, Babs called and asked if I wanted to go down town to see if we could get a glimpse of the King of Norway, who was visiting Chicago that year. She had seen on the itinerary that he would be touring the Art Institute. So we got gussied up and went down to see what we could see.

There were crowds of people lined up on the steps to the Art Institute, with a center 'aisle' cleared and bordered with red velvet ropes. At the bottom of the roped off area were a couple of limos.

I chose to edge over to the limos, so I could get a front-on look of the man. When King Olaf came out of the building with several other dignitaries, people clapped, and he walked very stately down the wide span of cement steps, and seemed to look straight at me. I somehow had gotten inside the rope, and was standing near the door to his limousine. I had a brimmed hat with an ostrich plume on it, and was wearing my wool tweed coat that sported a big fox collar. He walked straight up to me with a wide smile on his face, removing his glove to shake my hand. I bowed my head and said, "I hope you are enjoying your visit to Chicago, your majesty." Then, when the limo door was opened, he paused, as though I were supposed to precede him into it.

Now I wish I had. What would they have done…throw me out? But, instead, He bowed slightly and got into the Limousine and they drove away. A lady walked over to me and said, 'well, they certainly know their own'! (I assumed she meant I look Norwegian), and I was elated. Babs and I were walking back to her car, and a Tribune reporter came after us. He hastened across Michigan Avenue waving and shouting to wait. The reporter was Jeff Lyon. He asked me, "How did it feel to meet a King face to face?" I nervously laughed and said, " "I've never shaken hands with a King before" and then, "He really has nice hands"!! I clearly wasn't ready to answer any questions and it just fell out of my mouth. I had been pretty impressed when I saw King Olaf up close. His cashmere overcoat and fedora was without a lint on it, and when he ungloved his hand to shake mine, his hand was strong, smooth and beautifully manicured. He held the doffed leather glove in his gloved hand. His shoes were perfect, especially considering it was winter in Chicago. But when I thought about it, our city made sure that anywhere King Olaf went, it would be clean and dry, free of salt. Babs and I went home, and of course, my luck, the next day I was quoted in the morning edition of the Chicago Tribune. To make matters sillier, a week later at the skating rink, one of the other skaters brought the Norwegian newspaper with her, with the article circled by her husband and written across it was, "Is this our Judi?"...Oh, mercy! Now 'everyone' knew about my goofy remark. Ouch.

****

After a few years in our new house, I started teaching folk guitar in Deerfield. My husband had been complaining that I should get a job. I had gotten certified for teaching figure-skating, and I taught a few beginner classes, but it didn't quite do it for me. I expected too much. My kids were in school, and all I heard was that I should help with the bills. My husband said that other people's wives worked, so why couldn't I? Of course, those ladies weren't cleaning their own houses, either, or taking care of the yard. They were working for their husbands, just to get out of the house. They didn't need the work. Their husbands didn't gamble. Fred gambled 3 and four times a week, so far as I know. Once in a while he would grumble about losing a couple of thousand, 'but would make it up the next time', one night at the apartment, he came in as usual early mornings, and was mad at himself for losing seven thousand dollars.

I couldn't fathom it, but I felt it was his job to rectify that. I was taking care of the house in Northbrook. I loved it. There were times when he would actually call me downstairs to change the TV channel for him. Although we would joke about it, I actually did it. I had turned into a Stepford Wife. Although Bill and Johanna would help do most of the lawn mowing, most of our neighbors had landscapers who came weekly to spruce things up. I cared for the flowers and blooming bushes. I took care of nurturing the trees, too. Mom would bring me bushes and bulbs and flowers to plant, and I made the yard beautiful with her help. But the entire house— installing dimmer switches, and building necessary shelving where needed and fixing tiles, was something I took on.. I liked knowing that I *could* do it, and I would fix small plumbing failures. I installed new sump pumps and cleaned the furnace. My mother in law finally found something to brag about. She wouldn't dare to call me a burden again.

In the apartment on Sherwin, Fred did some heavy gambling every week, not just at the card room, but with heavy-hitters who would sometimes use our dining room as a card room. I would put the kids to bed in their bedroom, and then hibernate in the master bedroom, taking the time to do my nails and set my hair while I watched TV. The stench of smoke was devilish, but somehow we put up with it. A couple of times I would gingerly go to the dining room to have Fred answer the phone or to ask them to keep it down. One of the players, Jack Netchin, who owned Hollywood builders, and other high rises, along with a big hotel near O'Hare, had a 'small' three-screen television on the chair next to him. He was also gambling on other games. I'm not sure if I have his name spelled exactly right, but I want to say, he was a replica of Walter Mathau…in voice and in looks. Sometimes this group of men hung around with Shecky Green, Dick Shawn, Phil Tennenbaum, and other horse owners, Well, one night, when Jack was talking, and I could hear them from the bedroom, I would have sworn that it was really Walter Mathau. In my hair-rollers and robe, I stealthily crawled from the doorway of the hall, through the living room and hunched behind the corner of the console Television set to venture a peek. When I saw his face, I drew back fast, but couldn't contain my surprise, hoarsely squeaking, "It IS Walter Mathau"…and crawled back to the bedroom as fast as I could. Suddenly I heard a burst of laughter. I stayed in the bedroom with my kids for the rest of the night.

CHAPTER 16

WSSY

I was lead to a little radio station in Northbrook, Ill, after a cable company came to the Bristol to interview me. I was introduced to Gary Carlson, who said I should join him on WSSY, just to have some fun with a show. The station was only a couple of miles from my home, and I went over there during his program. The tiny building stood just below the overpass off Dundee Road and the Toll-way. It was easy enough to find with its two tall signal towers minimizing the already small facility.

I liked doing radio right away. Gary Carlson knew the mechanics of it and kept track of the time, all the while I yakked away. After a few visits, we had a 'show', and we had a big poster with the call letters on it, and the words, "Listen to Gary Carlson& Judi K on Sunny WSSY—1330 AM."

Soon, Gary was letting me have all the airtime I wanted, and I started asking guests to come on and be interviewed. The program had stretched from a half hour to nearly 2 hours. I started with interviewing some of the Northbrook people who I knew who were starting new businesses. One was Diane Pryde; a model who in her prime was one of Victor Skrebneski's favorite subjects. Victor Skrebneski is a world class/world famous photographer whose camera's eye has captured just about everyone who is someone. Diane lived on Cambridge Drive, the same block as I did, and she was a celebrity. She and her partner Beth started a business that taught me how to make some promotional material for work. That work included the arts, including being an extra.

When it came to being an extra, I was hired to work in a Cheech and Chong movie. It was "Up in Smoke." I was assigned to walk across a room just as Cheech was entering; our paths were to cross. On queue, I was to walk at an angle, crossing Cheech's path just before the mark at the center.

Over and over and at any point, the director yelled, "Back to One," meaning to go back to the starting point and wait for the queue to start over. I started wondering what I was doing wrong! Actually, they were taking several angles of the same shots, and I suspect many of the angles didn't work, whether we were doing the right or wrong thing. After going through it ten or eleven times, we had to do it again. Just past the center I heard a voice yell, "Back to One" and I turned and went back. Cheech grabbed my arm and jumped onto a table, pounding it and laughing, "*I knew* you'd fall for it," he said to me, and everyone laughed. HE had been the voice that said "Back to One" the last time, not the director. It was so goofy, I had to laugh too, and we did the take 3 more times before the director called the wrap. We all walked to lunch where the buffet was loaded with shrimp and crab legs along with several delicious side dishes. At one point, the scene was a nightclub, and Cheech and Chong's wives were a part of it. I was designated to sit at a cocktail table in the audience with another extra. We were so far back, and I didn't know the rules, and I kept looking over to where the camera was, not considering they might swing it past me for any reason. It was interesting to watch the machinations. After a while, the director walked over to my table and started yelling saying 'if you keep doing that, you're gonna make this whole scene go down the toilet'! I was clueless. He couldn't be talking to ME...I have no importance in this. Cheech said we were simply moving wallpaper for the movie. The guy across the table said, just keep your eyes on my face and let's have a conversation. I'm sure I should have been doing that throughout, but I am so naïve, and always relishing the experience, good or not. It was one of the coldest winter days in Chicago. After disappearing for a few hours, Cheech and Chong came back in with their wives, who they had just gotten floor length chinchilla coats for, from Evans furs on State Street.

Shortly after, I was in a pilot for "Lady Blue" filmed in Chicago, about a lady police officer.

I believe they had Angie Dickenson slated for the lead. During a "bank robbery" I learned what "Candy Glass" was and how it worked. We extras spent hours of waiting, but while doing so, I was with some of the Second

City students and actors, and was entertained while we all sat on the cold floor of the Daley Center waiting to be called for our scenes.

This time I could see myself on screen…. for a second. The brown winter coat I had gotten from Handmoor at a ridiculous price because the buttons were missing was how I found myself in the crowd. Cheech and Chong had called us "moving wallpaper", but this time the pattern in the wallpaper was clearer.

Then came a movie that gave me a couple of lines to read. I was sent by an agency to meet the directors and producers. I made the appointment so I could stop by the Bismarck Hotel on my way to my gig at Dick's Last Resort. I figured I may as well play the 'role' and wore my long white fox fur coat over one of my more subtle costumes. I dramatically swept into the foyer of the hotel where the 4 business-suited men were waiting. Ohhs and Ahhs corresponded with them getting up and shaking my hand. One of them spoke English. He said they all thought I was perfect and would I go to the corner of.. (I forgot, but it was in the loop…I want to say Washington and Wells)…on such and such a day at 2PM? Well, I knew my agent was honest, so I figured I'd give it a try. The make-up room, which was a trailer, was just inside the area of the street that was roped off for the movie. I went in. Two ladies said to sit down so they could get me ready for my scene. One ratted up my hair and the other removed my makeup. Then I was handed a bowling shirt and a baggy pair of jeans to put on. In those days, I was still quite thin and shapely, but obviously that didn't matter. They handed me a bucket with rags and a brush and sent me up to the third floor of the corner building. The scene was a dark, shoddy apartment. I was supposed to be cleaning a mirror. The 'star' was reflected in the mirror so that when I was told to look up I would see him. He spoke in Italian. He sounded angry and gruff and drunk at the same time. If he really wasn't, he must have been a pretty good actor. When he called to me, I was to look up to see his reflection in another room. I was supposed to say something like, "But what about me Giuseppe?" "What about me" (I just made that line up)…So, I said whatever it was, but I think I was way too loud. I had been in stage plays, and volume was important, but here, they had a mike right over me. Only two tries, and the director s Oh'd and ah'd again, saying I was just perfect and I could go. So I did. Later, when I got my check, my agent said they would dub Italian over my scene.

So much for glamour—At least a singer can try to look glamorous– even after she sets up the sound equipment and prepares for her evening. I have no idea of whatever became of that Italian 'movie'. I probably became the face on the cutting room floor.

CHAPTER 17

Back to WSSY

WSSY provided me with experience in Radio Broadcasting, filling dead air and enjoying the moment. I was barely into the singing business, but I used the radio opportunity to invite musicians onto the show, where they could talk about their business and where they were performing. The leader of 'Special Consensus', one of the finest bluegrass bands around, was a guest of mine. I had met Greg Cahill on stage when I did my very first concert with Jethro. Special Consensus has great harmonies and are top notch musicians. I also had the leader of the Buckingham's as a guest, and talked with him and played their music. I was just starting to get to know people in the jazz field, and I invited Jim Beebe and other musicians. I invited a 'Psychic' by the name of Sue Storm who was also a regular at the Bristol. With Sue's appearance, I got my first call-in during 'my' show. I still have tapes of almost all of my radio shows. Sue went on with her interest, then switched to angels, calling herself the "Angel Lady", and actually got a short spot on Saturday Night Live, and wrote a book.

After about 6 months, the station changed to all taped shows in different languages, but we were the very last live show they took off the air, and during those months, I had had a great time. Since then, I have often been a guest of Tom Macek, a jazz DJ for WRRG and the College of DuPage, who has a 5 hour jazz show every Sunday; and I sometimes guest on NPR locally in La Crosse. Once a year or so, Campbell Burnap of the BBC in Liverpool had called me to visit on live radio. Campbell passed away this past year and as a friend, a Traditional Jazz Trombonist and fine singer, he is missed. Steve Voce in England also interviewed me a couple of times. Ben Bennedetti (Madison Area) always supported my recordings, too, especially the "Wisconsin Memories" one; and the same with Bill Korst, who broadcasts from Beloit.

A few times I would get notice from some one who heard me on the Twin Cities Public Radio, and Chicago, and several remote stations around the many places I have lived. I could easily get used to doing radio. It's fun, you need to think fast enough to avoid dead air without getting in the way of another person who is conversing, so, that part is a challenge. I have no problem talking with people, and one certainly meets the nicest people in the Broadcast field.

My kids were on their way with their lives, and I was spreading my wings. I was about forty-four years old. Johanna was still in school, though, when I had attended Oakton College. I started out taking film appreciation classes and writing, and, of course music. Writing was always a favorite thing to do in my life. I went through the poet stage throughout high school and during college, I got a few poems published, and took a workshop with Gwendolyn Brooks while at Oakton. Gwendolyn Brooks had been awarded the Pulitzer Prize in 1950 for her second volume of verse, named poet laureate of the state of Illinois in 1968, succeeding Carl Sandburg. When it came time for Ms. Brooks to critique my poetry, all went well, and she was very helpful and polite. However another woman in the class was surprisingly upset over what I had written. I was embarrassed, surprised and then apologized...my little poem was disrespectful of religion in her eyes. Gwendolyn Brooks said I should not apologize. It was a short, powerful poem: Recently I found and read it and now I think it was written by an angry child. Actually, it *was* written by an angry adult/child! I'm glad I saved it; its meaning is dissolved except that it tells me more about myself than I could have had in mind when I wrote it. I bring some of this up, because, ladies and gentlemen, start writing down your experiences. Keep a journal, if you can. It doesn't have to be good writing, and it doesn't even have to be in perfect order. Just get it down and be surprised; pleasantly or unpleasantly...which ever way it goes, it's a learning tool, and it can be very enlightening to your offspring someday when they see themselves in you and want to learn what not to do.

The next workshop was with Harry Mark Petrakis. I took on a project at Oakton College that required interviewing someone, and one of my classmates suggested someone she knew. He was Harry Mark Petrakis. I set up an interview. I did my homework and read some of his works before my appointment, and prepared some questions that I robbed from some other interviews that I looked up, then set out to meet the Man.

H.M.P. was very gracious, and even though I stunk at interviewing. I wound up getting an "A" on the project in spite of my pretentions. But more importantly, I met an author whose writings could teach me something. I signed up for a workshop with him through DePaul University. After the workshop, in which he was able to pare down a page of writing into about 1 short paragraph, I started attending his lectures.

He is such a terrific speaker, I never got enough of his stories. His lovely wife, Diana was kind enough to sit with me, and she laughed when it got to the point that I could lip-sync his words verbatim. Such a story spinner! The beauty of his writing is that he brings the Greek culture into our consciousness through historical fiction. He spoke just like he wrote: casual, readable. Soon Diana was giving me tips on making Greek appetizers. At that time, I entertained a lot in my big house with the beautiful dining room, making hors d'oeuvres for cocktail parties, and I loved setting a pretty table. Actually, I liked serving people and getting their reactions. Besides, staying busy served as my buffer for not getting involved in any heavy discussions. I got to listen.

Harry Mark Petrakis is the author of twenty-one books, including *A Dream of Kings*, which was made into a major motion picture. He has held appointments at Ohio University as a Visiting Lecturer and at San Francisco State University as 'Kazantzakis Professor in Modern Greek Studies'. He was twice nominated for the National Book Award in Fiction, won the O. Henry Award, and received several other awards.

After reading Pericles on 31st St., I fell in love with it, and I wanted to own it. I started looking in stores for the collection of Petrakis' short stories. It was out of print, and I started scouting out used book stores and went to Delores Shay's ' rare books' store. She started looking for it; and, I put it on the back burner.

My 40th birthday was coming, and on that day, I received a birthday card from Jethro and Gussie Burns. I also received a package. The package contained the collections of Petrakis' short stories which included 'Pericles on 31st St. What a great birthday present, and the book is signed to me from both Harry and Diana, with Diana's little drawing of a birthday cake. That, and other books of Harry's, with his notes to me are proudly displayed on my bookshelf today.

Going back to school in the beginning of my middle age was very fruitful. I met up with a dynamic vocal coach, Dan Detloff, I met Harry Mark Petrakis, and Gwendolyn Brooks and I even wrote a play. The refreshing courses in voice gave me a new feeling about myself, and many good things started happening. I highly recommend any parent with grown children, or without for that matter, to discover themselves by going back to school. If I hadn't, these marvelous experiences most likely wouldn't have happened.

In the late seventies and early eighties, my guitar teacher, Mary Lou May, who had a heart of gold, got me into teaching guitar. I was good at it. My classes filled up. One summer she recommended me to do the music coaching at a nice summer camp on the North Shore. It was pretty good pay, and I enjoyed it, except for the heat. We instructors dressed as comfortably as we could, but our 'classrooms' were outdoors. I'm Norwegian, so the sun and I are not buddies. Many times I would have the class sit on the grass, around me and we would sing camp songs while I played my Martin D28. Soon after, I would buy a Martin 0018, which fit me better. Having a good guitar meant a lot to me, but having it in the sun made me worry about it. My guitars were also Norwegian- by affiliation—they didn't like the sun either. One day, while sitting in the grass, a felt a tickle on my bare legs. I looked down and there was one of my favorite creatures crawling on my leg. It was big fat Minnesota spider that reminded me of the house in St. Joe. Dang…how did it get all the way to Illinois? I didn't want to scare the kids, and I whisked it off, then quickly stood up and finished the entire day standing up, very often looking at my feet to make sure no more little crawly creeps were getting close. The next summer, the Tamarac Camp Director asked me to return, even adding more pay, and I had to say no. The popular Geraldine Armstrong took my place that year.

****

CHAPTER 18

My Mother's Daughter

When my daughter was young, nearing 10 or so, I snuffed out my unhappy marriage by *being my* mother for her. I sewed some outfits for Johanna and that made me happy, and she liked them, too. Johanna would wear her little eyelet-trimmed jeans to riding classes at Blue Ribbon, a nice riding stable in Northbrook, and I would use small checkered gingham for the letters of her name on the front of her bib overalls. I made matching gingham ribbons for her ponytails and pigtails. I loved working with her thick naturally curly hair, and I loved dressing her up and taking pictures of her. She had unusually long thick hair even when she was very little. Even though I had her hair cut short a few times, by the time she was a teenager, I could hardly wrap my hand around her thick ponytail so I would section her hair off and bring 2 side braids into it. I just hope I didn't pull as hard as momma did when she did my own hair way back in Fargo. Later, the bob came back in style, and I took Johanna to a salon for a cut.

The hairdresser literally drooled as he held his scissors ready for the cut. I knew this hairdresser was a precision cutter, but I think if I had just stood at the door with Johanna and simply shouted "Who wants to cut this girl's hair?" I would have had every artist in the shop lining up for the thrill of it. Lenny took his time snipping, relishing the long curly tresses hanging over the back of the chair. Lenny made a production out of his 'conquest', cutting slowly and purposefully. As the wet hair dropped to the floor and started to dry, it curled up to about 4 inches deep and after a while,

Lenny said, as he stepped gingerly through it, holding his rattail comb like a Sheppard's staff, "I feel like Moses parting the red sea." All the other hairdressers had been watching and they laughed, clapped and soon went back to their stations. Here's Johanna getting ready for a Bar-Mitzvah:

At Halloween, I would have the best decorated house in the neighborhood. The clanking chains and yowling sounds that came from a cassette tape were enhanced by some black fabric I put on the windows, with strobe lights flashing to make it look like lightning inside the house. I used a huge black caldron to hold the candy, but I had a screen under the candy to shield it from the dry ice below it. The smoke from the dry ice made getting the candy out a 'scary' experience for the kids. I had a 'famous' witch cackle, and used it over the intercom as the costumed kids came and left. Every year I would get some neighborhood kids who would return with a thank you note and a drawing they made for me. I have a couple of those drawings in my stash...can't bring myself to throw them out just yet.

One year, the Gloria Dei Lutheran Church in Northbrook asked if I could lead the summer choral kid's group and I accepted. Things went pretty well, little ones are easy going and want to please you, so I had time enough as to teach them a song to perform in the church as the end of the couple of weeks. It was so cute to see the rows of little suits and proper dresses. At the end of the song, the parents clapped and I was down on my haunches, eye level with the kids 'leading' them on, and a little boy that had been singing rushed to me and gave me such a hug that I landed fully on the floor while his arms were still around my neck. I will never forget the laughter of the parents and the sweetness of the moment. And I don't even remember their names. Ouch.

Early on in Northbrook, I signed myself up for figure skating. I learned fast, but I had taught myself some bad habits those years of skating on the Clara Barton rink in Fargo. I was fairly strong in jumping, spinning but I favored the 'wrong' side. I hadn't given a thought to which way was the norm...I just wanted to do it. I now compare it to be right or left handed, and taking the easiest way to learn. I wound up skating against the skaters who were circling the rink, outside right, warming up. You had to be strong in edges and crossovers going both ways, but most jumps are one way, taking off from one edge or the other. I think of a figure skate blade as having 4 edges: a front inside, and a back inside, a front outside and a back outside edge. The center, located just behind the ball of the foot is the rocker, the part for spinning and turning. In those days compulsories were strict on how the edges showed up on the ice after working a figure eight or circle. You watched for the marks the edges made so the teacher could tell if you were doing it right. When you spin, if you get a little off the 'rocker', or 'the center', the spin travels. The spin mark becomes little loops, like lower case script 'ees'. The mark on the ice *should* be just one 'O' over and over itself. It's when the general public realizes this that watching the pros and competitors skate becomes really interesting. It's like watching a proper tour jeté in ballet with full, strong extension, lots of air, no lax knees except for landing, and no limp arms and hands. It was hard to be a part of the skating team, but I managed well enough even though I did everything better in the opposite direction. I credited my dance lessons I had taken in Fargo for learning a combination routine quickly. Mom and Dad had me taking 2 classes and one private lesson every week. I loved it. Ballet dancing was very athletic. It kept muscles and joints strong, and I could dance on point within my second year.

In Northbrook, in the 70's, figure skating lessons were only $35 for a season of classes. Taking classes also allowed the student to use the rink at certain times without paying in between lessons. Northbrook was "the speed skating capitol of the world," because several medalists were trained there, and came from there. During this, my husband was not a happy camper. He grumbled about me taking lessons. It was too much money. I argued that one. I had found an outlet and was determined to keep it, and I knew I was frugal with most everything I had or did. At times, life was good. We would go to Colorado on ski trips and I fell in love with downhill skiing. The quiet beauty of the Rockies coupled with rhythmic shushing as we traversed the slopes was heavenly. At the end of the week, we participated in the Nastar races. It was exhilarating. We skied in Aspen, Snowmass, Vail, and Steamboat and Loveland Pass. We were always with a group of people who were used to having, and I enjoyed tagging along. We took Billy and Johanna with us once or twice, and they too raced in the Nastar Races and did very well. Bill was first in line right behind Spider Sabich, who was setting the pace/time as the paradigm for the run that day. At that time, Spider was the resident pro in Snowmass. After the races, we got ready to go home. By the time we got home to Illinois, we heard that Spider had been shot to death. I knew that none of us did it.

When I think about all the wondrous ski trips we took, I also think about the week in Steamboat Springs, CO. It was just about the time the bidding for the Olympics began, and Steamboat was against having the Olympics take place there, and the residents won the fight against corporate muscle. The residents were not thrilled with the prospect of buildings being built then emptied and taking away the rustic charm this isolated area had. They also were not the most accommodating ski patrol to tourists.

Steamboat has some really serious black diamond slopes filled with steep moguls; each mogul much taller than I was. But I wanted to do one extreme mogul run, just one; like on a bucket-list. I figured I'd get the hang of it if I had an instructor for one hour.

We started down the run. I had just done Heavenly Daze, which should have been the most for me to challenge, but I thought that with an instructor I would be safe on a little tougher mountain side. He wound his way down a mogul, then from there yelled for me to come down. I couldn't see where he was waiting, and yelled, "How?"

He said, "just come on down." I couldn't see him at all, but gingerly half skied, half slid down the side of the mogul and then another one...and one more. Not a word about shifting weight downhill or keeping my shoulders downhill. Then, I heard a crack. My binding had broken off. I tried to fix it on the spot, but he said he had no tools with him. He said to just go to the top where there were ski patrols and ask them, and suddenly my instructor whisked away never to be seen again by me. We had paid in advance. I started crawling up the mogul. It was straight up. I dragged the unusable ski with me. I made it to the top of the mogul and looked up, and still could not see anything except the next looming mogul. So I started crawling up. I couldn't see what was up or down.... There were just huge white moguls blocking my views. I crawled farther, and there, at the top, not of the mountain, but the top of the mogul patch, were two ski patrols lying in the sun, tanning themselves.

Now, In Aspen or Vail, the instructor would have done one of a couple of choices: he would have accompanied me to make sure I was ok, or he would have radioed the ski patrol to come and help. But, here... well, I showed the patrol the broken binding, and like Tweedledee and Tweedledum, they said practically in unison, "Just take the lift down".

In Aspen or Vail, the patrol would have most likely pulled out a trusty screw driver from his rucksack and tried fixing the binding then and there, so I could at least ski down and have it fixed permanently at the rental shop. The lift that the Tweedle brothers pointed out was another half mountain away. Up. So, I said, "Is there any other lift nearby, where I wouldn't have to climb to get to it"? They pointed in the direction of a mid-mountain lift on another run. It was sort of down and across. I made my way the best I could, carrying the skis, and headed through the snow to where I thought I would find the lift. I stayed to the side of the mogul run so as not to be in the way, incase another skier came along, but, didn't see or hear any. I sank deep into the snow that the groomers hadn't touched. By the time I got to the mid lift, it was too late. It was closed. Only the top one was still open. I started my journey down the mountain on foot. Two hours later, I saw the bottom. It was slushy, and my husband and two of his cousins were standing in the water/snow, watching and waiting. I was exhausted. We went to dinner and had some good food along with some good laughs. The next morning is another 'grand' memory.

We had rented a nice condo that was near enough to walk to one of the lifts. I got up earlier than the others and took a walk. The sidewalk leads to some kiosk where you could get coffee and a hot buttery crepe. I saw a popcorn stand and wished it were open, and when I reached it, there was a huge corpse lying on the sidewalk, shirtless. His white beer belly extended full of corpse gasses, like a big mogul. I looked around and saw no one else, so I dashed to the nearest door and had them call the police. I didn't stick around. When I got back to the condo, cousin Bob, who we had given the nickname "Bunkie" to (*referring to the commercial of a man who had aches and pains; and the commentator would ask "What's the "What's the matter, Bunkie, are you feeling left out?"…each commercial started with "What's the matter, Bunkie"*) well, Bunkie and his wife Roberta came outside and I asked them to come with me to the location of the dead body. When we got there, it had been removed. I turned around to walk back, and tripped and fell face first into a large, muddy, slushy pot hole. Bunkie said, "Oh, no!" and gallantly reached down to pick me up. He said, "What's the matter Bunkie" to me and we started laughing, then he noticed the front of me, my white suede jacket full of mucky, muddy water, and said, "EEUGH" then dropped me right back into the puddle. We laughed all day. Now I wish we had had a video of it, we probably would win a prize for 'America's Funniest Video'.

I like to believe that my children had a nice growing up life, even though Bill's was harder than Johanna's was. Fred allowed Bill to take classes at Columbia Fine Arts College and invoked strict limitations, even though Bill continued to work at the camera shop my standards were too high even for me. When I grounded him, I grounded myself, too. Now Bill claims it was good for him, but I know in my heart that I should have been more outwardly protective of him. I know I was happiest when he was living with me, as my little boy, in an apartment in Broadview. I was the one providing a home, his clothes and toys. I was in charge of finding the right babysitter, meeting the parents, and taking my son to kiddy land. He was such a good child, and I had the world by the string; working everyday at the county building, saving and having everything in order. Marriage changed that.

Just before he started his first year in high school, Bill had gotten himself a job at the Northbrook Camera shop, and worked to supply himself with equipment for a dark room in our basement. Bill had to buy his own chemicals and equipment, and working at the camera shop every day after school helped with that. I'll never forget the day he came home on his bicycle and announced he had gotten a job selling cameras at the Northbrook Camera Shop. I was so proud and actually didn't know what to make of it. Should I act as though it was the normal thing for a 14 year old to do? Glenbrook North's photography teacher would call on Bill to come to the photo class to assist him and help troubleshoot. Bill received work credit from the high school for his job at the Camera Shop. He continued that job every day after school and through the summers for the full 4 years and then some. All that time, Dave Beneventi, the owner of the shop and his sidekick Norm kept Billy under their wing and taught him about camera repair, picture taking, picture developing and retail. Later, when he went to Columbia College in Chicago for photography, he needed more dark room supplies, all of which are expensive, so he took another job to help pay for those needs. My friend Anna Levine from Chicago had a friend who's company needed help during tax season. They hired Bill, and it was Bill's introduction to computers. The rest is history. After his first year at Columbia, Bill was offered a job with a computer company called Tymeshare in Dallas, Texas. within two days he left for Dallas. Photography became a thing of the past. He went with nothing, lived in a cheap motel until he saved enough to go in with a roommate. I had lost my son too soon and too often. During our marriage, my husband, a lawyer, never offered or suggested that I go to visit Bill, either. Not once. I had to beg. Actually, I had to 'beg' for anything I needed. And when I did ask, his conditions were high. He wouldn't put out the price of airfare for me, so, one day, my cousin Kaycee came from Milwaukee with her van to help me bring Bill's bicycle and guitar and clothes to Texas for him.

Kaycee and I were chatting so much during the drive, that we lost direction, and started heading toward Ohio. When we realized it, we backtracked through miles of Midwest Illinois nothing. I was surprised to see that cotton grew as far north as mid/southern Illinois We decided to head toward Missouri to see Hannibal. In the middle of miles and miles of cornfields on all sides of us, her van ran out of gas. What would we do now? We had no idea of how far we were from anything. There were no cell phones, no GPSs.

We got out of the van, locked it up and started walking. As luck had it, at the very end of the tall cornfield was a span of grass that couldn't be seen until you were right at it. On it was a single gas pump, and further back was an older ranch style building. It happened to be a nursing home. The man in charge offered us a partial can of gas, just enough to 'get us to the next gas station' which was about 2 miles away. We took the gas to the van, and poured it in, using the attached funnel. And when we returned the can, I brought my guitar into the nursing home and we did a couple of songs for the residents as a thank you. "*...They call it that good ol' Mountain Dew, and them that refuse it are few...I'll shut up my mug if you fill up my jug of that good ol', good ol' Mountain Dew"....* The trapped audience loved it. I always had my guitar with me, no matter where I went. Kaycee and I felt good about our luck, and that trip provided us a lot of good memories.

After a few days with my son in Dallas, seeing where he lived which by now was a nice apartment, we headed for home, stopping in Hot Springs Arkansas to look around, then got back on the road again. Late into the night we got a craving for our favorite snack— fresh popcorn. I think we were in southern Illinois with five or six more hours to go till Chicago.

Back in high school, I was the popcorn popping queen for my classmates. At that time, I used my mom's pressure cooker, and under pressure, the popcorn was the fullest blown, no 'old-maids', just perfectly exploded kernels. But now, my cousin Kaycee can't be beat for tasty homemade popcorn. I have gotten to be a sucker for baby-rice popcorn, but Kaycee's popcorn-popping-prowess provides great taste, whether it's yellow large kernels, white or black jewel ones…and she uses a plain kettle. It's a knack.

During the trip, we figured we would be lucky if we found a tavern that had those little two-bit sized bags of popcorn hanging from strips of plastic hooks. There wasn't any store or even any gas stations to be found on the route we had taken. We did spot the lights of a tavern, though, and it was about to close. We sat at the bar and had a cold beer, and talked to the bartender about getting some popcorn. They didn't have any. Then, just as we were salivating at the mention of hot, fresh popcorn, the bartender walked over to the door that led up stairs and yelled: "Mom! Can you make these ladies some popcorn?" And after the smell of freshly popping popcorn made us crazed, down she came with a big bag of it for us. It was such a delightful surprise, I asked if we could pay for it. The bartender said, "Oh, make it two bucks." We gave him $5 and thanked him profusely, taking the big paper bag of popped corn with us to eat on the road. I took the names of the people and the bar, and later sent them a note to thank them again…the popcorn was absolutely delicious. It was true highway hospitality. Maybe they were members of the "Swanks".

After that trip, I wasn't to see my son for long stretches once again. I could hear Mom's voice whispering one of her 'slogans': "you made your bed, now sleep in it."

I buried my time in Johanna. She was a bright, hard working little girl who had the gift for good planning. At an early age, she was a strategist. She was asked to join the middle school track team, even though she was in the elementary school. She never missed a day of homework, and she missed very little, if any, school. Homework was piled on the kids. As a fourth grader, she would go to track practice early in the morning and then go to school. Her homework would be finished by 10 PM or so, and she would lay her clothes out on her bed for the next morning. There was no television in her life during school. She did, however love to watch Julia Child on Saturday mornings. Johanna liked Julia Child, Bill liked Jeopardy, and my grandson watched the weather channel each at the age when other kids would be watching cartoons.

When Johanna was in the 3rd grade the kids had to make cookies and bring them to school with the story of how they did it. Parents were discouraged from helping. I had to attend one of my husband's political functions that evening, and when we came home in the wee hours of the morning… there were cookies, laid out to cool… and the entire kitchen was clean! My little girl did it all by herself. I tasted the best sugar cookie I had ever had. Ever. It was perfect color, thin, with a slightly tan edge, and it melted in my mouth. When reading her little paper, it explained she didn't know where her mom's flour sifter was, so she (laboriously, I presume), forced the flour through some cheesecloth. I can't imagine how long it took, but it was obviously worth it. A few days later, she came home with first prize. A cook book awarded to her from the Henry Winkleman Elementary School and her teacher, (Mrs. Dugan?) It is in storage downstairs, with the boxes of her dozens of blue ribbons and many other ribbons and plaques from track and horseback riding; and many trophies I have no idea what to do with. I just can't throw them out, and I hope she will somehow display them someday.

Overabundant handing out of homework was prevalent at Stanley Field middle school. One night, she was crying from overtiredness. She wasn't getting it done before 11PM that night. I felt sorry that she worked so hard, and that the school was piling on the homework, so I said. *"Don't do it; Just don't do it. This one time won't hurt you"*. She looked up at me as though I had totally missed the boat, stopped crying on the spot and finished all of her homework. Can you imagine a parent telling a kid not to do their homework? I'm glad she didn't take me seriously although I was, but afterward when I thought about it, I laughed at how it worked out.

She and Bill both kept their own bedrooms clean, and their beds made. I rarely had to say anything more than once. They both kept their bathroom clean, and Bill helped with the laundry. They were good kids; my heart and soul. They still are. I was tough as a Mom, but they say they are glad for it. I was a bit clean-crazy, but they laugh about that, too. Thank God.

They are a mother's dream come true. There were many trophies and awards trophies for the sports they joined. Both of them got state wide recognition in at least one of their sports. They grew into marvelous adults. I'm a happy Momma.

CHAPTER 19

The Village School of Folk Music

As I said, I found Guitar teaching through Mary Lou May (later Hightower) a marvelous lady who I had signed up with to take lessons. She was multi talented, taught several stringed folk instruments and had a few groups that she would take out to do small concerts. She was soft spoken and always had something nice to say. Mary Lou is a great role model, and always gives someone incentive to learn. After only two lessons she had me playing one of my favorite songs: "Dust in the Wind." It's a picking pattern that I found much easier than I would have imagined. The beautiful combination of the violin and guitar chord changes in that recording haunts me. Mary Lou and I would sing with each song that we played. It was therapeutic for me. I was enjoying being a part of music.

Soon, we were harmonizing while we played and sang, and she was about to teach me a Country Western tune. She said, "Now, you can't use your pretty voice for this one, Judi".... She surprised me with that one, I hadn't thought about my voice being pretty. But since then, I realized that I always had to try my best to fit the voice to the style of the song. It's great fun and adds a bit of a challenge. When she said that, it was just around the time when my vocal coach Dan Detloff was getting through to me about finding my different voices. No more church voice for me! I was 'getting' it. I would use the church voice (upper register)for the higher ranged folk songs and ballads. Soon, Mary Lou asked if I would be interested in teaching. I had learned the Bob Gand method, which is quite clever, using a lot of tab in place of actual note reading. It made for faster learning and playing.

One day, Mary Lou asked me to sub for her that evening in Buffalo Grove where she had adult classes. She told me which songs to teach them. I was anxious to try. What I *didn't* know was that two of the adults in my beginner's class were staying behind from their advanced class they had just finished. After getting everyone's guitar tuned up, I started showing the class a few picking pattern 'tricks' for the song we were learning. Lynda Campbell and her friend would play it with precision and say…."Like this?," with mischievous grins on their faces. And I was totally taken aback. Had Mary Lou given me the wrong class? A couple of others in the class chuckled and asked me to show them again. Again, Lynda and her friend whipped through the measures. I felt my face turn red. By the end of the class, I thought I was a failure.

But before everyone packed up, they announced to me what they were up to. I was relieved and laughed along with everyone. Every last person had been in on it except me. Then we all went across the street to the Buffalo Nickel: a bar and pizza place. We goofed around and laughed until 2 AM. The evening had been a great escape, something new for me.

After that, I had some students who were in their teens and became serious players. When I got finished showing them the finger exercises and the number systems, and a bunch of basic songs, I would turn them over to one of our more advanced teachers for some heavier chording and, if wanted, rock and roll, something I wasn't interested in. Several students stayed with me to learn folk songs. I did garner a few letters of appreciation from my students. I might even still have them in my stash of scrapbooks.

My 38th birthday was coming up.

On my birthday morning, very early, I heard horns honking as the cars passed my house. I got curious. Even the garbage truck honked and the driver looked up at my window and waved. I looked down onto the front lawn. There was a long banner…Maybe 9 feet long…held up by two dowels stuck in the ground at each end. I went outside to see what it said. On the front of the banner was printed: "Honk…its Judi's Birthday"!!! I knew immediately that Linda and Mary Lou were the culprits. They had made a banner at the Village School on the old daisy wheel printer. They colored it in bright shades and went through the trouble of going out late at night to accomplish the caper. I kept it for good memories for a long time. The three of us became inseparable; we were mischievous and have always cared for each other as true friends.

I enjoyed teaching guitar, and had classes from after school until 7 PM, and on Saturdays. My husband said he didn't like that I wasn't home when he came home for dinner. He had to wait an hour before I got home. "You don't make enough money to make that worth it," he said.

I was damned if I did and damned if I didn't. I couldn't make the kind of money he did. We fought like we were from different planets...we were from right out of the book: "Men are from Mars Women are from Venus".

In Rogers Park, after Johanna was born, I got pregnant again. When I told my husband, he said, "I don't *want* another damn kid. Get rid of it, and I don't want to hear about it again!". Those were his exact words. I was reeling. I was living in a strange life, and felt I had no control over my own body or my emotions. I was in that programmed scheme of women acquiescing to their husbands. My daughter was only a few months old. My husband wouldn't go with me, so I went alone to see the Doctor. I told him the situation.

What had I done? I had fallen to the bottom of the pit. Any self-esteem got obliterated. My heart broke and I hated myself. I was a nightmare. There was nothing left for me but to live the life I had chosen. If I were any more cut off from the people I cared about, living meant very little.

******

CHAPTER 20

No Ordinary Recital

The Village School of Folk Music held its annual recital in a modern church north of Deerfield, Il, on Half Day Road. Each of us instructors had our classes grouped on the long wooden benches, and we would perform our songs directly from where our students sat. It worked out well. Bob Gand was an ace at running a good music school and we all had plenty of students. He would hire a well known guest every year, so that more people would come to the annual recital/concert, more than just the parents of the students. This year he hired Jethro Burns.

I had known of Jethro ever since I was 8 years old. It seemed odd to say his name without the "Homer and" attached to it. My brother Joel, my sister Jane, and I knew every word of the comedy team's Kellogg commercials, and would mimic Homer and Jethro often. When we lived in Fargo, we would watch their antics on the Johnny Carson show, the Ed Sullivan Show, the Dean Martin Show and on many other variety shows. Jane could sing their hilarious hit songs, and I would copy her. "Screen Door, What's that Secrit Yer keeping?" and… "She had nine buttons on her night gown, but she could only Fascinate"…. Oh, the laughs we had watching Homer and Jethro… And here he was; after all those many years, right in front of me. Just before Jethro came on stage, the recital had an intermission. The students had done their thing and the next on the agenda was a performance from Jethro. He asked me to come into the church kitchen, which served as a 'green room' for him. He said he heard me sing with my students, and would I like to try a song with him. I told him I only knew "Teach Me Tonight,"… (I wasn't about to do "I Ride an Old Paint")…and he said fine, now let's find a key.

He and Don (Stiernberg on Guitar) worked it out for me, and I went back to my group of students in a trance with the key of A flat in my mind.

Jethro came out to do his show. Then, he announced that he was inviting one of the teachers up to do a song. When he said my name, the other teachers gasped. I nearly fainted myself. I made my way to the stage, he started playing and I sang. Everyone hooted and clapped. He said, "I think I can put you to work." I didn't dare think even a day ahead, or what he meant by that, but those words soon changed my life. During the time I knew Jethro, he always called me Judi Kelinsky, "Jewdy Kalensky" bending the middle of Klinsky with a Tennessean lilt...

I went with him on some small concerts for park districts and other events. He was such a musical genius, and he could play off my naiveté in a way that the audience would think it was part of the act. He would stop right in the middle of a tune, and in his fake hillbilly accent make a straight faced crack that would be funny to everyone, including me, and even though I was giggling, somehow both of us would start right back up in synchronization. I guess I had mimicked Homer and Jethro so much as a youngster, the feel for that kind of vaudevillian humor came naturally. The audience ate everything up. After a show, he said, "You have something that the audience likes." Suddenly I felt like Judy Garland, standing with her feet shoulder width apart, holding firm while belting out "The Birth of The Blues." Jethro had whetted my appetite and given me some self-esteem, even a little hope. Had I a better marriage going at the time, I think my focus could have been stricter and I would have been more professional. But it wasn't, and I wasn't. I couldn't fathom that I just might go somewhere with this gift, but I loved the challenge and decided to grab onto it, day by day, however short and tenuous. Had I been competitive, things may have gone another way. But I wasn't. I figured this experience could disappear at any moment, so I clung to the moment I was in.

After a few concerts with Jethro, I started looking for gigs. I hadn't the slightest idea of how to go about it, but when I did get one, Jethro was very patient with the small amount of money I had negotiated. When I started to get more for the gig, he would say, "now, you're learning." It was all hit-and-miss. Jethro was kind enough to go all the way to Milwaukee with me just to watch me work at a kid's group home. He would patiently stand near me and play his mandolin for whatever tune I would sing for the kids. I didn't have to warn him of anything I was doing. He could read my mind. My aunt Antoinette and her daughter Kay made hand puppets for me to give the kids to use while learning a song. Each puppet was a different look. I used those puppets over and over, and one day Jethro asked if he could keep one. I was thrilled he would think like that.

I took mandolin lessons from him for a time, bringing my garage sale mandolin to the Guitar Works in Evanston, where Jethro had a lesson room. He would say, let's switch, and he'd hand me his expensive hand-made Mandolin with gold inlay, a one-of-a-kind that Washburn or Gibson made for him. Both companies vied for Jethro to use their instruments. Then he would tune my $25.00 mandolin and play it, making it sound way better than it was! He taught me some silly tunes-a la Homer and Jethro- that were parodies of songs that I could do while I played my guitar. One of them was "Daddy Played First Base.".. (a take on Daddy played Bass) and a line in the chorus would name the team, and then repeated… outfielders were "Brothers Art and Bart and Cousin Fargo too.".. And each time it drew chuckles from the audience. Jethro gave me a couple of his mandolin music books that he wrote, and signed his autograph to me on them. I've kept them through the years, along with many of my taped lessons with him. At that time, I went searching for every old Homer and Jethro LP that I could find, I would bring them to The Guitar Works and Jethro would sign them for me. Somewhere, during that time, I wanted to make a demo recording, and Jethro, Don Stiernberg, Terry Straker and I went a couple blocks away from Terry's store, The Guitar Works in Evanston. It was a studio in the lower walk-out level of a huge home on Ridge Avenue. A young man named Steve Rashid took care of the sound and we recorded 5 or 6 tunes; one of which I used 10 years later on my first CD with Jazzology. "I Can Dream, Can't I?" was placed just after "I Remember you" where I had used Dave Baney on guitar and Don Stiernberg on mandolin as the segue to the next cut. Although my voice on the Jethro demo sounds younger, the song fit the compilation well and the album got some pretty bright reviews from some pretty high places! These days, Steve Rashid is a two- time Emmy award winner with another one on the way, for his documentaries. Thank you, God, for giving me that experience of working with those talented people! There is only one regret I have from that experience: I thoughtlessly neglected to put Terry Straker's name on the album credits. He played the guitar on the songs I did with Jethro and Don Sternberg.

****

CHAPTER 21

More New Experiences

As I said, I was also taking classes at Oakton College while my kids were in school. I took more voice lessons than were on the class line up, and in order to continue with that teacher, whom I considered excellent, I would have to sign up for directing, theory, orchestra and whatever we could get away with just so I could keep learning what to do with my voice. It worked. When I discovered I had a lot more than a church voice, it was an exciting find. I soon learned how to use my mid voice, and belt voice. With a big thank you to Dan Detloff for being a top notch voice teacher, I could control my head voice and go into an isolation that I wish I had exercised more. But it scared me! I could do it at home, in private most of the time, but in public it stayed on the hook and only on a perfect night could I touch it. I worked on erasing the break between voices. I think more so than having a star like Jethro 'discover' me, the realization of my voices truly was as exciting, and it all came together. I would recommend Dan Detloff to any and all singers from then on.

Northbrook did a cable show interviewing me, and what it felt like to be a late bloomer. The North Shore Magazine's Art Shay managed to find a whole page to write about me, even though I felt as though I hadn't done much of anything yet. What the heck was going on? Now I was getting hungry to learn more while living in awe of this strange, new world, but I always managed to leave brake marks as it went a little too fast for me.

I called a talent agency in Minneapolis. I wanted to have a performance in the Twin Cities so that I could get my Mom and brothers to see what I was up to. The agent said, "I just happen to have your promo package in front of me"…He asked what I could handle, and who would be with me. I told him I would ask Jethro Burns and he said, "What?" Jethro's name carried weight. I didn't know how to handle a contract of any kind, so I turned it over to Jethro. Jethro handled it, and I asked when we could rehearse. He said, "I don't rehearse"…I was dumbfounded!

The combinations of notes that Jethro came up with for each change were positively awesome. He was a compelling virtuoso, and nothing could stump that man. Later, after I met Jim I wished we had all crossed paths while Jethro was well and out there. Jim would have loved playing with "TWGMP". *You just get up on stage and do it.* So I did. But,like a drummer or any other musician, if a singer doesn't have good time, the rush or drag could screw up the song, confuse the other players, and the speed can get out of control. I learned by trial and error, and soon I held my own. I learned to lead, front and sing and to know the notes I was singing, and where the bridges go; I learned to count the song out and feel the 32 bars and know where the band was…Most of the time.

CHAPTER 22

Orchestra Hall

The next thing I knew was that Jethro, Don and I were on an airplane to the Twin Cities to perform at Orchestra Hall. We were met at the airport with bronze sleek modern limousines…2 of them! I was in awe! I think Don and Jethro were surprised, too. Jethro said that 'they' probably assumed we would have some kind of entourage and equipment to fill the second limo. But as the two limos sailed along the boulevards to Orchestra Hall, I could see that people in other cars were trying to peer through the tinted windows and more than likely wondering who was in the limousines! We were taken to a lovely hotel near Orchestra Hall, and escorted to our rooms. At 4 PM we were asked to be at the Hall for a sound check. As soon as we got to the building we were escorted to our own dressing rooms. When the union workers were ready for the sound check, security came to our rooms, knocked, and escorted us to the stage. We weren't allowed any pictures even at the sound check, I was sad to find out. I did sneak one of Don though, in his dressing room, warming up on the mandolin and guitar. But that was all I got. The stage was glorious, it was all set up complete with dozens of untrimmed Christmas trees, depicting a tree sales-lot complete with warming cabin, and I walked up to the microphones for my very first real 'big-time'sound check. The sound was so clear and easy, and I was in love with the feel and shape of the beautiful hall and the magnificent stage. Afterward, the people at Orchestra Hall gave me a couple of lovely posters as souvenirs, and I had one matted and framed, and gave one to my cousin to do the same. The rich greens and purple iris bloom colors are perfect in each of our decors.

Back at our hotel rooms we had a small dinner, and got ready for the concert. We were in our dressing rooms, and when the stagehand knocked on my door saying "5 Minutes!," I pretty much felt the floor drop away from under me! Then, the security came to escort me, and they locked my dressing room behind me. I soaked it all in. I was back stage to wait my queue. I heard Jethro introduce me, I let some time pass, slowly, purposely winding and rewinding through the Christmas trees. He called on me again. "And here she is, Ms. Judi Klinsky" he said for the second time. I came out from the trees, pretending to huff and puff as though I were walking a long distance. "Now Judi, (Jeeudee) where were you?" he asked. I said, "I was lost in that forest Jethro, and I am sure glad there weren't any dogs around… *look* at all those trees, " I exclaimed with my best Goldie Hawn 'dumb-blonde 'expression. He burst out laughing with the audience, and I knew I would be all right. I sang my two songs and got paid a hefty check. Afterward, Jethro smiled largely and said, "Just like that!". So, this is what show business was like! I would learn later that it wasn't that simple. We all stayed over because Jethro had booked himself on Prairie Home Companion the following night along with his brother in law, Chet Atkins. I got to go and watch how it was done, and afterward everyone went out to dinner at a delightful restaurant in St. Paul. The next day we flew back to Chicago, and it was on that plane ride when Jethro informed me that he had cancer. We would do one more club date at "The Place" in Kenosha before he quit.

****

CHAPTER 23

Diving Into The Unknown

Jethro had introduced me to "The Place" in Kenosha some months before. He gave Bill and Josephine Andrucci, the owners, my 'story', and from then on they had me back with and without Jethro, taking me under their wing and giving me very useful advice. "Always look your best, Judi, even if the house is empty. You never know who might walk through that door." "The Place" was a retro nightclub–actually left over without revision from the flourishing live entertainment times of the 50's. It had a marquee and the old-fashioned red leather tufted door. The little stage was just big enough for a couple of performers, and a small house band, which then consisted of a grand piano and a drum set- with their respective players. The huge bar faced a wall full of headshots from the 30s, 40s and 50s; they were all the stars of the time that had performed at "The Place." The rows of pictures covered the entire length of the wall; every big name of the time. I knew many of the famous faces and even so, felt quite at home. The familiar faces of Dean Martin, Sammy Davis Jr, Joe Conti, Bill Bernardi, Helen Forrest, Mimi Himes and Phil Ford, and many others that I felt I knew of were comforting. For every show at 'the Place', I dressed like a nightclub performer: beaded long dresses and jackets, some props such as an army jacket for songs of WW1 and WW2, and some hats and boas to suit some ragtime/ Dixieland songs. Every moment was an adventure and I wasn't afraid to make mistakes. I wanted to learn and I was determined to do it better each time. I taped my shows and videotaped a couple of them. Actually, I had to use a home movie camera, because video tapes hadn't come out yet. So, we used an 8mm movie camera. Each reel was only worth 15 minutes of time. I learned a lot from those films, and could correct *some* of my bad habits.

Jethro Burns bravely refused treatment for his cancer, and he died about a year later. He was only 67 years old, but had been in the business for so long that people, including me, thought he was older. He and Homer had been performing since the age of 16. What a lot of people don't know is that Jethro's real name is Kenneth Burns; and that his wife's twin sister married Chet Atkins, therefore Chet and Jethro were brothers-in-law. It surprised me to find that Jethro's home was in Evanston for many, many years, and his everyday speech was without much accent at all. He was born in Conasauga, TN, raised in Knoxville TN, but lived most of his adult life in Evanston Illinois with his wife Gussie and their children. One of Jethro's stories about his grandson Kelly was that he and Kelly went to get some groceries, and the check out lady asked, "Your grandson is so cute, Jethro, is he spoiled?" And Jethro responded: "No, all little boys smell that way".

Now, somewhere in this mix of experiences, my husband and I went for dinner at Biggs, a lovely French restaurant near Rush Street. There was a strolling accordionist playing to the customers at the tables. He stopped at our table and started playing a standard ballad.. I automatically started singing along, and the accordionist asked if I would be interested in giving a try at singing with his band. It turned out to be the Jerry King Orchestra. Jerry comes from a musical family that spanned the entertainment decades of Chicago's live music. His dad worked at the Green Mill in the Capone days and has some wonderful stories to tell. At that time Jerry was a young boy and witnessed some stories that most of us have seen in movies, but it was real. Jerry hired me to sing with his orchestra, his wedding band and in his jazz band and I had a great time with this versatile assignment. They were excellent musicians and I could jump right in with a rock song when needed, or with dance tunes and even the Julida Polka! Whatever I knew, they did with me. It was a gas! Jerry had me sing on one of his Orchestra recordings. I think it was a demo, but he used the best studio. Columbia was plush, unlike many of the other studios I have used. He lead me through two thickly padded doors, that sandwiched a small step-through of just dead air space, then into the sound room. I was asked to stand in a specific spot, and a large octagonal microphone slowly lowered from the ceiling. It stopped just at the height I needed. All I had to do was sing along with the pre recorded songs. These days, Jerry and his wife run an accordion repair shop in Berwyn called "Buttons and Keys". I am sure Jerry knows every single moving part of each accordion that is brought in for his expertise!

After Jethro died, I figured I would go back to Deerfield and continue teaching guitar. It wasn't to be. I moped around for a couple of weeks until my Norwegian neighbor asked if I wanted to go to have a drink with her at the Scandinavian club in Arlington Heights.

I should say that several months before that, these neighbors and my husband and I had stopped in a restaurant in Algonquin for a nice dinner. It was the Iron Skillet Restaurant, and when we walked in, I peeked into a huge dining room that was filled with enthusiastic diners who were enjoying one of the best bands I had ever imagined at the time. It was the Celebration Dixieland Jazz Band. It was just a short term peek at the band before we went into another room for dinner there, but I was hooked. I couldn't stop thinking about that band.

CHAPTER 24

Everything Happens at Once!

But, now, months later, my neighbor and I were at the Scandinavian club, enjoying some homemade Norwegian glogg, a strong mulled wine drink. We walked into another room where there was some music, and she bought us another drink. I looked at the band and realized I was looking at the same group and with the same bass man I had seen months before in Algonquin. Although I didn't know it then, he had also been one of the Treniers that I had seen downtown on Rush Street approximately 12 years before. The band was swinging, and tearing up the audience with great music and comedy.

The next thing I knew, my neighbor Babs was talking to the bandleader, and soon he came over to me and asked if I wanted to sing something with his group. I could feel my face burn, and I told him I only knew two 'Dixieland' songs. It was a guess…I didn't know if I knew any. But, he asked what they were, and I said "Alexander's Ragtime Band" and "The Preacher." I found out later they were good choices, as Gary Miller, the bandleader was actually a preacher by profession. He said to com'on up and 'try it'. Gary said to do "The Preacher" first. I had learned it the way Bing Crosby did it, and used the same ending. Thankfully, the band knew what I was doing, and it went over really big. Then, I sang Alexander's Ragtime Band, and the audience was on their feet. It was exciting. Gary said, "We found our singer!" He asked me to come back that very night (It was a Sunday), to sing with the band at his gig in Algonquin. I went. Again, the audience was incredibly enthusiastic. Gary said, "I want to consider you my singer for any gigs I can get that can use a singer, including here at the Iron Skillet".

Two days later, I received a letter from him saying the same thing. It was a commitment. I was flattered, I was in awe and I was scared. The next time I was to sing with them was only a few days later, and that night, I was told that a bandleader from New Orleans needed a singer to travel with his band for a tour.

Connie Jones needed a singer to take the place of a girl singer who backed out of the pending tour at the 'last minute'. He sent me a tape of 9 songs and told me to learn them. I had 3 weeks. I wore my Sony Walkman daily for those three weeks, even to and from my son's wedding in Alabama. A week later I was on my way to meet a group of strangers and my Mom was on her way to Hawaii to marry her fourth and final husband. Mom had endured the deaths of her three husbands. Besides my dad who died very early, the next two were very nice men, good for my brothers, but they both died from cancers. This last one was a couple of years younger than she was.

****

CHAPTER 25

The Wedding in Alabama

My son was getting married to his sweetheart all the way down in Alabama.

I got up early before the wedding and 'secretly' went downtown Brewton Alabama, and knocked on the Jeweler's window. Nothing was open, and I was lucky he was there. He unlocked the door and I went in and bought a 14k gold 'K' charm to give my new daughter in law. From the rehearsal the night before, I had learned that once she and Bill were man and wife, the program scheduled the groom to stop at his new mother in law's pew and kiss her cheek. Glenda would do the same with me, her new mother in law, and at that time I would give her the little box with the gold 'K' in it. I hoped she liked the idea and it did turn out to be a good move. After the reception, the newlyweds were off on their honeymoon and the tour dates with the band from New Orleans were approaching quickly.

Johanna was in college, and I was ambivalent about going on the tour. I didn't think I knew enough and I was right about that; I was still an unconscious singer, except for the lyrics and melody. I always felt that the composer had a story to tell. I had no idea if I could actually do a tour! Now I know that if I hadn't gone, I would regret not having done so and I would have missed out on many great learning experiences.

But first, I sat down with my husband and we talked about being empty nesters; I was trying to do this right. I knew he had his hobbies, he was still living like a bachelor, but if I were going to go on this tour, it had to be ok with all of us. I told him I might just like doing this, and he should do more than watch television when the kids weren't around the house. He said to go on the tour and have fun.

****

CHAPTER 26

A Crash Course in Touring

It was time to leave for Aurora. My husband chided me about trying this; grinning at my audacity to answer this awesome opportunity to live life. He said not to worry about him, that he would be all right. He drove me to a house in Aurora, where I would then ride with Warren Felts to meet up with the rest of the band who were coming in from New Orleans. The musician, his tuba and I rode to Iowa where we would meet up with the rest of the band at the concert site.

I packed too heavily for this kind of trip; I actually packed a different outfit for each concert… Not figuring that because each concert was in a different town… I could have gotten along on just 3 or four costumes, I figured that out afterward… Savvy Me… One of my outfits was slacks and a tunic, the slacks were solid sequins, black, and the top was black sequined with gold trim. It was quite a stunner, I had gotten it at Sax Fifth Ave, and it fit really nice. When I came out on stage, Connie Jones announced: "And here she is, in her suit of lights." (Laugh, applause) And I did feel like a toreador up against the unknown, needing to be tough enough to survive this experience.

Every review that included me was good. It was far more than I expected. Several small towns published 'glowing' reports on my performances. I had a cassette tape recorder with me…the old cumbersome kind, and would record every concert, to see what I was doing wrong…or right. I tried to learn to do better each time. And I did. On a night that a note just wasn't coming out right enough, I went back to my room and nearly cried while I tried to find the answer. I finally made a long distance call to my vocal coach, and he told me what to do. It worked. He could have been one of the "Car Talk" guys...he knew right over the phone what was wrong and fixed it. If he had a 'call-in' show, it would have been called "Voice Talk".

The answer was that at that pitch I had to change the shape of the vowel. When I got home he recommended the 'Singers Guide to Diction' to me, and it is very helpful. I would recommend that book for singers, and strongly recommend that every singer or player records himself often to critique themselves. Several years later, I would see even the very best in the business do just that. At times, Franz Jackson would bring a small tape recorder with him, and so would John Young, a masterful pianist. John would also write himself little 'queue' cards that would read: "Are they enjoying the music?" or, "Are they smiling?" These wonderful musicians were always striving to be even more creative. That mentality helped make them the great musicians they were and their actions taught me some stratagems.

****

The tour was tiring, but when it was over, Connie liked to tell people that I was no trouble; I was the only singer who carried her own luggage and never asked for anything. I knew my limits and figured if they would put up with me, I'd try to carry my own weight. I sat alone in my room after a concert, and while listening to that night's tape, sewed loose sequins and beads back on my costumes. The band and I warmed to each other, and we started having fun. Actually they all knew each other, and they had fun all along. I was the outsider. We celebrated 'Dickie' Taylor's birthday with pizza and pop and a lot of laughs. We shopped in South Dakota where I fell in love with a pair of the goofiest slippers I ever saw. I bought them. They were soft sculptures of a male farmer for the left foot, and a female farmer for the right foot. The open mouths let your feet slide in. I still smile when I think of those puffy slippers.

We got into Canada, and there was enough snow for me to badger the guys into getting themselves some boots and gloves, etc. They were from New Orleans and snow was pretty rare for them. They didn't get the things I thought they needed, but, a couple of them found a thrift shop and Les got himself a heavy woolen pea-coat. The sleeve was torn and the lining needed repair, and since I had a sewing kit with me, I fixed it. Connie's van had no heater, and I was odd man out, so I spent a lot of time sitting on the floor between the seats. I should say here, that most of the time one of the guys sincerely offered his seat to me. Sitting anywhere else was my choice. I wore a fake fur jacket with large padded shoulders that were the fashion in 1987, and Les Muscut tagged me "The Smurf," although the jacket was pink, not blue. Connie Jones Crescent City Jazz Band with the pink Smurf.

When most of the guys opted for the more comfortable, warm ride in Dickie's van, I napped on one of the bench seats in Connie's van. When he put on the brakes, I landed on the floor. Les said, "Oh, look, we're playing "roll the Smurf." He was a wonderfully funny person whose roots were in England but who had been living in New Orleans several years and the French Quarter was his home for many years. I remember one of the concerts was held in a small Church with a vaulted ceiling that had fans hanging down from long stems. As we were bringing in the equipment to set up for the evening's concert, Les stopped in the center aisle, put his banjo and guitar down on the floor, looked up and sighed. "They'll never get it off the ground" he muttered of the propellers spinning overhead. Another time, we were scheduled to stay at a worn-down little motel somewhere in the Dakotas. It was dark, and the driveway to the motel was long and crooked. With the cold air and leafless trees, the entrance was foreboding. The sign hung slightly tilted and was missing some lights. Les quipped, "I wonder if Norman is up"… (referring to Norman Bates in "Psycho.") I didn't sleep well that night. I hated that movie.

17 concerts in 21 days on the road, and everyone was fun and copacetic. I felt like a school girl with 6 mentors. Throughout the tour, and though I was a rookie, things lightened up more each day. It was Connie's first tour with his Crescent City Jazz Band. His mother was very sick, so being away was stressful, and he called home often. He told me that his wife Elaine was a nurse, and she stayed home to help take care of his mother. I doubt he would have accepted a tour if it weren't for Elaine. When we all were in a souvenir shop, or truck stop, he would pick up a small item for Elaine, and I picked up a cute little nurse sculpture and bought it for him to give her. Later, I found a joke book for nurses, and bought two of them, one for

my Aunt Vera, who also was a nurse, and one for Elaine. Things seemed normal. By the end of the tour, we were all exhausted. I was torn between not wanting the tour to end and getting back to Northbrook to see what was in store. My son and his wife were getting settled in Texas and my daughter loved UW-Madison and was studying hard.

My husband was busy being an estate lawyer for my friend who lived across the street. Her husband was dying of cancer, and she had asked my husband to take care of her legal business.

CHAPTER 27

Not a Women's World Out There

I had just returned from the tour, and I was anxious to get back to my gig with Gary's band in Algonquin. He had me come in because he was celebrating his 7th anniversary with his band performing at the "Iron Skillet"…the restaurant where I had first seen him, and where I sang my first time as 'his singer'. My repertoire had grown, and I was feeling pretty confident for a rookie. (I called myself a rookie for years, feeling like one, until finally Jim told me to stop that; he said, "you are a professional so act like one.") But I know my limitations. I went into the restaurant, and everyone knew who I was…or it felt like they did. The tour had been with musicians that were a lot better known than I thought, or knew, and I had created a stir. I felt it was too much. I was not equipped to handle the responsibility. But, with straw hat in hand I went up and took my place on stage. Gary had asked two widely known musicians to join his band that night as a salute to the anniversary. When I sang my songs, the two guests were included in the band. He announced them as Jim Beebe and Barrett Deems. I had never heard of either of them before that, but when they were playing behind me, I knew it was something special.

Years later, Barrett would pay me a great compliment, saying "If Jimmy hadn't gotten to me first, I would be singing with *his* band." But Jim did get me first, whirlwind fast. I didn't even know it. After the sets were over at the Iron Skillet, Jim approached me and asked if I wanted to give singing with *his* band a try. He told me he was out in Oak Brook at the Bristol Seafood Grill.

I went out to Oakbrook and listened to his group, while sitting in a corner, enjoying a lovely lounge furnished with leather couches, interspersed with little two-person cocktail tables. The band was playing old songs, the ones I had 'grown up' with. Jim spoke into the microphone, and dedicated a song to me. It was Sultry Serenade. Years later, after my first album, Delmark had Jim add to his own discography another album that featured me on 5 songs. Jim named it "A Sultry Serenade". (Jim's Discography is quite long, having recorded with the Dukes of Dixieland, Bob Scobey, Little Brother Montgomery, and several albums with his own bands, and my discography is simply 4 CDs at this time.. Of course that is more than I had ever thought of having!)

*****

As a kid, I loved musicals and the wonderful hit parade, along also with Louis Armstrong, Ella Fitzgerald, Frank Sinatra, Bing Crosby and all the smooth movie star singers and dancers. It was a totally other world that I only dreamed about. And here it was, right in front of me: Ragtime, Dixieland, and old pop tunes that had become part of the jazz repertoire. I saw it first at the Iron Skillet, although I had experienced it with the great Jethro Burns, I hadn't really identified it. It was beginning to take shape in my mind as Jimmy Johnson was singing "Caledonia," and the audience was eating it up. People were raising their arms in unison to the chorus of "Yellow Dog Blues". Everyone was happy. Jimmy Johnson was also the bass man in Gary Millers' band.

It took me three weeks of hemming and hawing before I dared sing a song at the Bristol.

CHAPTER 28

Pipe Dreams

When I first sang with Gary's band, I thought I had died and gone to heaven. Gary was a preacher with his own congregation. Shortly after I returned from the tour, he called me to say he had a friend who was opening a new club, and wanted me to sing there and 'run' it. He had heard that I was downtown with an investor looking at places to put a new Jazz club—one of my pipe dreams. I found a great spot in Printer's Row. It was then a rundown area, even though it was near downtown Chicago, so the building owners were anxious to give deals. So was the City. I could have had a gorgeous old bank building that was marble and granite; and I fantasized emulating the "Raccoon Club", a period club started and run by singer Jan Hobson. Her lovely 'speakeasy' was classy, all acoustic, a grand piano that was always kept in tune, a semi circular stage with a short 'runway' type of aisle jutting from the front center. The tables were small, with long white linen cloths, and the coffee was served in European press pots. But, my one investor wasn't enough, and he offered to talk to some others. I had no idea of what to do, even though he was a lawyer, he wasn't a restaurateur either. And I sure was no business person! So, I chickened out and waited to make another opportunity.

****

CHAPTER 29

Meanwhile, the Advent of Divorce

Just about the same time I was starting at the Bristol, I was due to have a hysterectomy. I missed one weekend of work, and a corporate job that Jim's band had, that I wished I could have worked. He used an excellent singer, and I am sure, an audience pleaser. The following weekend I went back to the Bristol. I was very sore from the incision, but I was happy to have an excuse to stay away from my husband. His idea of sex was that if he was happy I must be. Of course, that caused my husband to demand it. He pushed me down on the bed. I told him "I can't; I'm not healed". He put his entire weight on top of me and forced himself on me. The pain was excruciating, and I half screamed "Stop it!" It didn't work. It took all my strength to pull my knees up under him and use my feet to push him off. He caught his balance and yelled, "You bitch." And I moved into my son's empty bedroom from then on. I was so angry that I wished I had kicked harder and that he had fallen backward through the window. I imagined myself being led away in handcuffs and trying to explain what had happened. But I didn't say anything about it to anyone. He was my daughter's father, and we were a family.

I moved into my son's empty bedroom. Soon, we decided to get a divorce. He is an attorney, and I knew that while divorcing, the only ones that get anything out of it are the attorneys. I didn't want to drag anything out like that, I needed to put it behind me and get on with life. So I let him sort it out rather than bring in another attorney. (Savvy Me)…Well,

I was tired. My kids were gone, and I wanted to get away too. He would come into my son's room where I was sleeping and wake me up. He would stand at the foot of the bunk bed and shake it loose so I would not get back to sleep. He would scream that he would live better than I would. He was right. I don't know why he made such a ruckus. He already had his next pick to marry. He took care of himself. But I've learned that sometimes getting money isn't worth the fight. I found that out, although it made some difficult years to follow. As a lawyer, he made a settlement that I would get the house in Northbrook. But that was all. I did want it. It had been my only long-term home since my Dad died. I thought I would spend the rest of my life in that house, and that I could someday have my children and their children come there to visit me and spend holidays. Pollyanna Grannie.

Meanwhile, he told me to use the equity checks from the house to buy groceries and whatever I needed. To keep peace, I kept right on keeping house and cooking as usual. I didn't want anyone else to be nervous about an impending divorce. HELLO AGAIN! I was so dense about trusting him; he was also using the equity to buy himself expensive golf memberships, and putting his own salary away in anticipation of the divorce. In exchange for the house, he kept 100% of his salaries, his pension, his IRAs, and he didn't take any responsibility to make sure I had any insurance or money for my other needs. He called it splitting it 50-50. We agreed not to make it final until after his nephew's wedding which was coming up soon. I said to please don't tell his brother and sister-in-law until after the wedding. Their son's wedding was supposed to be a happy day.

But, of course, he just *had* to tell his family the day *of* the wedding... *at* the wedding. Of course, they blamed me. M ex's friends had gotten his version, and had no idea of what the truth was. Instead of telling them my side, I let them close me out of their lives. Not much loss there, but not even civil contact was made. For the year we stayed in the house until the divorce, my ex had me use the equity checks for groceries, and all the bills. The equity also went to pay Johanna's tuition through 3 years at U W Madison. I didn't stop to think he was actually depleting what was supposed to be mine. I figured the lawyers would take care of that. And they did. My husband's best friend represented him, and he and his friend Mel charmed, or whatever lawyers do, the female attorney I finally hired. I thought my lawyer was supposed to protect me. As it came out, she was only interested in running for judgeship. I remember how when she proudly told the judge how easily she completed this divorce and I remember how the judge shot her a disgusted look. As I look back, I can pretty safely say the judge's face was saying "What are you so cocky about? Don't you see you are leaving your client with nothing?" I wish now that I had trusted that reaction or *someone* and reneged on the divorce until I could get good, realistic representation. But after nearly 24 years of marriage, I didn't think I should have needed it! A thought of fighting with legalities made my head fuzzy. With over 23 years of marriage, I got no part of his pension or his savings and I didn't even get health insurance, and, within two years, I lost the house. He still had his practice **and** was still getting paid from the county as a title examiner. A month or so after our divorce, he married our neighbor— the woman who had hired him to do her husband's estate. My female attorney went on to become a judge. I'm sure she got an extra two votes from my ex husband and his lawyer. He said I would get half of his Social Security, but when that time came SS told me he hadn't put much in, as it went into his pension instead. So I am stuck with what little Social Security I get from my own jobs.

CHAPTER 30

Getting Through It

I continued working with Jim's band at the Bristol and at Dicks' last Resort. Jim Beebe was a wizard at getting gigs for his players, and we worked, for long terms of 5 and 6 nights and days a week. Sometimes we would do a Coldwell Banker breakfast gala, and on the same day, an employee appreciation day at Motorola, or at Salerno, or Nabisco. The nights were regular gigs in jazz clubs. The players in Jim's band became my family. I worked with them daily, nightly and many other times when one of us had our own gigs.

Jim always told me "never go to a gig that another singer has, to find a job…you have to create your own gigs." And I did. Of course, I wouldn't have been able to go out to see other singers anyway as we were always working. I had my own world, my own learning process as it was, from the very best musicians that Chicago had to offer. As I got more confident, I did look for more between gigs, but I never, ever went to another singer's gig looking to sing. That kind of aggression is just not in me. Why should anyone have to get knocked off their tracks because some cocky performer thinks they're better? Everyone has a talent, and everyone should be allowed to have it and allowed to enjoy it as long as they don't use it to abuse. It was during the times I had my own gigs that Jim would hire Polly Podewell to sub for me. It was an honor to know someone of that caliber would fill in for me.

CHAPTER 31

Don't Mess With Shirley Temple

What I didn't know was, that while I was burying myself in the work Jim had, and expanding my own repertoire, people elsewhere were gossiping, and other singers didn't have half the gigs I had. They would come out to the Bristol, sometimes with their musician husband, or their boyfriend 'manager', just to compete. And Jim was always gracious to all of them, and never failed to introduce them and bring them up on stage to sit in, if they were pros, and even some who weren't. It was very common with our band, and if I knew the singer or player, I learned to do the same thing. But I had to go through Jim and it depended on his mood or plans for the sets. Singers as well as players would come in to test the waters and some were unethical and aggressively so.

I had known one of these women from north side. Sometimes I would stop in at the Railroad Inn to sing a couple on my way to the Bristol, and we had always been friendly up until then. When she found out where I had been going to, she came out to Oakbrook. I invited her to sit with me, and I introduced her to Jim and mentioned that she sang a good "What a Little Moonlight Can Do". He let her come up. She was a fairly good singer. But she had no ethics. She came in the next night and walked past me and straight up to the stage. She schmoozed with the band, and got herself invited up to sing. After that night, she would come again, with her friends, and wearing glitzy stage clothes. After a few more of those kinds of nights, I sat down next to her and her friends, and told her I really didn't appreciate what she was doing. I asked her why didn't she go and find her own gig. I said I wouldn't come to hers and she should stay away from mine. She stuck her finger in my chest and threatened… "Judi," she squinted her eyes and said, "If I can get them to have *me* sing here, I am going to do just that."

Now, I got frustrated and clenched my teeth as I whispered "Try it." I relayed the experience to Jim, who had been watching. The next time she came in with her entourage, and it was time for Jim to announce me, he was mischievous enough to say, "And now we want to bring up a very fine singer who we met recently." The woman sat up with expectation. He let her wait. I was feeling pretty uneasy, because basically, I wasn't very sure of myself. Jim said, "And here she is…. (pause)…JUDI K." I never saw such chaos at one table. She started crying and her friends put their arms around her.

Often during the week, many odd things happened. I was there less than a year when I met a woman that went by the name of Margot Teagarden. She befriended me, and I enjoyed her stories. She was a big woman with a speaking voice that had been destroyed by smoke. That didn't stop her from talking, smoking—or coughing—or clearing her throat loudly though. At that time, cigarettes were allowed to be smoked in bars and restaurants, and no one made anything of it. Margot would sweep in the room and Jim would introduce her as an ex-wife of Jack Teagarden's. He would ask the audience to say hello to the 'wife' of his idol, Jack Teagarden. When he said Margot Teagarden, She would stand up and bow, and enjoy the applause, throwing a kisses. Sometimes he would say, "Please say hello to Mrs. Jack Teagarden". I think he liked believing it was really her. She had a way of telling stories about herself that no one knew if they were true or not, so they gave her the benefit of the doubt.

Then, one day, we started to see the light. I am going to insert Jim's story here; written in his own hand as an explanation to some calls he had gotten from a musician in Canada. He also submitted it to the Jazz Institute along with some other experiences he had put in his writings. Although Jim spells Margo without the 't', I was told by her she spelled it with a t.

****

Margo (Mrs. Jack) Teagarden— by Jim Beebe

The Chicago Jazz scene has always been a rich and flavorful one with wonderful musicians and bands of every stylistic description. This has been made possible by the many venues—from nightclubs to dance halls—that have used jazz music as for entertainment. From bands that feature very early traditional-classic style jazz to very contemporary jazz modes, all seem to find venues in which to strut their stuff.

Supporting this vivid musical palette has been an exotic cast of jazz fans, and out and out characters, who fill the jazz clubs and to whom jazz has become a core part of their lives. One very colorful fan was Margo Taft (Mrs. Jack) Teagarden. Her love for jazz took on a life of its own. I found myself right in the middle of it. Let me go back a few years....

My phone was ringing off of the hook. I finally answered it. "Is this Jim Beebe?" "Yes it is," I replied. "Is this Jim Beebe, the bandleader?" I assured her that it was. "Jim, I'm sorry to have to tell you that your vocalist, Margo, has passed away. We found her in her bed this morning."

I was completely taken back and said, "There must be some mistake, I don't have or know a vocalist named Margo, and my vocalist, Judi K is here with me." The caller insisted that she had the right Jim Beebe and that her tenant, Margo sang with my band at the Braxton Seafood Grill in Oakbrook. Again, I was taken aback as I did, indeed, work at the Braxton with my band but with Judi K as vocalist.

The caller told me that she was in Forest Park and that Margo and her husband rented an apartment from her there. The caller gave me Margo's last name, but it was one that I didn't recognize. Margo had told her that she was an entertainer and sang with my band. She was going through Margo's things to find relatives and friends to contact. She said that Margo's husband was ill and could not help. As we spoke things finally started to click and I finally realized that this caller was talking about Margo (Mrs. Jack) Teagarden. I had not seen Margo 'Teagarden' in some years and I was sorry to learn of her passing.

Margo was one of those wonderful colorful characters who were such a lively part of the Chicago Jazz scene. She surfaced in Chicago somewhere in the late '70s or early '80s. I remember her as she began attending, seemingly, almost every jazz event.

I had a band in the Flaming Sally's room at the Blackstone Hotel and she began to come there often. She presented herself as Margo Teagarden, and as I am an ardent Jack Teagarden fan, we became friends. Margo told me that she had been married to Jack Teagarden in the early '40s. I knew that Jack had been married 3 or 4 times so it seemed quite plausible to me.

She knew a lot about Jack and this added to her plausibility. She liked to be introduced as Mrs. Jack Teagarden. Later she disclosed that she was from the Taft family and she would often refer to herself as Margo Taft Teagarden.

Eventually, I took my band into the Braxton Seafood Grill in Oakbrook for a Friday and Saturday gig which has continued to this day...14 years. Margo became one of our regulars. She was a vivacious, flamboyant woman and looked like someone straight out of the early '40s nightclub scene.

She often arrived in a limousine or someone would bring her. She wore large colorful hats and would usually make a Maria Callas entrance. I began to introduce her to the audience as Mrs. Jack Teagarden and I would say something about her having been married to Jack in the '40s. The audience was thrilled with a real jazz celebrity in their midst and Margo loved it. These introductions became a regular bit.

Margo began calling me a lot and was also calling my vocalist, Judi K almost every day. There were some musicians who didn't believe her story of having been married to Teagarden and thought that she was a fake. I had some doubts myself and I asked both Bobby Lewis and Barrett Deems about her, as they had both worked with Jack. Neither seemed could recall Jack ever mentioning an ex-wife named Margo.

Margo seemed to know a lot of well known musicians on a first name basis. During her phones calls she would say, "Oh, Buck just called me and he is doing such and such..." or "I talked with Zoot today and he is going to England," etc. She seemed at the center of many jazz happenings. Every phone call was like this—it all seemed on the level, as many of the things that she related did, in fact, take place.

At one point Margo told me that she was from the Taft family and intimated that there was old money there and there was an estate on the east coast. Every now and then she would announce that she was going back east to visit the estate and we wouldn't see her for several weeks. She said that her housekeeper would look after her retarded brother who was in her care.

She told me that after the divorce from Teagarden she had been married to three pilots—two military and one commercial—and that each one had crashed and died, leaving her with their pension money.

As these stories became more embellished and outlandish, I decided to order a Jack Teagarden video from Joe Showler in Toronto. Joe is a Teagarden enthusiast who puts out rare Teagarden recordings and videos. I wrote a letter to Joe and mentioned that Margo Teagarden was a regular where my band was playing. Joe fired back a letter in which he said that I had opened a can of worms in mentioning Margo.

He said that he believed that Margo was a phony and was never married to Jack, and that he wanted me to find about the truth about her. I wrote back that Margo had become a friend and that I couldn't pry into this, but if I found out anything more I would let him know.

Judi K is the one who inadvertently got on to Margo. She had befriended her but was puzzled. Margo had presented a very affluent picture of herself—with Taft money, an estate, pensions etc. One day she called Judi and asked her if she would help her by taking her to the bank. She gave Judi directions and Judi went there expecting a residence that would reflect Margo's lifestyle. Instead she found a shabby upstairs apartment that hadn't seen a housekeeper in years. I remember Judi's complete bafflement as she told me this.

One day, just after Judi had finished reading a *Chicago Tribune* article about some piece of jazz history, Margo called. She started relating almost verbatim the same information that was in the newspaper article. But with one big difference...Margo was now 'in' the story. Judi told her, "Why Margo, I just read about this in the paper." Margo coughed, sputtered and hung up the phone.

Judi called me and bells went off as we realized that a lot of the things that Margo had told us were things that Margo had read that had become part of her personal history. She would read about some jazz musician or event and would interject herself into the story, ala Woody Allen. I realized that the marriage to Jack Teagarden was a fraud. Actually, I really didn't care.

Margo never called or came to the Club again. I don't believe that anybody in the jazz world ever saw her again. There was a brief period that got rather ugly as Margo started calling some musicians who work with me trying to spread negative, false stories about Judi. That soon stopped and we never heard of Margo Taft Teagarden again until her landlord called me.

Sadly, the landlord said that she had contacted a daughter and cousin but neither of them wanted anything to do with her. A cousin said, "Well this explains why she would never play the piano for us. She had us believing that she toured the world as a singer and pianist." Margo's retarded brother turned out to be her husband who had worked in a factory.

This seems a sad ending to a jazz life. But I look at it in this light. Margo had invented a vivid fantasy jazz life for herself and she lived it to the fullest. She seemed to have a genuine love of good jazz and knew quite a bit about the music and the musicians involved. She added a bit of zest and flavor to our already rich Chicago jazz scene.

As Jack Teagarden sang so many times, "Who's going to know…a hundred years from today."

****

There were a few years when there wasn't enough time to do all the gigs Jim's band had! We were handling our three nights a week at Dicks, our varying 2 and 3 nights (the 'third' nights there was a Wednesday) a week at the Bristol/Braxton, and a few weeks at the Chord On Blues, Goose Island Brewery, and many more venues that wanted us, along with having my own gigs with trios and duos. Jim always managed to start a new gig in a new venue, and open it up to other bands working there. I liked doing artwork on the Computer, as primitive as my computer was, and I made a special flyer for Jim Beebe Chicago Jazz Weddings, as we had a great number of newlyweds who wanted the sound of our band to envelop their wedding day. I loved having my own dinner concerts at Korebels, where they would sell a package deal of dinner and my show for one evening a month. Although they had dinner concerts with other performers, Brian, who organized the dinner shows said I was their biggest money maker. I really had a great time there, mostly because it was just myself and piano and that gave me a ton of leeway to stop and start with the audience and involve them. I used Jeremy Kahn, and not only was I lucky to have him, he was just right for the gig. One night, I was about to sing Rainbow Connection, and the young man in charge of entertainment sneaked in a Kermit puppet, and 'hid' behind the plant stands that separated the customers while they ate. He 'sat' Kermit up on the wall for all to see, and started harmonizing with me. The young man used a perfect Kermit voice.

It was just wonderful! Using the microphone, I talked to "Kermit" when we were finished, and he carried on a conversation with me in Kermit's voice. The audience went wild. I had to have that again, so I asked Brian if he would join in again the next date I had at the restaurant. He did, and it didn't go as well, although we gave it our best effort. I won't forget how good the first, impromptu upstaging was and I cherish the memory.

W I D K I (not WIKI) = what I (didn't) know is

Having so much work was unusual for a singer. I didn't realize that, because being busy, I figured everyone was doing that. I found out that wasn't so. I hadn't been downtown Chicago for anything else except to work a gig I had gotten, or with Jim's band or some corporate event or our regular nights at Dick's.

Jim taught me to be conscious. I knew I was conscientious, but, I mean he taught me to be *conscious*; mostly in singing, but in regular life too. 'Don't be an unconscious singer'...meaning: know your notes, your pick up notes, where the bridge goes and how you are going to handle it. Good lessons.

****

CHAPTER 32

My House

After my divorce, I rented my house out to a family from Holland. After a year, I moved back in it, made repairs and found a couple of people who were being transferred to a new computer company in Northbrook. These people needed a place until their own homes were ready to move into, and then they could bring their families. I rented two of the 4 bedrooms out as 'sleeping rooms'. I would only allow someone who needed a room for sleep, I didn't want strangers in any other part of my house. They would only use the one bedroom that they rented, with the hall bathroom. I provided the clean furniture and bedding, and towels. I had no bedroom set in my master suite, My ex had taken it, so I slept on the floor. I had given half our things to my ex, naively believing 50-50 was really 50-50. No matter what he did, I needed to do my part right. I didn't stop to sort it out realistically; I just separated black from white. I had no one to talk to who would direct me. If it meant splitting 50-50, he got 8 dishes and I got 8 dishes. He got the Henredon furniture, stereo, television and armoires and the master bedroom set. I got the kid's bedroom sets, the formal living room and half the kitchen supplies. Savvy Me. And a month or so later, he gave all the furniture to his brother and married our old neighbor and moved in with her. Savvy Me.

A wife of one of our friend's told me after the divorce that she and her husband had always thought that my (ex) husband treated me like 'another appendage'. Not a partner. Those were her words. I was glad someone had noticed.

Neither one of my kids really knew what was going on during the last year of marriage. I like to say that. but it's a bit more complicated,

My daughter had a tougher time with the divorce even though she was in college and out of the house. She was closer to her Dad, and she wasn't prepared to see her parents divorced. She blamed me for a long time. I let her do it, she'd never have believed me anyway, and her father was very convincing. I cried a river. Like her mother, she didn't ask her dad for anything. She worked to pay for her own master's degrees, and she bought her condo out of her own money. Same way her brother Bill made his own life. Johanna could have asked her dad for help, but she stood on her own two feet. Bill wouldn't have gotten it even if he *had* asked for it. Both of my kids have retained their humor and I am proud of them for their strength and self sufficiency. My children and I are now closer than ever, and I am content.

****

CHAPTER 33

Too Fast, Too Soon

Back at the bandstand, Jim's marriage was breaking up. His wife had thrown him out of her house, and he came to work in distress. I didn't know then that he was suffering from emphysema; I didn't know much about his private life, I didn't know he was sick then because he put on such a strong front in that department. I would learn that if the industry learned that he was sick, they tend to not hire, and choose one of the many others waiting in the wings to replace him. I didn't know much about Jim's past and that he had married a singer from Gary's band some years before. This caused a rough path for a while where I was concerned, because of the first couple of gigs I had gone on with Jim's band. Gary was livid that I would join Jim's band. I wish I had known more about Jim's and Gary's history, knowing would have helped me understand some of these events. But they didn't know about my private life; so why should I know about theirs? My focus was to become a good singer. I also knew I was adding a lot to the band, to the show. Gary wrote me a letter that nearly burst into flames as I read it. It left me shaken. What had I done? After all, the same musicians played in several bands, so why couldn't I take jobs with other bands? It just didn't make sense to me. These things happened very fast and I didn't have an understanding of them. Should I have talked to Gary before working with Jim's band? Savvy me.

One night, I was leaving the Bristol and Jim walked me out to my car. Since I lived in Northbrook, I had to take the toll road each night. I opened my door, and he leaned in and kissed me lightly—on the lips. I could feel the electricity creep up from my feet to the top of my head. I said good night and left. I didn't sleep very well that night.

******

Things went on routinely for a few more weeks, and I felt I was getting better at this new craft I have been handed. I never really felt I had it except toward the end of my years in Chicago; even though I had a ton of formal voice training before going public. In my youth, I sang in plays and choral groups, and took voice and piano, but Mom made it sound like everyone did, so I wasn't too interested. The nuns taught us to attack a note in a very square way. The real interest came when I decided to take voice lessons as an adult. Even after some years of training, it took a while on stage to actually summon up all I *could* do.

Learning how to use a microphone, and trying to understand what the jazz musicians were doing, and keeping up with the caliber of musicians that I worked with took a lot of energy and concentration! Of course, *they* had been doing it all of their lives. They knew more theory, style, of history than you can get from a book or from years of college. By all accounts, I was a newcomer; a rookie; considered myself one for a long time. But, on the way, I found out I had more of a background than I knew. When I study my habits as a youth, I remember bringing my piano lesson home with me and doing things with the chords that weren't asked of me, or weren't printed in my lesson book. I toyed with different sounds; new harmonies and relative harmonies. Playing thirds and fourths, and arpeggios were exercises that I fingered up and down the keyboard, crossing over each octave, imagining myself at a concert grand, raising my limp wrist high into the air with each chord. I dreamed more than I learned. Years later, I wrote a few songs that are still in my file cabinet. One was put in a big band format; and a couple of others are just piano and voice. I wrote words and music to a song that came to me from the experience of my close cousin, Kay. She had just found out the name that was given her daughter that she had given up in college. The nuns convinced her. For many years Kay wondered where her daughter would be, and got in touch with the adoption agency. Back then information was closed. But, when a change was made, she found out her daughter was ok, and lived in a good family. And she found out her daughter's name was "Julie". She called me from Milwaukee to tell me. Her call was so moving, I immediately started writing "And Then There's Julie". The words and music came to me at the same time. It was exciting. I sent it to Kay, and she hung on to it. 50 years later, Kay got a phone call from a stranger by the name of Julie. It was her daughter. After all the years of worrying and wondering, Kay could take a deep breath and find some peace. Right away, Kay sent her daughter the song I wrote. I had forgotten all about it. But, there it was. At the reunion of mother and daughter AND grandson, she asked me to sing it. It was better than I remembered it. It is darn good. So, recently I had been trying it out, with the story as a segue, while volunteering at assisted living facilities. It makes a nice addition to a show.

CHAPTER 34

Returning to the Band Stand:

Dozens of musicians always wanted to get on Jim's roster of players, and over the years, dozens more from out of town would stop by to sit in because they knew he would be gracious and bring the best out of them. Jim knew of them all, as they would come from the East and West Coasts, from Minnesota and far south, and be welcomed in to sit in. It was the sign of a well read, well bred, and self-assured talent in Jim to welcome other players. Franz Jackson and Jethro Burns were much the same: secure with themselves that they allowed other players with them, who would walk away feeling good about themselves, not realizing their success was <u>because</u> of the strength of the elder musician. Now that I have the time to reflect, I realize more, how very fortunate I was all those years. It was so much more than singing. It was healthy, happy, studious, and soul saving.

CHAPTER 35

Flashback

We were at Dick's Last Resort. We were the first band that Dick's hired in Chicago. Jim Clark's was the second. The reason was that Dick's Last Resort headquarters in Dallas had sent Tommy Loy, their house band leader, to Chicago to hire bands for the new Dick's Last Resort in North Pier Terminal. It was the second facility of what was to be a chain for Dick's. Tommy Loy's first hire was Jim Beebe's Chicago Jazz Band. Jim then talked the Chicago Dick's people to hire me after he had been there just a week. I was new to the scene; I was thrilled to have two regular gigs. The one night at Dick's developed into 3 nights a week and after several months, dropped down to 2 nights a week, and went on for nearly 5 years. Meanwhile, the Bristol had us in Oakbrook 2 and 3 nights a week, plus occasional events and holiday brunches. We were busy for more days and nights than there were in a week. For a short time, it was Wednesdays, Thursdays, Saturdays and Sunday Brunch at the Bristol. Then it would switch to Wednesdays, Fridays and Saturdays, but no matter how many nights a week, it was always Friday and Saturdays, week in and week out. Jim almost always managed to sell me as part of the package. I didn't get hired to do the brunch because there were no mikes, the trio walked around restaurant, parking temporarily at an assortment of tables of diners. He did ask me to come over one Sunday, just to do a song or two, though, and when I walked in, the three of them sang to the tune of "Hello, Dolly"…, "Well, Hello, Judi, well, Hello Judi, it's no nice to have you back where you belong…"! I basked in the attention!

I had become a 'pro'. But I also had to be reminded of that. I never really felt like one until several years later….

The regular band during my first several years with Jim, was Joe Johnson on Piano, Jimmy Johnson on Bass, Greg Sergo on Drums, Bob Neighbor on trumpet, Franz Jackson on Reeds, and Jim leading with his trombone. I was the featured singer. Whenever one of them couldn't make it to a gig, Jim only had to pick up the phone to call his first choice; most of the time it was whomever sat in the most recently. It was the right thing to do. At the Bristol, later the Braxton, the band started out with Andy Johnson on piano, and later an assortment of wonderful piano players would come and go, but the great Duke Groner was our regular bassist. Joe Johnson and Franz Jackson would join us frequently, as they were the regulars downtown, but Greg Sergo was our drummer most regularly. Greg later got busy with his own group, the "Ellington Dynasty", using Joe and a variety of great musicians. More often than not, Bob Neighbor would work with us, and often Steve Jensen. Sometimes Warren Kime, and, although for some years Charlie Hooks was our reed man, later, Franz Jackson would be the full time member. When Duke Groner retired, Jimmy Johnson took over the job full time and stayed until he died in 1994. Truck Parham filled in often, as he was then with us at Dicks, and how I enjoyed Truck's stories, his antics and the sound of his big painted standing bass. How he would wow the audience with his own "Truck's Blues", slapping and spinning that bass wildly!

One of the nights at Dicks, I was surprised to see the band switch places on stage, taking each other's instruments and doing a pretty darn good job of performing. Jim and Franz could both play the piano and Joe Johnson took over the bass while JJ went up to sing. That lasted three or four tunes before they resumed their usual places. But the fun of it lasts much longer in my memory. Those guys were awesome!

****

CHAPTER 36

Discovering Jim

After 48 years of life as I had it with all of it's bad decisions, I finally found something, someone who would teach me something; who would give me some self worth. Early on at Dicks, another life changing situation unfolded: we were all on stage at Dicks Last Resort; and in the middle of a set, Jim staggered to the back wall of the stage and leaned against it. His skin was turning gray. I had never witnessed an asthma attack before, and Franz said I should take him to the hospital and that he would keep the band going. Jim said he used the VA in Brookfield, so I took him there. They kept him overnight. The next day, a fellow trombonist told me not to let him go back to Warrenville, where Jim was living with a fellow musician in an older house. Jim had moved in with a single banjo player/guitarist after Jim's wife 'threw him out'. (What a strange way to put it). Besides being a very talented musician, the owner of the house was a physically healthy man, he was against smoking and had a clean house from what I know. That was good for Jim. But the house was on low land, and there was standing water in the basement. Another trombonist, who also had asthma and severe allergies said that the house had mold spores in it and he himself couldn't get near to– "even the back door"…and Jim should not go in the house again. Jim's COPD Medic, Dr. Draga, agreed. But, all of this was foreign to me. I had never heard of mold spores indoors or out. I come from healthy, farm people, who never had allergies and basically were rarely sick.

******

This was during the time I had two renters using two of the bedrooms at my house. (Sleeping rooms). I saw Jim as someone who could use a place to stay, and I sure could use a third renter. And, since no one seemed to care that Jim was alone, that he was barely able to take care of himself. Jim was nice to me; I looked forward to having him around. Jim said his current landlord was charging him $60 a week and I said that would be ok with me. So, he moved into my son's room, a clean bed and clean-air house, and Jim got well. He said that he would like to stay, and that was ok with me, too. We ate together in my kitchen, and after a couple of times taking separate cars to work, we started to divide the expense of parking and the driving and tolls. I took care of his laundry and cleaning, because I wanted to. He sure didn't know how, and I had a washer and dryer in a room next to the kitchen.

I went over to the house in Warrenville to see if anything was retrievable. The other trombonist specifically said to leave Jim's clothes, shoes and 'even' his luggage behind and 'don't bring anything back into my house, as the mold spores would travel along'. I asked him what about the boxes of newspaper clippings and programs Jim had there? In my mind this was all pertinent history. I was told that the drugstore sells an acidic solution that you mix and spray on the infected objects, even newspaper, and then you lay it in the sun to dry before you pack it away. I went out and got a few large Rubbermaid storage boxes, and did whatever his friend trombonist suggested. Jim owned very few clothes, and I left them back in Warrenville for the time being. I had a few bucks from my renters, and I was making some money working for Jim, and so I went to Sam's Club and stocked Jim with socks, underwear, shirts, a jacket and tie. Some of his things were perfectly good after I had them dry cleaned and/or washed. My husband had left a couple of windbreakers behind, and they fit Jim too.

The upshot is that Jim and I admired each other, we had the quite the same tolerances and later, I found out we were both from the same area of Wisconsin. I found that out in a strange way: at a gig. He used the term "biffy" when he went to the restroom, and I laughed and said, "My mom used to say 'biffy'...where are you from"? "Wisconsin" was the answer.

And, I couldn't forget that kiss.

CHAPTER 37

$cientology.

I really hadn't heard of it before Jim entered my life. Nor did I have much interest in UFOs. But, with Jim's background having dabbled in $cientology, he had an interest in both. He had joined Scientology because of another musician's involvement, but before a year was up, Jim has seen and heard enough to figure out the scam.

His time became limited in music, and as I took over more responsibilities of the band. He got more involved with the people who helped victims of cults find some secrecy and deprogramming. "Savvy" as I am, my thought was, if these people want to stay in, let them. I didn't know how grave being caught up in a cult could be. Jim brought me with him to one of the meetings, mostly I drove him to where he needed to go because of his health. I had to pack snacks for him to keep up his strength, and handle the oxygen tank, etc. But the meeting of all these family people who were tortured by knowing their loved one was pretty much captive of Scientology or any cult started to get to me. They feel helpless, their own children or parents or siblings and friends are completely blocked from their lives through these cults. So, I started helping Jim.

I helped him make phone calls, drive him places where he could have a covert meeting with one of the deprogrammers, talk to some poor souls, one of who turned out to be a mole for Scientology, I would take Jim's many letters and envelopes to the post office…and pay for postage…he would send tons of links to my son in Dallas and ask him to print them out on hard copy (computer use was not like today's)…and Bill would mail boxes of printed paper back to Jim. Time Magazine did a column on Jim and his efforts and reasoning, and after that we started getting harassed by Scientology 'thugs'. The first one that I was involved in, was meeting two of them at one of our regular gigs. These two came in to warn Jim about going public with what he knew. They came into Dicks Last Resort and made a couple of threats. I think Jim enjoyed the confrontation, but I didn't. I was sorry I had ever heard of these horrible people. At the time other countries blocked Scientology, and those countries, I feel are smarter than we Americans are about what can and should be called 'religion'.

In comes Germany: one of the more notorious leaders in blocking Scientology at the time. They had contacted Jim after seeing Jim being interviewed in Elkhart, Indiana, I believe. The German videographer and interviewer came to Chicago to stay with us and talk to Jim at my townhouse in Northbrook. It was an interesting couple of days. There is a series of 6 of those interviews with Jim on You Tube. They are off the cuff, and Jim is already on oxygen, and his answers come from his heart.

While the German media was at my place, filming, I left the house to go to my day job, which at the time was real estate sales. I came home soon after to a chaotic scene, where there were a bunch of $cientology 'thugs' meddling around my townhouse. Now Ancient Tree, where I lived is a high end area, with hills, golf course, club house, winding streets, lakes and streams, yet here are a bunch of non residents milling around the bushes at my neighbor's house and at my place. The German camera man came out and videoed the nonsense, and went back into the house; Jim called the police to explain what was happening. Luckily the police came and shooed the 5 (FIVE) cars and men out of the community. The German media asked if we would 'escort' them to the expressway so they could safely get back downtown and to a hotel. They had other appointments to fulfill on the subject of America and Scientology. The problem was, that they had been 'hijacked' before and had their videos stolen from their car by those thugs. So, in our naivety, Jim and I said ok, but didn't know what to expect. If we only had had cell phones. So, here is the two cars, ours and the German media thinking we could get the job done. We got to Landwehr Road where the entrance to my subdivision was, and what do you know, directly across Landwehr, facing us was the string of cars with their thugs waiting!! We turned toward Dundee to lead us out to the expressway. Too bad it was 'rush hour'.

The Scientology thug cars were right behind us, as we were in the right lane on Dundee Road heading to Edens Expressway. Right away two of the cars got beside us, the second one hogging the lane making us slow down. There was a lot of traffic as it was, so the going was slow to begin with. The first thug car maneuvered in front of us while the one on the side hugged us. The third car got in front of the German media's car, and the fourth car got stayed at their side; the fifth car got between the Germans and us. Eventually, the first and second cars forced us off the road, and the other three cars ushered the Germans past us and down to the Expressway. There was nothing Jim and I could do. I was aghast at what had happened; I was, unprepared, as was Jim, although he wasn't surprised. Eventually we went back to the house. Later, we got a call from The German reporters, who said they had reached the hotel but were still harassed in $cientology's hateful ways. The doorman had gotten security to bring in the videos and deposit them in the hotel's vault. The two Germans were very grateful for our 'help'…and said they brought disguises along so they could go out for dinner in peace. They would use the back door of the hotel. The videographer told Jim that the same bunch of thugs had 'followed' and harassed them all the way from Clearwater…the headquarters of Scientology. Scientology had gotten wind of them doing their videoing in Florida, and knew they were in the states to get the story. The Germans had had plenty of experience with the 'thugs' as I call them, because Germany was smart enough to not allow this cult into their country. Jim posted the pictures of the thugs who had been milling around, trying to hide in the bushes when the camera came out AND when the police came and asked for identity from viewers. Sure enough, some people who had had the same experiences came forward and were able to name 3 of the 5 thugs. For a time after that experience, I was bothered. We had the police come and check to see if my place had been bugged somehow. From then on, our area security checked on cars that did not have a resident's sticker on it. I was leery of every repair vehicle near my townhouse in Ancient Tree, and had the security check on it. Jim told me that is exactly what Scientology wanted to result from their harassing. So, the fear faded, and so much more happened.

For one thing, when we returned home, two Scientology thugs were rummaging through my trash can. Jim said they do that and look for bills and other things that they can use to bother you with. I hoped they grabbed a handful of snotty Kleenex. So, things moved along rather routinely, and Jim is doing his thing on the newly acquired internet that at that time was through the phone lines. He found the name of one of the young 'thugs'- Greg. Jim went to his house in Barrington, and attempted to talk to him. Greg was already at the 'auditing' stage of Scientology's game. And he was a Scientology soldier.

He did seem to come around, slightly, though. He worked for a large advertising company downtown Chicago, and softened a little toward Jim, and Jim made some headway with him, as Greg was younger and seemed to like Jim. Scientology got wind of the relationship, and one day we found out Greg committed suicide. It's not uncommon with members of a cult they cannot escape from...especially after attending 'audits'. A little research and you can read more about it. Jim met with Greg's dad who was so distraught he wrote an ongoing, prepaid article in the Chicago Tribune about how Scientology killed his son. He asked, "how can a group call them selves a 'church' when there is no charity, no love, no family, but only fear and hate.".…. Jim got the Chicago Reader to do an expose on Scientology and it was quite the journey, as those writers and their reporter suffered threats while in the process. They followed through beautifully, but later said no to Jim continuing or elaborating on the story. I still have a copy of that story, albeit the paper is getting very old. It is now online, courtesy of the Chicago Reader. I also have one of Scientology's publications that abhor and reject psychiatry and any mental health doctor. They have their own, of course, their own security forces, their own lawyers, doctors and people they call ministers of the 'faith' who are all unwittingly in the circle of the cult. As you know, Scientology "church" has no God of any kind...they call their founder the Messiah...a broken down, cunning science fiction writer turned leader who has his empire on another planet, and you can only join them if you are audited and full of their alien nemesis's that are supposed to be attached to your skin. Because of this Greg spent many sleepless nights, believing these things after being audited. Auditing is a 'level' of their plan, putting you a step higher in the chain.

As a rule, cults are cruel and destructive and Scientology is the worst. It is powerfully rich; there are some big names who contribute to their immense 'war chests'.…. some of who are high on the ladder in the corporate world and even the news world. Jim continued his work diligently until he got too weak. Many people have thanked him over the years, and I am glad to have had the experiences, such as they were. Personally, I am more of a country bumpkin, curious about everything, wanting to know, but unable to grasp thoroughly.

In a short time, Jim and I found out we were very good for each other in many ways. Our temperament was the same, and we sounded off at the craziest things. When I apologized, he would say "it's ok, we all have to let go of some charge every so often." When Jim sounded off, I think it came from his medication for his condition. Prednisone made him ornery and aggressive. (I remembered when Jethro got sick with cancer, *his* personality changed too). Simply stated, it's just brain chemistry, and drugs along with the immune system seem to play 'dirty tricks' on their host. Jim was so smart; he could explain his own outbursts to me. He was in touch with himself and the effects of his medications. My own outbursts came from ignorance and frustration with myself, catching my mistakes too late and realizing I had lived a whole lifetime without Jim or this music—and then realizing I was *with* Jim for the rest of my life. Our relationship was unlike any other that I had ever had.

We talked about getting married, more than once. Although he brought up the subject of marriage, Jim admitted up front that he would never have any money to take care of me. He had two younger children, and other obligations, along with three older children and three ex wives.. I didn't mind. He was needier than I was. And I was healthier. At the same time, Jim showed me that *I* needed someone around who could teach me to be better than I think I am. It has worked somewhat, even after his death. We both had similar goals, one of which was to keep the band working.

In fact every other year; it was like reevaluating our status. Every year it was pretty much the same; with his debts, and my need of independence, it turned out we were better off without the legalities. The only time that backfired was when he was getting ready to die.

Though, from the day we met, our relationship was to become a really true love, full of giving and caring and learning. I don't think many people are so lucky as to have that. Leslie Johnson, the editor of the Mississippi Rag called Jim and I- "a Great Love Story".

CHAPTER 38

At the Bristol

Kim Cusack was the band reed man, and then after, Charlie Hooks was our regular reedman for the first three-or-so years at the Bristol. His wife Lornetta would sometimes come along to a gig and bring her flute. She is a beautiful young woman with shiny dark hair that reached well past her waistline. We all had many grand evenings and wonderful memories as part of Jim Beebe's Chicago Jazz. Later, when Franz worked more often with us downtown Chicago, Franz took Charlie's place with us at the Bristol/ Braxton. The restaurants were cutting down on band numbers, Charlie had his Sunday Brunch. So, Franz came in and took Charlie's place on the stage at the Bristol, and then was with us all week long for years to come.

Franz played 3 horns and was very strong with all three. He and Jim had always gotten along well, and had worked together so often that they were one. Jim knew how Franz worked and accommodated him; they belonged to the Mutual Admiration Society. Franz was already with us 3 plus times a week, both at Dick's, and other events. So it was natural that he would come on board with us at the Braxton. It was a trip working with Franz who had no trouble letting me know what I was doing wrong or right. Sometimes his comments didn't sit right with me; but he was always right, and he made me think. He took me along to sing on his gigs, too, as did Truck and Sonny Turner. Duke Groner, our first bassist at the Bristol, had 'mentored' me, too. He went with me on many single gigs; always classy, great posture, and his suits and shirts were always crispy clean. I was so lucky. I'm thrilled to have some of these great men on my first recording, "It's Been a Long, Long Time".

****

CHAPTER 39

Franz And Me

Actually, it was Franz who first encouraged me to sing with a jazz band. I feel so many people had so much to do with my good luck in singing; but my loyalty to Jim makes me default to him because he always made sure I was working and he gave me the most time because we were a pair. But before Jim, before Gary Miller, after Jethro and after having my own trio, a friend, Stu Godwin, had taken me to Andy's. He wanted me to experience Jazz-At-Noon. When we got there, he asked John DeFauw, the leader of the group that day to have me try a tune. Franz Jackson was playing in the group. I had no idea that Andy's even existed or did I know any of the players. John came over to our table and began the longest lecture about how many singers wanted to sing with this group, and couldn't make it, and how much money it would actually cost to hear this band in a concert, etc, etc. and continued with so much information, I lost my nerve; but I had to try a song. (years later, after I got to know the players and John, John's widow Vi and I would have a chuckle about it). But that afternoon, I was so scared of getting up on the stage that when he did ask me to come up, my legs turned to rubber. I sang Alexander's Ragtime Band; it was one of a few songs I knew. I could tell the audience loved it, until I lost focus and twisted the words. Then I just wanted to disappear. Or start over.

At break, Franz came over to my table and sat down. He complimented me on the necklace I was wearing and chatted gently until I relaxed. At the end of the next set, he invited me up again. It went much better. A couple of days later, I got a note in the mail from Franz Jackson. All it said was: "Give it another try. I'm playing at the Rib Exchange in Schaumburg."

Underneath that he gave me the dates and time. All of this was BEFORE meeting Jim.

I went to the Rib Exchange. Here was another wonderful group playing 'my' kind of music! Franz had me sing. It went well. I asked Franz for his autograph. He wrote on a napkin: "to Judi K- a voice that is true, mellow and soothing" and then signed it. He folded the napkin and handed it to me and said "here's a quote for you." I still have that napkin in my scrapbook. I recently showed it to his daughter Michelle, and the quote is now on her Dad's website. I am using the quote on my website, too. Franz's death in 2008 put me back in connection with his family. His daughter Michelle and I started to email each other. For years, I would sign my emails to my kids with Ellington's "Love You Madly," and used the same sign off with Michelle. Michelle then told me that her mother did the same thing with her and her brother Robert. That revelation gave us a little extra bond. Later, I changed the sign off with LYM, and Michelle would respond with the same. I was/am very impressed with Franz's daughter Michelle and with her family, and Franz's son Robert and his family. I wrote this for the Mississippi Rag Bulletin when Franz died:

FRANZ JACKSON— "DIDN'T HE RAMBLE"

Franz was the only singer I know who would sing <u>all</u> verses and words to that song; and then some. He would make up some extra lines just to amuse himself.... and us.

Now Franz is with his wife Virginia and with all the wonderful musicians who went before him, and because of that, now I am sure the other side is a better place! And it's looking better to me all the time. The music must be...heavenly!

A couple of weeks ago, 9 days after Franz died, I was honored to join Franz's daughter and her husband at the Chicago History Maker awards dinner. Franz received yet another award for his part in Chicago Jazz. That night the room was filled with achievers unlike any others, including entrepreneurs who bring in millions and even billions of dollars in revenue. But Franz—he was the richest one 'there'. I saw him in his daughter Michelle. Her presence at the podium and in her speech brought tears and awe from the 350+ attendees. Like her father, she brought the audience to a standing ovation twice. Franz was proud of his whole family...he was as proud of them as they are of him.

As for me, Franz's legacy is as marvelous in the rearing of his family as it is in his incredible music he has left us with.

When I was with Jim Beebe's Chicago Jazz, I got to work with Franz for several years, regularly three nights a week at Dicks, alternate nights at other clubs, 2 other nights at the Bristol Seafood Grill (we were there for 16 years), and so many corporate events and weddings that I was with that band more than with my family. That band was my family in many ways. We stuck up for each other and sometimes would fight like brothers and sisters. But mostly we loved each other and enjoyed each other, and respected each other's talents. We often would play for a corporate breakfast, then an afternoon corporate picnic and then our regular gigs at the clubs at night. I often referred to our calendar as the 'Agony and the Ecstasy'.

Jim kept his band working so steadily that sometimes we would have to form a second band to cover a gig. They would jokingly call themselves the B band. But Franz was always the tops in any of our groups. He could cover every song, any key, any tempo, and I have several stories about some memorable events, one of which we called "The Wedding."

*Franz Jackson was always the pro; he didn't drink or smoke, but focused on his music every minute. When we were out of town, he was up the earliest and doing his laps at the pool. I would pass him on the elevator on my way **to** the pool, and he would already be heading back to his room to get ready for breakfast. Franz was the best role model for me and he would tell me which players were best for me to learn from, and he would tell me things like, " don't sing it like that…" and even one time he said… "Don't ever wear a turtle neck again"*

Franz was the start of my best music experiences. He gave me my first attempt at Andy's, as a total neophyte singer, then wrote me a note to come and try it again with his group at the Rib Exchange. He encouraged me, told me what not to do, and told me what was best. He gave me a ton of experience and knowledge over the years, and I thank him with all my heart.

I also thank my Jim Beebe for having the smarts to have Franz in the band. My Jim was a long time friend of Franz's and no one respected Franz more than he did. He and Franz worked well together, and as Jim's breathing grew more difficult, Franz, understood his predicament and would play all the harder to cover for him. I know that Jim was waiting at the pearly gates with open arms for Franz to join him and the others once again.

As our talented friends leave us for the next level, it isn't really the end. Franz, Jim, Steve, Andy, Jimmy Johnson, Joe, Truck and the many others live on in our great musical history, and they live on in our hearts. End of Tribute.

****

CHAPTER 40

Early Days at The Bristol

During the earlier years with Jim's band, and all too often, I would have my 3 or 4 songs prepared for a set, and Jim would ask what I was going to 'call'. I figured he needed to know so he could decide where the song would fit the best. When I said what it was and counted it off, the band would start and Jim would stop them and say, "no, no, not that one, do this one." I think he did it to get my dander up. In the long run, it was good exercise for me: I learned how to be ready for anything. Finally, Greg Sergo, our regular drummer at that time, who knew Jim's personality better than I did, suggested that I call a tune that would be in the same vein, but the suggestion would make Jim name the one I was really planning on doing. He said it tongue in cheek, and amazingly, it worked. (Sometimes). It became a game, and I learned to be ready for anything, and Greg and I exchanged many smiles. Sometimes it was hard to have something in my head, all ready to go, only to change hats and start a different song that Jim decided to call. I believe Jim did that because his nature dictated he should; he liked to stir things up now and then. It actually was an exercise for my brain. But, as Jim's disease progressed, so did his push-me-pull-you personality. But that would be later. I fell so deeply in love with him that he could do no wrong. Ever.

I tried some Real Estate sales, fell in love with my Real Estate listings and my heart ached for the people who had to sell their homes. Probably because I had to sell my own dream house and move Jim and I into a small townhouse. The hardest part then was coming home from a long day of showing houses, shower, redress, redo hair and makeup, and then change hats to be a singer, manage gigs for the band and other incidentals that Jim asked me to do for the gigs.

As the years went on, Jim got weaker. He finally acquiesced to using oxygen at gigs, but only if he could enter the gig before me, and I come in later hauling the tank, and hide it under one of the nearby tables. When he felt he needed oxygen, he would give me a subtle signal and I'd take over on stage while he sat at the table. I was good at fronting the band. Having observed Jim, Connie and Jethro and other band leaders, I discovered that I was able to handle a lot.

I would often get good paying gigs through my real estate company or through my job as a corporate executive secretary, and I'd hire a lot of the players I knew. One event for Kahn Realty, I hired Paul Asaro. I knew that he knew Bessie Smith's "I've Got What it Takes But it Breaks My Heart to Give it Away". The gist of the song fits a realtor's life running around with 'customers' who drain you by asking many questions and telling you to take them to see several houses, but don't stay loyal. The other realtors loved the analogy.

I knew that I could I keep the gigs stable, but as Jim's health declined, I felt myself wanting to stay at home with him. Jim insisted that I continue to go to the Braxton without him.

On a couple of occasions, he started to panic as we were getting ready to leave for work. He'd say that I had to go on alone and take care of things. He couldn't control himself; the panic attacks came on more and more.

It didn't feel right without him, but I managed to deal with those feelings by calling him on my cell phone while on stage and in the middle of a set, holding the phone up to the audience and asking them all to say, "Hi, Jim!" in unison. So as not to rattle the musicians who thought <u>they</u> should be leading, I had each of them pick a song for the band to perform; I called it "player's choice." Sometimes they would take over a bit too much, but Jim told me how to curb that. By now some of the players who had joined the band in the last couple of years were salivating at the thought of having the gig for themselves. They couldn't bear the idea of me staying there, and made it as difficult as possible. Jim seemed to keep an eye on things from his bed, while three of the band members shot down chances of my working.

On one of those occasions that Jim couldn't leave the house, I was afraid to leave him alone at home while I took care of the gig. He called Tommy Bartlett to sub for him. It was going very smoothly, I was comfortable with Tommy, but suddenly I realized I didn't want this without Jim, and the realization was so stunning, that I started crying and left the stage to spend a good deal of time in the ladies room that night. My friend Sue Storm followed me into the 'biffy' and with her expertise, the "Angel Lady" brought me back to the moment and relieved me of a splitting headache. Sue knew Jim from his Reike sessions.

When Greg's band "The Ellington Dynasty" got busy, Jim started using a variety of good drummers. Toward the end of the run, we acquired a drummer with a warped sense of ethics. The last time Jim fired him is when Bob Cousins finally became our regular drummer, and he stayed with us for the rest of the run. Shortly afterward, the fired drummer vowed to take Jim's job. He decided to blame me for his own inability to work with us and he vowed to end my work. He nearly did, but he didn't do it alone. He sent his 'fans' and cohorts in to the Bristol—now renamed the Braxton—to sit in front of Jim and puff on cigars, knowing Jim's lungs were weak and knowing one of us would say something. Then those same customers would complain about us, and we would get scolded. We knew it was a set up and the new, inexperienced management fell for it: these troublemakers were people who had *never* been around during the years we had the gig. They only came in *after* the drummer was fired. We were very familiar with our audiences and Jim's memory was sharp. He remembered everyone and everything. I knew most of our regulars, too, and no one who was new to the room would have honestly found anything to gripe about. They always got an evening of great entertainment. This selected fake 'audience' were put up to it and many of them were blatant enough to tell the management they would rather have (so and so) there. These were people who found the least thing to complain about: (shoes or not…under my floor length dress), or we didn't smile at them; or the one time I asked the mom of a bunch of kids to keep them away from the vulnerable instruments on stage, and the mom went ballistic and told me off; meanwhile, her little ones were scrambling in an out of the microphones and horns on stands during break. One time, one of the cockier non-regulars looked at the guy next to him after calling the manager and after having the manager apologize, and smiling with a success grin asked, "How did I do"? They all laughed...and enjoyed the free meal the management provided them because of their bogus complaints. Not all musicians are kind or loving.

Pretty soon, the newer, younger management was getting snotty, both to Jim and to me. They had endured several visits from our ex-drummer who wanted the job. He literally cried "tears" publicly about many things he imagined people were doing to him. (Throwing glass in his swimming pool, hitting on his wife, purposely blocking the audience from seeing him drum...and the list goes on)...The thing was, he had an acting ability that, the first few stories, made you feel sorry for him. During the entire run, none of the other management groups had ever given us a bad time. They respected the business we brought them and the way that Jim handled interference and continuous announcements. He always made sure that the businesses that we worked for were mentioned in magazine articles and other written pieces about us, and that they were always placed in our programs at the many jazz festivals where we performed. When you think of how much that kind of publicity would cost, it was priceless. The wait staff liked us, but when the young, lifeless new management came in, they had a strange, needy hunger for attention and control— and to make changes. On our last night at the Braxton, the wait staff brought me an exquisite bouquet of flowers. I will never forget those young people who worked there (or the staff at Dicks Last Resort). They enjoyed happy times, and they too didn't like the changes the 'new' management was making. When we left the Braxton, some went on to other restaurants to work.

****

Under the previous several managements, we were allowed and even encouraged to include the wait staff to join in many of the tunes. They happily came into the lounge once a night to do a 'line' dance to Jimmy Johnson's *Caledonia*. Jim Beebe's Chicago Jazz was not entirely Dixieland or "Classic Jazz" as he like to call it, and it changed with the players who had different styles to offer. But Friday evenings were entirely dedicated to Dixieland. And every Friday night, the audience would look forward to the New Orleans style parade he would conjure up during the last set. I would bring the beaded umbrellas along to work, and Jim would designate a couple of people to lead the parade, twirling and dancing with the umbrella. While the band played, the line of customers would snake throughout the huge restaurant before returning to the lounge. The patrons loved it.

Many of the wait staff 'trained' in the lounge before they served the upscale dinners in the restaurant. Sometimes we would set up a new waiter or waitress by telling them that when they graduated to the dining room from our room, they had to first sing with the band to make it official. The bartenders and experienced staff went along with it, making the new guy sweat it out. It was fun, as sometimes, a candidate would hide on us, but Jim was persistent, and they would finally come up to the bandstand to try it. A couple of them were very good singers, so we would sometimes call them in from the dining room to show off to their customers. Their customers loved it and tipped them accordingly. And us.

The new management, however, wanted to change things. They were weird about having a band there longer than they were. The fact is we lasted through *several* management changes. The newest management hated to hear that. The previous managements would take that line and run with it, turning it into something funny and superfluous and everyone would love it. After all the patrons were coming there as long as we were. But the current management would squelch anything we were having fun with. The gig got harder to go to. The band members became watchful, waiting for the end. One of them would sit at the bar and discuss with the bartender how much better the music would be after we were gone. I physically walked right into that conversation; because I wanted to be sure I was hearing it right. I was. Jim was betrayed some of the very people who he had kept working so long and often. One who hated the idea of me working so much, even though he was hired by me for the gig at a banquet hall, that he deliberately stepped on my new eyeglasses that had fallen to the floor. Then he twisted his foot on them, like he was putting out his cigarette. Losing that weekly job at 2 plus nights a week was...For me– traumatic...how would I make enough money now to pay my bills, and to keep a roof over our heads? That was never Jim's problem, it was mine from well before Jim and I connected.

We always did a lot of outside work for the places we had gigs. As Jim gradually gave up the responsibility of the band, I had become a secretary/manager for the band, making sure the restaurants we worked in got billing and advertising from us, whether it was in a program, or a newspaper article. I did whatever Jim told me to do to keep the band working. They could never have worked for so long and so often if it weren't for Jim's business sense. My friends, fans and two of the staff kept me posted for a couple of years after it was over at the Braxton. But, after a while, I got tired of hearing the same old gossip. A couple of the friendly bartenders quit, one of them just after we left. Some of the wait staff went elsewhere. Fifteen years later, I still get Christmas cards from fans who remember the good old days at the Bristol/Braxton.

CHAPTER 41

2 Years Before:

I was working at Baxter Healthcare during the day as a temp secretary, and after 8 years of selling real estate, I had given up my license in 2000, as it was too grueling. I was tired, and lost. There was no income coming in from music as it had been, and Jim was getting sicker. My townhouse was only about 15 minutes from where I worked at Baxter, and I would feel compelled to run home at noon to make sure he was eating something, and sometimes I would find him sitting at my computer, with his oxygen hose running under or too close to the open flame under my hot water heater. I would tell him, but I knew he wouldn't remember anyway. But heading back to work and worrying about him *and* my home...made for a difficult focus as a secretary. I was nearly 60 years old and I was getting very tired of the stress.

On February 23rd, 2002, my aunt Vera died. Vera was one of the 'four' cousins' Mother. Kaycee's Mom Vera was the oldest of my moms' sisters. She had been failing, and her time had come. A funeral was planned and I did my part. I was to see my Mom for the first time in many months. Two of my brothers were walking at her side as she approached the coffin with her big sister in it. Mom looked so frail. I was there alone, and it dawned on me that I couldn't let my Mom go back to St. Paul alone right after her sister had died. Now what do I do about Jim?

In the Twin Cities, My brother Jimmy was staying in Mom's home, taking care of her. He had been taking care of Mom's husband during the past two years, while Jack had colon cancer, and Mom was too weak to handle such a challenge. Jack had died about a year before, so after Vera's funeral, I went with mom back to St. Paul to spend a week with her, and it was a true blessing that God gave me that week. We had each accepted a set of Vera's PJs from Kaycee, and wore them while we slept together in her big bed and we chatted late into the night. We went shopping together, and had our hair done together, and even our nails. I hadn't had my Mom to myself like this in over 40 years. With 6 siblings and so many other people around, few of us rarely did. So, it was my blessing.

In Northbrook, I had two neighbors looking in on my Jim during that time, and things seemed to be going all right. It was one of those times when I wished I could have had someone in his family take over during my absence. But I couldn't. My friend Darlene, and her associate, Cookie, along with my good neighbor, Lynne Adams from across the street checked in on Jim when I was gone.

A week with Mom seemed to invigorate her. She started feeling like doing things again. She had been slipping toward dying before that, and I thought I could change all that. I would have moved to St. Paul to live near her, if I could have found a way. Just to nurse her. She was a great Mom, who had always taken the high road.

The next weekend, I left St. Paul and headed back to Northbrook to be with Jim. I hadn't called in to work, and I didn't have much interest in working anymore, even though I needed the job. I had no sooner gotten into the house when the phone rang. It was my sister. Joan said Mom had had a massive stroke and I should get back there. I immediately called Darlene, Cookie and Lynne and told them I had to leave again. They said they would continue to look in on Jim.

I reached St. Paul, and Mom was in the hospital. I didn't get it. I was in denial. I wouldn't accept it that it was her turn to go. When I left her just a couple of days before, she was better.

CHAPTER 42

When It Rains.....

Of course when things don't go well, things just seem to keep not going well. My car's transmission needed replacing. It was at Vera's funeral in Arcadia when my car broke down. A kind, local mechanic fixed it well enough to barely make it back to Northbrook, clunking along. So on this trip to Mom's, I had to use Amtrak. And I was about to get another beautiful blessing. The best way to describe it is with this article: This is where the last installment comes in of the earlier story that was published about my Dad's death. I can reprint it here. This is where I decided to name the two stories together as "May the Circle Be Unbroken":

The Arcadia News-Leader:

> *"May the Circle Be Unbroken, Bye and Bye Lord, By and By."*
> *Submitted by Judi K*
> *The Circle IS Unbroken. With the death of my Aunt Vera, this past month, and subsequently, of my mother, my heart grieves for our families. Not for the loved ones who died, but for the rest of us left behind. Last February 25 I found myself in Milwaukee, consoling my cousin Kay because her mother had just passed away. Vera had had a full life, she was wise, the pillar of the families—her own family and my mothers' and their sisters.'*
>
> *I say my mother's family, because my father was killed in a car accident 45 years ago, leaving 7 children behind and my Mom, with all her god given strength took care of all. It was Vera, with her husband Ben who brought us the news and the big shoulders. About 30 years after Dad's death, I wrote a short story about that experience that allowed me to talk about something I had*

avoided talking about for all those years. It was published in the News Leader, and copied again and again. Dad's sudden death left a huge hole in my Mom's life and in ours. I would like to honor the closing of the circle here.

After the services for Vera in Milwaukee, I stayed overnight with Vera's Daughter Kay, and rode with her to Arcadia the next day for Vera's wake and service and burial. Kay gave me a couple sets of Vera's fancy pj's as a remembrance. The Matriarch was gone. Her sisters in their frailty were taking the loss hard. We worried about Vera's husband Ben, now alone. He had lost his wife: his best friend.

In Arcadia, my brothers brought my fragile Mom to the wake. The passing away of her oldest sister would leave a big hole for Romona: mom's younger sister. Their youngest sister, Antonette, was in Milwaukee, her health too precarious for her to make the trip. After the funeral, we gathered at Ramona's house to be together. Then, I went back with my Mom and brothers to Mom's home in St. Paul. We dropped Jon, my second to the oldest brother, off at his car where he had met up with Jim and Mom to ride with them. I wanted to be with Mom to support her after Vera's death. We had a grand visit.

I was very fortunate and blessed to have had the quality time with her alone. Younger brother Jim needed a break from all the care-taking. He had also taken care of Mom's late husband who had suffered with colon cancer for over a year. He continued to take care of Mom, being her companion, her caregiver and errand runner and driver. My being there was a chance for him to have a little space for himself. And this way Mom would have some girl time, too. So, I helped her bathe and dress. I got to cook breakfasts and help clean up the kitchen and bathrooms and bedroom. Doing these things was a privilege and something I hadn't had the opportunity to do for her in many years. I am nearly 60 years old at this writing (March 17, 2002), and I can say that during that visit, Mom and I shared feelings, gossip, memories and private talk that I hadn't had with her in over 35+ of my 60 years or ever. It was only after Dad's death that she and I had those moments. I was the only daughter left at home after Jane married, and mom and I had a camaraderie and special relationship that I will cherish always. That last week with her just before her stroke was a gift from God that fills my heart with eternal gratitude. And there were more gifts to come.

I have always felt I have been the luckiest person alive! Mom was starting to rally after congestive heart failure. She had been recuperating, and the last

3 days I was there, she was evincing an appetite and even talked about cooking and cleaning again and getting back to her Church projects once again. Things seemed to be getting back to 'normal'

I left her home and took an Amtrak from St. Paul on March 3. I hadn't been home but a day or so, when my sister Joan called to say Mom had had a massive stroke early AM on March 4th, destroying the dominant side of her brain. I was shocked; hadn't I just left her in great spirits? Could this be happening just a week after her sister died? We left Chicago immediately to go to her side. At the hospital, I wanted to scoop Mom up and take her home with me and try to heal her. I felt such closeness that we could become one and my energy would be hers. I did that often with Jim, and he said touch healing was very strong. I would have given up everything to be physically closer to her AND to Jim, so I could take care of both of them. I was good at that. Then the Neurologist talked to us, giving us the prognosis. The truth panicked me. I didn't want to believe it. Mom was supposed to live forever. The other members of the family seemed to understand but somehow I didn't. I had just shared a week with her. She was feeling 'fine' when I left. She would heal. My siblings seemed to have been better prepared. It turned out that I hadn't read through all the paperwork that had been sent to me. I was in a mode that Mom couldn't, wouldn't die, and those preparations of hers were just more of her paperwork we were supposed to store. I didn't take the paper work seriously; I would have time to read them later….

Panic struck and I started running through the hospital corridors looking for my siblings. I found them in the cafeteria. The next day the neurologist called a family meeting, and we were encouraged to ask questions. He gave us the straight facts and once we were all on the 'same page', we became more of a unit and we worked together toward fulfilling Mom's list of wishes. We agreed unanimously and we all did all we could to take part in her journey.

I like the word journey for the dying process, including 'crossing over'. This is where more gifts come in:

Her journey provided us with time to get everything in order. She had organized her dying process, just as she had organized the many clubs and foundations she was responsible for. Her list of accomplishments is long and successful. I feel she knew we needed this time to be a part of her journey because we were so brutally denied this with our father's sudden death.

Mom loved music and we took opportunities to sing to her. She seemed to respond. When I was alone with her, I would sing songs that were like lullabies to her. I sang softly, "You are My Special Angel, sent from up above, the Lord smiled down on me and sent my mother to love"…. She would look at me with her soft blue eyes. "Sail, Momma, Sail, out across the sea, only don't forget to sail, back again to me…" Then I would sing "Going home, Going Home…." Which was one was Jim's and my favorite tune to do when we performed memorials.

I mustered up all I could remember about being a nurses' aid. When I was in high school, I took a course at St. Cloud hospital and became a nurse's aide. Little would I realize then that I would utilize some of what I learned on my own mother so many years later. Mom was very modest, and I watched that the nurses wouldn't leave any part of her uncovered while bathing her or changing sheets. Later, I asked the undertaker the same courtesy, and his kind and gentle answer calmed me. I whispered to Mom while bathing her that I was doing the best I could.

I know she heard me even though she could not respond. I wanted her to feel just as clean and presentable as she was used to being. I described her to the nurses as the perfect "Kool-Aid ad Mom," meaning she would wear a pinafore apron over a polka dot or checkered dress, with a perfectly tied bow, with a white collar, nylons and high heels…as a daily routine!

(I remembered one morning in Fargo; I awoke while it was still dark out, and went down to the kitchen to get a glass of milk. There was Mom, already up, dressed, hair combed and that slight touch of mascara on her lashes, and she was ironing. She never stopped working, and dad never saw her not looking prim and proper).

That evening at the house, and away from the hospital, we were going through old pictures, and there she was, in a picture of her standing over a mix master, with her pinafore apron on, starched and pressed, hair in place and surrounded with little children.

I brought that picture to the hospital to show the nurses what I meant about her being a "Kool-Aid ad Mom"…

During her hospital stay, one of our shifts included my sister Joan and myself to stay the night. We each had a place on the sides of Mom's hospital bed. We were in the hospice section of the hospital.

The nurses were doing their usual busy time, but when we were alone with Mom, we took to saying the rosary with her, her lips moving slightly with our spoken prayers, as though muscle memory were taking over while the prayer was in her brain. Mom's eyes had grown dim, her body temperature had dropped; she was cool everywhere to the touch. She seemed restless and her eyes moved around the room, resting on unseen things. I said, "Something is happening, Joan, she is looking around at more than just us here"…Nervously, with tongue in cheek, Joan said, "Maybe she sees your reflection in the mirror." I looked over my shoulder and saw that indeed whenever I moved, it did look like another person. But, were mother's eyes that good at that time? They were glazed, and the blue was muted, and yet she was seeing something. She got onto one elbow and looked around the curtain to the door. A move like that was miraculous in itself, as the stroke had left her immobile. Her eyes darted here and there, resting on each image she was seeing. I felt I was witnessing one of the greatest events I could ever be a part of. We tenuously continued on with the rosary, Mom's eyes were busy. Sister Judith, from the hospice staff came in to pray with us. She led, but after partial decade of beads she stopped and said, "There is activity in this room. There is something happening." I looked at Joan and I knew immediately what it was. Mom was "crossing-over." Our brother Jimmy came into the room and Joan and I took a break. We talked about the experience with awe and caution. After a while Jimmy joined us. He said, "You know, I think Mom is seeing angels today." That sealed it. We hadn't mentioned our experience to anyone else, and Sister Judith had left to attend another patient much earlier.

I was elated to know that Mom was going to that better place. I had just had proof positive that there is one. Janie brought her scapular for Mom to pin on her gown. Mom was always in the 'state of grace', but now it was more than evident, and she clutched her rosaries and her scapular with determination.

I stayed overnight again, sleeping in the pull-out chair next to her bed. The next morning, Mom surprised everyone, including the hospital staff. She awoke with bright blue eyes and was able to communicate in her limited way that the stroke had left her with. She seemed happy and peaceful. She looked younger. But that lasted a short time.

Then, later that day, she was ready to go. The hospital told us to get the family together to be there. With dread and anxiousness we gathered at her bedside, being told that this would probably be the last time we would see her alive. We prayed and prayed because we knew that is how Mom wanted it.

Her beliefs carried her through many hardships. Tears were shed and hymns were sung. We tried not to make too much commotion so as not to disturb other patients in the hospice. Many family members were there. The evening wore on. The next day, Mom was put on morphine. It was part of the Comfort Care that was requested by her in her living will. No artificial means to life. She couldn't swallow, and at times would close her lips tightly when I tried to put a wet sponge near her lips. She was ready. Her family was there. There was just one more request: to die at home. Another amazing feat took place. I said, "Mom, it's ok to leave us. Everyone is here, we have done all of your requests". Her facial muscles slightly contorted to try to say something. She worked and strained and finally a hoarse, moan came from her lips that sounded out "HOME". It was clear that she wanted to go back to her house to die.

The hospital transferred her to her home with the aid of hospice, and after a couple of days, her dear friends came to say good-bye. Then her children and our children and Mom's stepson stood around her deathbed holding hands. We prayed the Rosary and Mom's favorite prayer, the "Memorare." Then Mom took her last sigh and her spirit left her body.

When Father Mike had come into the hospital room the first time, he asked if there were any other prayers she preferred. I remembered her teaching me the Memorare, and told him it was her favorite prayer. As a little girl, I bought a blue plastic folding compact for Mom on mother's day. It would open like a book and stand, hinges holding it like a partly open book. It showed a small Blessed Virgin on one side, and the words to the Memorare on the other. She kept it for many years, displaying it on her bedroom dressers. During Mom's journey, that prayer immediately became a routine prayer along with the prayers of the rosary. During the days of the hospice care, I had written it out for the others to review, and I would find some of the siblings practicing it. Joan had copied it to her 'blue book' in order to memorize it. The blue book was a pamphlet that we were all to read to learn about the dying process. At the cemetery, as the priest turned after saying prayers I quickly reminded him: "The Memorare, Father?" Immediately we all said the prayer in tribute. Everyone joined in. I can pretty much guarantee that we will all be saying the Memorare in Mom's memory for the rest of our lives. At the very end of the burial service, I sang "Going Home" for my mother.

To talk about experiencing those hours when Mom was between this life and the next, I can only determine that many loving arms were on the other side, ready to receive her from our loving arms. It was too real a happening, and so beautiful, I would have walked right there with her in a flash. I felt that I was as close to her and those who were waiting as I was close to the people who were physically in the same room where it happened. It was as physical as it was spiritual and it's a feeling that I hope to experience again. I think she had come back just for the short time it took for us to bring her home to die.

So, there it is; a list of gifts Mom left us with. I don't have them bulleted, but as you read this, you will find those gifts are throughout this document. Thank you to a wonderful Mother. You will always be in my heart.

****

Mom died on March 15, just about three weeks after her oldest sister Vera died.

On the way home from Mom's funeral, I drove through Milwaukee so I could stop in to visit Mom's little sister, Antonette. I called her "Anty," not 'Auntie'…but an old nickname of hers, "Anty" short for Antonette. Later on, most everyone else called her 'Toni'. Except me. To me, she's always 'Anty'.

She was sitting on her couch in her living room, with a permanent IV—a PICC—in her arm.. Her arm was infected, and she was trying to get well. She wanted to know about Mom's funeral and she was so sad. I gave her a big hug after our visit, knowing how empty she must feel, having lost two sisters within less than 3 weeks.

When I got home to Northbrook, all seemed well with Jim. He seemed to have liked having the townhouse to himself, and both Darlene and Lynne had dropped by and tended to his meals and errands. I got-up-to-date with laundry and news, and we invited a couple over for dinner. Things were 'routine' for about 3 days, and when the phone call came, it was the news of Anty's death. It was April 8, 2002. Anty had already beaten death more than once. One of her close calls was when she was open for a second open heart surgery, something went terribly wrong, and they had to leave her open for over a day in order to fix the problem at hand. She was comatose. We didn't think she'd make it out of that one, but she did, along with a few other close calls. Those Fernholz girls were tough! But, this time, the PIC infection was the final strike, and sometimes I think she gave in because two of her sisters had just left her, telling her it

180

was ok to leave this world, that she wouldn't be alone; they were waiting for her. Once again, the four of us girl cousins were attending a funeral joined by Anty's family. Now, two younger girl cousins were part of the grieving-train. Of course all the male cousins grieved as well, but there was a special tie with the girls. The four of us plus the two newly added sisters are lifelong friends. Vera's, Mom's and Anty's funerals all blended, we hadn't had a chance to grieve each of our own mother's passings before we had to grieve another. It was overwhelming. Antonette died just three weeks after momma died.

****

CHAPTER 43

"Going Down Slow"

After leaving the Braxton, and after the death parade, I was living in a dense emotional fog. So many things were lost to me: my home, my friends, my work, my favorite people, and the knowledge that the love of my life was dying of emphysema. I tried to go to my day job at Baxter Healthcare, where I was a secretary-jack, (working in and out of several departments) but I couldn't focus. One day I went to the copy room and I couldn't remember how to get back to my own desk. My energy was sapped and I couldn't think straight. I blacked out and found myself on the floor of one of the departments, not knowing how I got there. The managers seemed to be very understanding and kind, but I knew I had to stop working. They were getting nothing out of me. I went home to bed and didn't get up unless my Jim really, really needed something.

On May 6, 2002, Jim's granddaughter, who had contracted cancer at the age of two just a year before, succumbed to the tumors that ravaged her tiny body. Once again, we were at a church, attending a funeral of a loved one and this time witnessing the pain of two loving young parents. I stood in that Church befuddled. What town was I in? What Church was this? Who died this time? Certainly not little Caitlin. The folks who had left me had had a long, great life. But, this little 3 year old? Why would God do this to these *young* people?

On June 5, 2002, my favorite bass man, Truck Parham, who I had worked with and recorded with, died, and Jim and I attended his funeral service.

On July 5, 2002, my Dad's oldest brother, Ervin passed away from old age. I went to Arcadia for the funeral. Dad's side of the family is Lutheran.

I attended this funeral by rote. By this time, I had sung "Going Home" so often it had become a ritual; a must-have:— **"And now: the#1 song on the Funeral Hit Parade: "Going Home" Sung by Judi K" (applause)**

My car had broken down, although somewhere in all that chaos, I had a new transmission installed; Jim was sick, I had no job, no income, and I was losing my house. It was all I had left. What in the heck happened to that little farm girl who thought the world was only made of love? Where has it gone? The physical world was crumbling. I had come to find the words of Mildred Bailey in the song "My Last Affair" were true for me: "…I'm not the same as I used to be….my happiness is misery…"

The only alternative I could think of was to move to a place I thought would be less expensive and near family that would let me rest now and then and give me a break from care-giving. I didn't want to be away from Jim. Jim and I were not married—on paper, anyway, and I had no legal say so in his care, even though both of us thought I would. My idea was to find another townhouse that had one floor living, with enough space to hold his oxygen compressor with ease in pickup and delivery. My Cousin Charlotte found 'just the right place' for sale in Onalaska, and so I took a quick trip up there to make an offer. I had just returned to Northbrook from having found another townhouse on the south side near the bluffs. That neighborhood looked a bit more like the one I was leaving behind, with winding streets, hills and trees. But there was a condition in the offer and my house in Northbrook wasn't sold yet. So, on return to Chicago from that find, I had to come right back to La Crosse to see and make a bid on the one Charlotte found for me. I was starting to fall asleep while I drove.

The young couple accepted my offer, and then I added another two thousand if she would let me store my furniture in their garage and basement for the month it would take for them to get into their new house. It was an impulsive, stupid decision on my part, but I was so overtired and over stressed and continued to make quick decisions just to get something over with without confrontation. "I see a pattern here…" (Joe Mantegna)

Then I went back to my place in Northbrook to start packing. By then Jim was even a needier patient. He didn't want to move from my place. He didn't trust, me, he thought I was bailing out on him. He had been told that by his family. Nothing was farther from the truth. There is no way I would have taken the easier road, and taken care of just me.

No way. I've never done that and I never will. I kept thinking, somehow this will work out.

(*Oh, Pollyanna, you albatross!*)

I was accused of 'bailing out' by some in his family, when all I wanted and desperately needed was a reprieve, time off for good behavior, a boost for my own well-being, having been the sole caretaker health-wise and financially, for Jim for nearly 8 years. The offer of just one week or even weekend off would have done wonders for my health and the need to be appreciated. But that was not to be. His families had come to the conclusion that my home was Jim's and that HE was supporting ME! "you would be nothing if it weren't for him" his older sister told me. And, now I was 60 years old and figured I had no future whatsoever. Not that I cared. I had made the choice. I would live with it the best I could. The stress put me in the hospital for 11 days and ravaged my health. My stomach insides were raw and I had 5 small ulcers circling a larger one. The pain in my stomach and esophagus was unstoppable. The only thing that gave me a short reprieve was a drink of Novocain. But they wouldn't let me have more.

Finally, I just plain stated to Jim's family in La Crosse that I got a place for the two of us, but because I couldn't get into it for 2 months, Jim would have to stay with one of them, and I would have to stay at <u>my</u> brother's house for those two months, or until I could have the new house ready and clean enough for Jim to live there. I needed the first month because the 'owners' couldn't get out right away, and the second month or less would be the time I would need to clean it up for Jim to move into. No one helped me. I didn't think I would have to ask. So I didn't.

It saved the worry of being yelled at and the worry of owing someone.

****

CHAPTER 44

The Overwhelming Chore of Moving

Jim's sister and her husband met me in Madison, Jim had to get away from the chaos of moving. It had been hard on his breathing, and it was going to get worse with boxes and furniture in the way. It was hard for me too, I couldn't maneuver around his equipment, and I couldn't pack up the bedroom because he needed it. Jim had become the love of my life, and my heart broke again as I said good-bye to him. I know he was convinced that I was abandoning him. He looked so frail and gray sitting in that strange truck with his sister and her husband. I stood in the rain and watched them leave with Jim. That picture of him sitting in the truck with a sad, distrusting look on his face will forever be etched in my mind. I drove back to Northbrook sobbing all the way. The windshield wipers worked very hard through the whole trip.

A few days later, my son Bill drove up from Texas for a week and helped get things sorted out; boxing almost all of Jim's things for Jim's son to pick up to keep until we got settled.

Bill put shrink wrap around all the furniture pieces to protect them until I could actually move into my next house. The Van lines were costing me a fortune, and I was trying to lighten up the load. Jim's son Jeff came over to get a truckload of Jim's belongings saying he would be storing them. My son packed the things that Jim would need immediately: his computer and books and clothes went into Bill's pickup to bring to La Crosse. And we packed my own 'immediate' necessities along with my own computer, into Billy's truck too, and we made the trip to La Crosse to deposit Jim's things with Jim at his sister's house, and leave the things I would need for the next month at my brother's home.

I had booked a really nice gig in Madison, that turned out to be on that same date we were driving up to La Crescent/La Crosse. So, on the way, Bill detoured to the gig and I went in and got ready to perform. Bill kept an eye on the truck and belongings while I performed for the corporate event. Dave Remington, Nick Tountas and Bob Cousins had come up to accompany me. It would be the last time I would see them for a long while, and the very last time I would ever see Dave Remington. He passed away just a couple of years later. The gig was a nice escape thanks to the music; it went beautifully, and afterward, as I climbed into my son's pickup truck loaded with computers and boxes, in my long beaded gown I thought of the contradiction and laughed as it must have been a sight. But it was only two and a half more hours to La Crosse, so after the gig, Bill and I continued on to La Crosse to unload the things at my brother's home. Jeff and Beth put us up for a few hours of sleep, and my son drove me back to Northbrook Illinois and we both packed until the movers came a few days later.

My daughter Johanna came on the last day to help pack boxes with her brother, and then, weeks later, when unpacking in Onalaska, I would find funny labels and would have a nice quiet laugh to myself. One of the boxes was labeled "Stuff." Another was labeled "More Stuff." I was glad to see some humor during all of the chaos. Later, another box would be opened that said "Office Crap" and then, "More Office Crap. So much for a Mom telling her kids to label the boxes! I love my kids! Thank God they can make me laugh!

The last day in Northbrook, I went to the closing before we even finished packing, and after the movers finally left that night, Bill stayed one more night and then left to return to Texas. What would I have done without my son, or my daughter? 15 years earlier, I had done *all* the packing from my big house when my husband left, and had done it without ANY help. At that time, Bill was in Texas, busy with his work and new family, and Johanna was in England at college, and I assume neither one of them was very happy about losing the house. Basically, I didn't ask anyone anyway. Back then, I was looking toward the music, and I kept thinking about one of mom's slogans, "When life hands you a lemon, make lemonade". But, I hardly had the strength to lift the pitcher.

This time, moving from my beloved Northbrook to La Crosse during this very dark span in my life was a difficult expense and change.

When the Movers got to my new address, I was already staying at my brother's house. My youngest brother and his wife had provided a private place for me in their basement, and even made a place for my computer. My sister in law had just started real estate work, and while I was there, I tried to help by cooking, cleaning or getting the children around in my car. I knew how full a Realtor's day could be. I spent time at my 'new' twindo (colloquial for duplex) getting it ready for Jim and I to move into.

****

Within a week, Jim was being shuttled between his two sister's homes. They had decided to trade him off every week. I know that was hard on Jim, and I also knew he was a handful. *I thought...see that? Not even a month has gone by, and TWO people can't take it. I had been doing it alone for over 8 years! And I didn't even have the title of wife or sister, or anyone else to take care of me. I know Jim was needy and could be demanding, but he was sick; you have to make allowances!* That's what went through my head without saying it out loud.

Before I even finished preparing my new place for Jim, his family decided that Jim 'had' to be in a nursing home. You can't handle him, I was told. I believe they were trying to be understanding in their way, but something wasn't right...it was more of a control issue...and I was in no position to argue.. It had been nearly 20 years since I had had any kind of break from work, including weekends.

I had made the move with the plan of taking total care of my sweetheart in my home; having family closer so they would come over to give me a reprieve when needed. Somewhere between the exchange with his sister at Madison and now, he lost hold of that; and he agreed to go to an assisted living facility. I didn't argue. My house was empty and so was my heart and my voice.

After sending dozens of resume's and query letters out in the area, I finally found a job...at a grocery store. At much less than I was making in Illinois, Jim was in a nice two-bedroom apartment in his home town of Sparta about 22 miles away, and had almost everything he needed. His uncle was down the hall, and many of the residents had known his parents. He managed to get his brother to foot the cable bill so he could have his computer going. That had been one of my responsibilities while we were living in Northbrook. The computer was his connection to the outside world. He always said I taught him how to use it. I helped, but he was so smart, and once I convinced him he could not wreck it, he dove into it. When he got into trouble, I could help him, but many times, it was my son who he would call to get him out of a computer jam. Bill is an expert troubleshooter and he willingly spent hours with Jim on the phone going through the problems.

His sisters swapped laundry days, unless I was there. I would do his laundry while I stayed with him, rather than take it home, as they did. Jim's sisters helped furnish his apartment, adding to the couple of pieces he owned.. Together we would get him to the grocer, and keep his cupboards stocked.

Just as it was a challenge to get him to start on oxygen some years before, I coerced him into using an electric shopping cart at the store. And, just as with the oxygen, he liked it once he tried it. Before that, he would ask me to get him a cart or a stroller so he could just lean on it while he struggled to slowly walk. But now, with the self riding cart, shopping was a whole lot less stressful for him, and he looked forward to getting out of the apartment.

I spent many nights with him and relished our being together physically again. How I wished we were in my house. Things would have been closer to normal. I knew just what kept him comfortable and clean and nourished. I no longer had that control. I would lie next to his frail body in his little bedroom of the assisted living facility. The staff at the home got to know me; and would greet me as though I lived there.

****

When I first moved to Onalaska, before working at the grocery store, I found a job working at J. C. Penny's. There, I found we employees could purchase used display tables, racks and chairs. After a few months, I thought to myself that as long as I was making near nothing working for someone else, I might as well make near nothing while working for myself.

Actually, the money wasn't bad, now that I know more about the area. But, I set out looking for a storefront. Right there, in Onalaska, near the corner of two main streets was an empty storefront. It was an omen. Within less than two years, I had moved two people, sold a home and bought one, did a good amount of fixing up on the new place, including landscaping, had a job at Penny's, opened a new store, closed it 10 months later, and worked at a Grocery store, buried my mom, aunts, friends, uncle and took care of my partner, and here and there, I had a few gigs in this quiet area.

I loved getting the store ready and couldn't wait for opening day. I still had excellent credit and was depending on my credit card to start the store. The owner of the storefront was a kind soul who had started fixing it up for a future art showroom for his artist son. He had put new walls, lighting... all but the floor. He was simply using the building to store things and rent the second floor at that time. I talked him into letting me rent for a year, and then if all was well, I would try another year. We had an agreement, and I started moving in. I discovered that under the glue, dirt and linoleum floor was an original floor of beautiful tiles; small hexagons that I wanted to refurbish. I scraped and scrubbed and scraped some more, then called in a couple of flooring companies to see how much it would be. It turned out to be an impossible job because the machines couldn't handle the swaying floor that was jacked up here and there from underneath. So, I bought a wall to wall carpet and the owner installed it. When it came to winter, I tread-carpeted the roomy entrance so customers wouldn't slip. I found a marvelous young woman who made signs from her house. Paula made lovely window signs from my business card logo.

As most people know, a lot of us people in the arts are basically lousy business people. Too often, we give our talent away just to be able to exhibit it. That doesn't work in retail. I used my credit card, and what little equity I had left in my new home. Darlene's calligraphy was the base of my inventory, which I bought and paid for immediately, but I tended to give too much away from my store. I converted the showroom into a three-part store. Basically, it was a gift shop that showcased Darlene's artworks and other gifts. I am proud to say her work is now sold in Neiman Marcus and other prestigious stores, and her art work is being made into fabrics.

In the very back of 'Judi K's Place', there was a counter that I converted into a coffee bar; and I added a few tables and chairs for comfort and ambiance. In the center, I fashioned a 'living room' look and feel that included my piano from home, placed next to an oversized potted palm tree. The palm and the piano were placed in front of a huge brass framed mirror, 4.5 ft. by 6 ft). that resembled a large palladium window. Near the piano, I put chairs and a coffee table that held copies of the Mississippi Rag, Rhythm& Blues, Jazz Beat and the Chicago Jazz Magazine, the four magazines that I am affiliated with. Against the pillar next to two chairs was a nice electric fireplace that helped give the area a welcoming feeling. A two story room, the vast walls displayed the dozens of framed and matted pieces of Darlene's extraordinary works, each one unique in colors and calligraphy. I had live music every Friday night for 8 months. I gave away coffee, music and prizes to get people in to the store. Small 'crowds' came. Smaller towns seem to resist changes and new people. I remembered that Jim's sister had told me how cold La Crosse people were in general. I got the same story from my cousin who lived down the road from me. I was told the same thing by others who had moved here from other places. I would ask why they stayed. They would ask me the same question. Anyone who did come into the store would ask if I were a "local". It sounded as though they wouldn't shop there unless I was a 'local'. So, I would answer, 'well, I do live here'. It became a regular, expected question each time the door opened. The local television stations announce to "Shop Local", making it sound unpatriotic if you shopped where you didn't know the owner, unaware of how some people's brains interpret that type of command. Do they mean don't leave town to shop, or to go into a store in their town and ask if the owner was born there? Hey, for pete's sake, my store was an only one, a kind of a 'mom-sans-pop' operation, and taxes and the expense of it was spent in Onalaska/La Crosse. My home is in Onalaska, where my Real Estate taxes go, my shopping is done in Onalaska and La Crosse, including clothes and groceries, yet, I haven't been accepted as a local. I support local entertainers, and volunteer at the schools and various other places.

I have found many nice people in the places that I volunteer in; one of which is RSVP who sends us out to blood drives, schools, concerts and volunteer events. It's taken me a while to get used to the small town gossip, which at first was most unsettling. Now, it's expected.

Several musicians that Jim had known over the years lived in the area; and most of them knew my situation, or I figured they should have. But this town is pretty isolated and self contained. The move, and the store was a last ditch effort. It was a do-or-die situation for me. It had been very recent since Franz Jackson was quoted in the Mississippi Rag that I had done a noble thing, referring to taking care of Jim and forsaking my Chicago home, friends and my singing to take care of Jim…for taking the high road. Didn't they read that stuff? I was on the cover of an international jazz monthly, and I knew it had a huge readership throughout the country and the world. My store was out there for everyone to see, including billboards. Yet, I was alone. Alone and unaccepted. But I loved having my own store, I gave my customers more than their money's worth in hopes they would come back to shop. Al Townsend, the local jazz icon stopped in twice. Al is a good person, and he has a swinging band. He had married Jim to two of his wives (at different times, of course!) and had a long history with my Jim. Al came to the grand opening of my store, and I had hired a piano player to play the piano at the store every Friday evening for the next several months. It was an easy gig; the piano and sound system was top notch, I supplied free beverages and paid decently. I was as happy as I *could* be… living in strange surroundings, missing my friends from Chicago.

In a corner of the store in the coffee area, I had an old console TV and all day long, I ran a continual string of videos of old Louis Armstrong performances, along with concerts by Ella Fitzgerald, Peggy Lee, Judy Garland, and others. I figured the coffee drinkers might enjoy watching the films, and I liked having the videos available. They kept me company during the empty hours. The front third of the store was the gift shop, and at the checkout, I also had the use of a very nice glass case to display jewelry. After a while, I purchased a second one for the expanding inventory. Local artists came with their wares asking me to sell it for them. I provided the display and whatever customers I had for them. So that the water at the store would provide tasty coffee, I called a couple of water delivery companies, choosing the salesperson who took the time to explain why their water was the best. He showed me the 'numbers' of chemicals and minerals in the water, and explained that the water in the La Crosse area is well water; full of minerals. Having come from the North Shore of Chicago, I am spoiled about good (surface) water. Here, you need water softeners and the water plays havoc with clear glass. The company I did business with was from Winona, and is as excellent in service and knowledge as well as having good water. I felt good using their product for the coffee I offered.

A few weeks later, the local bottling company came in and told me I should be getting my water from them because, after all, I would be losing local customers if I didn't support the local businesses. What the heck? I thought to myself that he would be smarter to have brought some customers *with* him instead of threatening me! Reciprocal support helps, not hurts. Three weeks later, he barged into my store and went straight to my coffee counter at the back and said, "I see you still have the other company's water". Of all the years I lived in big, bad Chicago, I had never gotten any kind of bullying like that. I will temper that experience with the fact that the local coffee service, Stanfield's was just great. They supplied the coffee, hot chocolate, containers and deliveries all for the affordable price of delicious coffee. I still go there to get my supply of coffee pouches just to use here at home. And I still get compliments on it too. Fine coffee and fine service: a nice combination.

Every day, the store got classier looking. I added several nice mirrors; for the walls, and had a couple of custom mirrors cut to fit the backs of my counters at the checkout. I was enjoying the upcoming Christmas season. I love to decorate, and from the curb of the sidewalk at the front to the very back of the store, lights and decorations glistened. I filled the window with dangling strings of little mirrors mixed with tiny lights and tube lighting. I made up a recipe for Judi K's Jazz Java, a hot coffee drink. It was rich, like a dessert, and expensive to make, and it was mine. There was a tree at the curb in front of my store, and I wrapped it with shiny gold foil rope... the whole trunk and every branch as far as I could reach with my ladder.

January came and the heating bills soared. I called the energy company and there was nothing I could do. The landlord generously offered to put a new furnace system in that room that would be more efficient, but for me that was too late. I couldn't borrow on my house any more, and the bills were getting bigger. The income from the store didn't meet the amount of the monthly utilities.

After bankruptcy, I took a few classes at the university downtown, and that got me out of the house and away from the ringing phone. The colleges in Wisconsin have classes that cost seniors only 5 bucks a class. I had a few gigs, and then I gave up on the local setting. Yes, I was spoiled, and I missed the hot musicians in Chicago and I was very tired.

One summer day, just a couple of years *before* I moved to Onalaska, I was in the La Crosse area visiting, and I took a walk through a food and music festival downtown called Riverfest. Al Townsend invited me up on stage to do a number with his group "The Wonderful World Jazz" band and there was a piano player I hadn't met yet. He was darn good.

I selected a common standard, "S'Wonderful," in the key of Ab, and all went well even though I do it quite up tempo, which makes it a challenge, but I was pretty comfortable with the piano player. Eric has a little group called "Swing, Inc., The Best Little Big Band in Town," and, with meeting him, I started enjoying the 'locals'…except that Eric is from Winona, so saying he is local is not completely true. He also plays the calliope, which talent takes him to New Orleans often enough. He has a big heart and a lot of talent, and a wonderful counterpart by the name of John Paulson. John plays a really fine saxophone, and directs the St. Mary's University music department. Eric is also on that staff. John featured me with his University Big Band for their Christmas Concert. It was a cold blizzard that blew that night, making for slow driving, but the music was hot, and we had a sizable audience. Weather like that would have had many other public places empty! Winona seems to be a warm, friendly place, and they immediately took me to their hearts and them to mine. A few years after moving to Onalaska, Eric and John's band Swing Inc hired me to sing with them at one of their venues. I truly enjoyed it, and drove to Winona on those weekends to sing a few songs. A couple of years later, I joined a local Classic Jazz Band here in la Crosse, The Seven Rivers Jazz Band, and we are now nearing our third year of a steady venue.

****

From *JazzBeat Magazine* by permission of Paige Van Vorst:

"JIM BEEBE— 1931– 2004

"It is with a broken heart that I tell you my Jim died this morning. The hospital called to say he had taken a couple of hard falls during the night. When I arrived,

he said he wanted me to go with him in the ambulance. I rode with him from Sparta to Gunderson Lutheran Hospital in La Crosse. He has been very ready to die for a long time now, and now the struggle to breathe is over for him."

"*Thus read an email I received on August 29 from vocalist Judi K, Beebe's long time musical and personal partner. Jim Beebe was an integral part of Chicago's jazz scene for over 50 years, and even after his playing career was prematurely curtailed by emphysema, he remained on the scene, contributing his knowledge to the Jazz Institute of Chicago website and keeping up a voluminous online correspondence on the Dixieland Jazz Mailing List and elsewhere. Jim Beebe grew up on Wisconsin, the son and grandson of physicians. His musical talent manifested itself early when he took up the drums while in grade school; he switched to trombone while in high school, and his interest in music was sealed when a neighbor took him to Chicago where he heard Bill Reinhardt's Jazz Limited band and Art Hodes' group…*

"*…He enrolled in college, intending to follow his father into medicine, but he left after two years to enroll in the marines at the height of the Korean War. He was a member of a Marine band stationed at Treasure Island, a base of the coast of San Francisco.…"*

Paige goes on to illustrate Jim's musical career, covering his 'discovery' by Bob Scobey, and subsequent recording with him, touring with the Stars of Jazz, which included Wild Bill Davison, Hillard Brown, Eddie Condon, Barney Bigard, and Rail Wilson, replacing Freddie Assunto for a time in the Dukes of Dixieland, when Freddie was stricken with cancer, and then Paige continues:

"*…Jim was a fulltime bandleader, and kept his bands working fulltime for the rest of his life. Extended gigs included more than a year at the Rib Exchange in Schaumburg, Razzles in the Holiday Inn, 4 years at Dick's Last Resort (I say it was Six Mardis Gras—nearly 6 years.) and 17 years at the Bristol/Braxton Seafood Grill. He also had his band for a lengthy run at Flaming Sally's.…etc…*

"*He began using Judi K as a band vocalist near the beginning of his run at the Bristol, and she's been a regular ever since, even taking groups out from time to time after Beebe retired.*

"*It was hard to see a man like Jim Beebe retire from music when he was relatively young. Judi K put on a birthday party for him about 3 years ago, and while he looked good and was in excellent spirits surrounded by friends and fans, he was tethered to an oxygen tank…*

"We'll let Judi K tell the story of his last day:

"Paige, I was blessed once again, this time to have had the opportunity to be there for his last breath of life as we know it. He had a sound sleep without medication the day before he died, waving the nurses away every two hours. I came into his room to find him peacefully asleep. He awoke to say he and an epiphany. He kept exclaiming, "Am I dead? Am I here?" He said he died and found that he and I are one, and that my mother and I are one He said the revelation was so satisfying. He then said he had to go to sleep once again.

'I left him at about 9:30 PM to go home, and during the night he got out of bed and fell. He was 'quite confused'. The fall resulted in a huge black eye and a cut just above it (Rocky- style) but he said he didn't feel it. The hospital called to ask me to come there and ride with him in the ambulance to Gunderson, the La Crosse hospital, where he asked my permission and that of his sisters if it was all right to leave. I told him it was ok for him to go, and he said,, "OK, I am now going into oblivion; I want to go. And his breathing became much labored. He said it hurt physically, so I asked for morphine, which they did administer. He died with my arms around him. How I loved that man…

"It was a dignified death for a dignified man. His journey has been a long and hard one, and he was a brave, wonderful man who I love very much…"

Jim Beebe personified Chicago jazz for over 50 years— even though he's gone, it's hard to remember he's not out there on the Internet tossing in acerbic commentary and well written reminiscence."

–Paige Van Vorst

****

When my Jim died, I lost the last bit of heart for singing. The few gigs I did had no meaning without him. I was asked to perform in Decatur, for the prestigious Central Illinois Jazz Fest. I was no stranger to that festival, but the timing,—so soon after losing Jim— was wrong. I thought I could do it. But I was empty. I hadn't seen any of the musicians since before we moved away, and rarely heard from any of them. I was excited to sing again with Don Stille at the piano; and I was anxious to work once again with Connie Jones, Kim Cusack and the others who I missed heartily. I was looking forward to seeing my old fans that were so faithful in Chicago and elsewhere.

I did ok, although I felt panicked, and was warmed by the reception of the people.

I had endured Jim's funeral and dying with no one around to grieve with. By the last day of the jazz fest, things were going along, and so many familiar faces were in the audience. I looked at them and started to dedicate my last song to Jim, and just uttering his name opened a floodgate of tears. I sputtered out the song; Connie was disgusted and I fell apart. My fans were feeling it. They came right up to the stage to hold me. Peggy Andruss told me, "Judi, don't worry, this was due. It was bound to happen. You haven't been able to share your grief with any of us for too long a time." "We love you, Judi," came up from someone in the audience, and I loved them, but I just wanted to disappear. The whole scene hurt from all aspects.

Before I left the festival that weekend, I felt so bad about letting my emotions get away from me, I went into Maggie's office to offer part of my salary back. I hadn't behaved like a professional; I was weak and hurting. I just hadn't expected Connie to be so thoughtless about my emotions and the stress I had been slapped with over the last few years. I threw myself a complete pity party: How would he have felt if he had lost Elaine and no one cared? He and Jim got along, and so did Elaine and I. One of the times that Connie and Elaine were my guests in Northbrook, Elaine could tell how sick Jim was getting. She said, "Judi, when the time comes, you are going to need help." She said it again as they left to return to New Orleans. As a nurse, she understood what was in store.

The jazz fest in Decatur had been only 4 months after Jim's death, yet, nothing was said when I finally met up with all the players again. How quickly they forget. I was mad at the world.

I returned to a drab and meaningless winter in Onalaska. My driveway was filled with 2 feet of snow. I was too tired to shovel, so I went inside and went to bed. I didn't unpack for 2 more days. I felt as though I were on a deserted island with no way to get off. It rarely stopped snowing. I was still repairing what other people broke. The yard, the porch, the shutters and screens...and more.

CHAPTER 45

My First Mother's Day Alone in Wisconsin:

The phone rang. The voice on the other end said,

"Judi?" It was Sonny Turner. Then he said in his easy, purposely slow manner, "Just a minute now," and I heard him walk gently over to a (table?) and pick something up. It was his trumpet. Then he started to play "Young at Heart," the entire song! And then I heard him put his horn back where he had gotten it. I heard his footsteps head back to pick up the phone and said, "That was for you, Judi." My heart swelled. Of all the people who worked with us, Sonny was the most thoughtful, and that gesture was the perfect example of his big heart. I will cherish that memory forever. He is a great entertainer, and we always had more fun when he was in a gig with us. One of my favorite pictures of him is one that I took from when he was with us at the Bristol.

Another person in the small handful, was our often-times drummer, Rusty Jones. We were the same age, as were Greg Sergo and I, and we always had our own brand of fun going on and off stage. Rusty would call me off and on just to say hello, and always called on my birthday to sing Happy Birthday to me. I pretended he was calling on behalf of all the other players.

****

The next year and a half was a struggle. There were no jobs to speak of, especially for an outsider in a town this; but the beauty is unmatchable. All towns are nestled in the nooks and coulees of the bluffs flanking the mighty Mississippi. Often, I want to stop the car and just stare at the awesomeness of the views, and I often do. The soil is sandy, and good for growing Evergreens. Around here the evergreen trees rarely have brown spots or have any sparse branches. They seem to be perfectly shaped Christmas-card trees, lush all the way to the ground. Around Chicago, you couldn't depend on an evergreen tree ending up full and perfectly shaped, so when they were, it was noticeable. I remember wanting one in my front yard when we built our house in Northbrook, and the landscaper mixed sand with the soil, knowing the roots of an evergreen need ease in spreading. Evergreens have to be nurtured more in some areas; but around here they do beautifully au natural. In my walks these days, I have to stop and examine the many enormous, lush evergreen trees in some yards. I cried when, across the street from me, the owner had an entire row of gorgeous evergreens removed from bottom to midway up, just so the mower would have it easy...dummies didn't realize that there would be no grass growing under the branches brushing the ground?.... ARGH.

CHAPTER 46

A Stretch of Good News After Moving

Soon after I opened my store, I got an email from a highly respected Jazz historian, Scott Yanow. He said he was interviewing singers for a book of "The Top 500 Jazz Singers of All Time," and that I am one of them. I asked if he was sure he had the right Judi K…he replied that he never had a doubt that I would be in it. I would be in the "Swing" section. Suddenly, it was a great day!

My spirits were buoyed for a long time after that. Of course, I had to brag to everyone I knew, as it was quite exciting for me. He said I would be in good company. I checked with him then to see what 'of all time' meant, and he said, from the beginning of jazz. The book would finally come out in October of 2008, and during the nearly 3 year wait, the Hal Leonard Corporation merged Backbeat Books to its own corporate name and of course, now the book has even more prestige. The cover has changed from having Billie Holiday on it to additional pictures of Ella Fitzgerald, Louis Armstrong, Frank Sinatra, Diana Kroll, and Nat King Cole. While waiting for the publication to take physical form, I was realizing that I would be lucky if I got just a few-words-mention. I am honored to say I have a half page even though my profile isn't as important or interesting as most of the other singers in it. (Note: the book's name changed from "Jazz Singers—the top 500 to its current title, "Jazz Singers—the Ultimate Guide).

****

Backing up a few months:

Jim's funeral was just what he would have wanted. Al Townsend officiated, using his band to play appropriate songs. Except for my children, my brother Jeff and his wife, and Bonnie Kolac with her husband Bob Wolfe, and my four precious cousins, who all showed up for the funeral, I was completely alone as soon as it was over.

After the funeral, I went back to Onalaska feeling abandoned and alone in the house I wanted to have Jim live with me in. If he had been able to live with me here, maybe he would still be alive—so says my wishful thinking superego. I had been beaten. Entirely.

Inevitably, the first 2 years after he died were the worst for me. I would wear his pajamas at night, and I wore the down jacket I had given him a few years before, I cried during the day. I was cold even in warm rooms. I heard his voice many times, and had vivid dreams of us talking and holding each other. I could actually feel his arms and legs and kiss his face. One bleak day I decided I didn't want to be alive anymore. I was desperate to join Jim. I called Doug Black, a wonderful scholar of the afterlife, who had studied how to 'cross over' and return again. He helped find other spirits for people who asked.– (a precursor to 'Ghost Whisperer?'). He is highly respected and well known at the Monroe Institute, and Jim had learned the 'trick' of crossing over from reading Doug Black's manuscript, and speaking with him. I felt I could do this with no training, I felt so strongly about it because of my experiences with my mom's death and recently Jim's. I took Doug's directions and simply soaked them in. I read them, and saved them for another day. I was able to see and talk with Jim on a couple of occasions. One of these occasions was so vivid, that when I 'returned', I was feeling so peaceful, so sure that all would come out well. I will cherish that experience always. Jim told me to look ahead, and go get back on track. I have realized that I am the only person who can make that happen. But that's easier said than done.

Another time soon after, I saw my mother, clear as day. She seemed to be telling me everything would be alright. My brother Jimmy, who listened to my spiritual experiences, told me about meeting up with Mom in a dream. He said he was 'flying', (he and I both do a lot of 'flying' in our dreams) and who did he meet up with but our Mom, who was also suspended but carrying a suitcase! (A picture of Mary Poppins came into my head). He asked her if she were going to come back with him. Her response? "No way, I'm not going back *there* again!" We were silent for a few seconds and then my brother and I shared a hearty laugh.

Another time, in one of my dreams, I met up with Mom at a bus stop. I think it was in Fargo. One second we were there, and the next we were crossing the street to approach the bus stop. She had a suitcase with her then, too. As the bus came to the stop, I said, "Mom, I want to go with you. I'll go with you. You shouldn't be alone." She answered, "No, you stay here, I have to go and visit Vera now." Vera was her older sister who died only a couple of weeks before Mom did.

Occasionally, I drive to my birth town, Arcadia, mainly to visit my aunts and cousins, and to spiff up my parent's gravesite. My brother Jon was in charge of that task, and did an excellent job; but there was always bird droppings to clean off the tomb stones, and dried up leaves and grass to tend to. The drive to Arcadia is breathtakingly lovely. Deep valleys with rolling fields can be seen from the winding roads in the high hills. Color changes are awesome, and Arcadia itself sits low, surrounded with hills The town has gotten old and changed a lot, but I remember that quaint downtown with the one department store, one dime store, one movie theatre, and several bars, full of friendly people who knew your name and cared. Where my grandma Liz's hat shop stood is now an empty storefront, old and ready to be razed.

Sometimes I drive out to the farm, and still feel the warmth and contentment of it overcome me. It's one road into the coulee ends at the Erickson farm, then another shale road juts into the hills to the side. I never thought of myself as a farm-girl; I'm not, but I believe I could enjoy living out there in that beautiful valley and create some kind of retreat if I owned it.

My blessings have been many. I was able to be a stay-at-home Mom except for the first few years of my son's life, and raise two incredibly wonderful children. They are thoughtful and giving, they live life to the fullest, they are contributors to their communities, and they always bring out the best in others.

****

CHAPTER 47

Carrying On-back in Fargo After Dad's Death

Mom taught us to stay busy; one of her slogans was: "When you wake up, get up"…. Well that was easy back then as all of us kids shared bedrooms, and we all went to sleep at the same time! The three girls had one bedroom at the front of the house, and the four boys had the main bedroom, which was big enough to hold two sets of bunk beds with plenty of room between them. Mom and Dad took the smallest bedroom. On waking up, we immediately hopped out of bed and started our day. Mom wasn't one to even sit down to watch television or listen to the radio without some kind of sewing or other project in her hands, and since I am my Mom, I do the same- not as well, maybe, but I try.

After my two older sisters left for Chicago and subsequently got married, I had the bedroom to myself for a year or so. During my freshman year at the Catholic High School, I sprained my ankle. In my Martyr's eye, I 'should just bear it', don't complain, keep walking on it. Even as I stood on the school bus, getting pushed and accidentally kicked in the midst of the students who were struggling to move around. I never told any of them to watch out for my ankle! My ankle swelled up like a hard black balloon, turning to shades of dark blue, and when I was in bed that night, and until it healed, my Dad would come in and sit on the bottom corner of my bed and asked how I was doing. He would say, "how are you feeling, Heart?" Sometimes he would try to cover my foot with the sheet, but the weight of the cotton sheet was too much to bear. And, after he died that year, I still experienced his sitting on the corner of my bed in the dark like he was watching over me. I would whisper to the darkness, "Daddy, is that you?." There would be no answer and the 'pressure' on the mattress corner would lighten and the bed would return to its regular height. I believe it was him.

When my daughter and I talk, I am my mother talking to me, and sometimes it's hard for her to take. I know the feeling. I try to remember the things Mom might say that I didn't like, and then avoid that. I am free with encouragement and give my kids plenty of kudos in case they inadvertently inherited any low self-esteem. There is a quote from one of my favorite movies "One True Thing," with Meryl Streep and Renee Zellweger with William Hurt as the husband/father. After trying to fill *her* Mom's shoes, Renee's character cried; "It's hard being my mother!" I relate to that, and I think it often.

As for myself, I am at the crossroads of enjoying life as it is—and knowing I am losing family and friends to the next world! I just hope I can do as good a job as my parents and aunts at keeping up the spirit of the 'older generation'!

Meanwhile, I was recently lucky enough to do a concert in New Mexico, when the great Houston Person joined me onstage, among some other gigs, such as fundraisers for the Minnesota Arts, and a Christmas Concert at St. Mary's University in Winona, I was flown once again out to New Mexico to entertain at a very special event at the Tamaya Hyatt near Albuquerque. Also, I shared the Great Franz Jackson's 95th with him, onstage in Michigan, just a few months before he died. It was so special, and later, when I went back for his memorial, I was made to feel special, too, for he was a huge part of my musical life, as was Jim Beebe, Jethro Burns and other great artists. On the first anniversary of Franz's death, I joined another fan of Franz' in Chicago, at 'Pops for Champagne', in downtown Chicago for a tribute to him with Lisa Roti who is a beautiful lady, inside and out; and she loved and respected Franz, too. In October the Singers Book finally came out. Originally named "Jazz Singers– the top 500 of all time," it is now published by the Hal Leonard Corporation, under the name of "Jazz Singers–the Ultimate Guide." It's authored by

Scott Yanow, a noted jazz historian from the West Coast. I was interviewed for the first edition and have been waiting anxiously to see if this honor is real!

My vocal coach from college got it and is using it for his music classes as a referral book–his brag book! Pardon the recap.

I just returned from Chicago, where I invited 5 musicians to join me at Delmark to make a new CD. Well, I must say, we had a ball, and a lot of laughs. Jeremy Kahn (musical director– "Wicked" and Ellington's "Play On" among many other credits), graced the piano, and old friend Leon Joyce of the Ramsey Lewis Trio was on drums. Older friends, Kim Cusack and Tommy Bartlett lent their horns to flavor the appropriate tunes, and newcomer Chris Carani joined in on Bass. I haven't listened to the roughs yet, but whether I use the session or not, it was worth the effort just to be singing with them again!

By the way, I have been a feature writer for the Mississippi Rag. This is a 50 page monthly paper that has been around nearly 35 years, offering mounds of jazz history to the public, and listing countless concerts and festivals for everyone's information enjoyment. My series is called "Jazz Warriors" and it is a tribute to all the volunteers behind the scenes that do so much to create venues for the performers. So far I have profiled 9 Jazz Societies. Writing is a nice outlet and keeps me in touch while I sit here looking out the window at snow, snow, and more snow!!!

A highlight this late fall was when my sister Janie came to stay with me while her husband Ed was hunting in the area. Jane and I spent many hours laughing and reminiscing about our cherished childhoods and precious feelings for one another. She helped me edit (what was so-far ready) of my Memoirs and we both laughed and cried at the anecdotes and memories. I hope to finish it this winter, and then find a publisher. It's a lot of work, but hey, I'm in Wisconsin—there's time! (That was written almost 8 years ago, and only now I am back at it).

Well, it is now late Summer, a year later, and I am still editing and adding and dropping. It is nearing a year since Janie was here visiting.

CHAPTER 48

Musical Beginnings: a First Tour

I've been going through the many scrapbooks of pictures and great memories. One whole scrapbook was dedicated to the tour with Crescent City Jazz Band.

Those 6 wonderful men were easy going and fun, and made each day something to look forward to. Of course, everything was so new to me that I was pretty much in awe of everyone and everywhere! We had two vans, Connie's old one that I nicknamed 'the terrorist van' because it was the model of Volkswagen that was used by what the movies showed as Terrorists' transportation (or Hippies/ i.e. the Grateful Dead followers).

Connie's van had no heater…I guessed you don't need one coming from New Orleans! Well, I was the 'odd man' out, so I rode wherever I fit. Dick Taylor, the drummer for the group had a nicer, larger van with a bit more comfort. Sometimes I rode in that one. Most of the time, though, when debarking at a stop, we did look like a 'Motley Crew'.

Snow made Connie a nervous driver, and he wanted to make sure everyone was on time for the concert in the next town, so when he knocked on all our doors early in the morning, you had better get up and get ready to leave. We did one-night concerts in each of the scheduled small towns from Iowa to the Dakotas, into Canada, Minnesota and Wisconsin and Illinois. Some of the motels that we had to stay at were pretty cold and lacked any amenities. Of course, with our schedule none were needed, there was no time. One of our stops we made, (I think it was in North

Dakota), we approached late at night. The driveway was long and curved, no trees, just a thin layer of snow, and the sign was hanging haphazardly with part of the neon broken spelling out 'Mot l'. Les Muscut, who played guitar and banjo for the band, was also one who kept us giggling with his dry English humor, said under his breath, but just loud enough for us to hear, "I wonder if Norman is still up". By the look of the motel, we knew immediately that he was referring to the movie "Psycho." The rooms turned out to be clean and comfortable enough.

At another motel in Harvey, North Dakota, when we pulled up to it, there were was a dog sledder's event going on. Trucks full with cages of barking Huskies. We got to our rooms, and left doors open to bring in our suitcases etc. I stood looking out the window at an endless flat span of snow, wondering why I love North Dakota. It wasn't deep or drifting snow, just flat and shallow looking. Les saw me standing there, looked out and in a minute asked, "Judi, is that a Tundra?"...I had to laugh, figuring he was joking...but I answered "Uh-huh" anyway.

Everyone was anxious to get some sleep as we had many miles to go next day. The next morning, Connie got us all up earlier than usual because it was snowing. Actually, to me it was just slightly blowing snow that seemed to hover over the road and change sides as it wisped across the asphalt. We got an early start, Connie was white knuckled, not having experienced driving in snow. He thought it was a blizzard. I laughed. I thought it was nothing. He explained that when they saw news of a blizzard, they figured people froze instantly, just as us Northerners think about a hurricane or typhoon drowning everyone that it touched. He was right, I would be afraid of any sized hurricane.

After a few blocks, Les looked over his shoulder pretending to 'long' for the sight behind him, and squeezing out a soft moan as he said in his English accent, "I wish I had been kinder to the dog sledders." We all laughed and relaxed.

A few of the concerts were set up in gymnasiums and churches. One of the churches was small, with long stemmed ceiling fans turning slowly. We filed in with the sound equipment, and Les stopped, put his instruments down, and settled his hands on his hips while looking at the spinning propellers. Then he shook his head and mumbled "They'll never get it off the ground."

When we went into Canada, there was more snow. I talked to the guys about getting some boots; Les found a used pea coat with a torn sleeve and missing button that I mended for him. I took pictures of all of us, and we actually looked like a group of hobos. Bundled in winter caps and earmuffs and scarves, we went to our rooms and got ready for the concert. The Manitoba audience was just great. Lots of college students, and since Steve Martin was one of my favorite comics, I copied him by bringing my camera on stage and taking pictures of the audience telling them to 'hold still', etc, while they were taking pictures of us. They got it, especially the students, and laughed with knowing heartiness. The concert went very well. I sent the pictures back to the school after they were developed a few weeks later, and got a nice letter from the music professor saying how much they all enjoyed us.

I had a tape recorder along, and taped each concert, and then, back in my room I would listen to the songs I did. I did the same 9 songs each night, so it was easy to note what could be improved on, and to see that I *really was* improving. I got good reviews from every paper throughout the tour. I wish now I had believed more in myself. My ego pops up at strange times but not when I need it!

While I listened to the tapes alone in my room, I would sew the loose or dropped beads and sequins back on my costumes. One of my beaded skirts was a bit long, and my high heel would catch in the fabric and I could hear the crunch of the glass bugle beads under my heal. I wondered if the audience could hear the same thing. I was naïve enough to bring a different outfit for each concert, not realizing that each audience would be different. I could have gotten by with only 3 or four 'costumes'. But I did carry my own suitcases and years later, Connie would mention that to people. I never was a prima-donna, even in my ignorance. I enjoyed being one of the band.

****

CHAPTER 49

Going Down Slow

As I said before, during my mother's and my aunt's deaths, and Jim's health getting worse, I tried to keep doing my gigs, even though my focus was unreliable. I shouldn't have taken the jobs, but I needed the money, and I needed my music. I accepted a nice gig at Chicago's cultural center and picked up Buddy Charles to play with me. It was a noontime gig, and the place was full. With my own emotional health getting in the way of my ability to entertain, I was lucky to have had Buddy there. I wasn't happy with my performance and wished I hadn't taken the date. But, the people loved what we did, and we got through it, thanks to him. I drove us both ways, and when we got back to his house, I went in for something cold to drink. He and his wife had many projects going, one of them was making rosaries! Dozens of them in a heap on the kitchen table would be donated to places that could use them. It was the first time I saw anyone do that. My Mom would have loved the idea. We had a glass of tea while I looked at the rosaries. Over his shoulder, I saw a picture of a cartoon cleaning lady with an 'aura' of a guardian angel with just a suggestion of wings. On closer look, there was a caption under the angel: "Fuck Housework".

Later, I would have Buddy with me at the Bunny Berigan festival. I knew he was best at soloing, so I asked him to do "Three Little Words", where he stands up and yells, "You're Under Arrest" at the appropriate time. That was in his element. The audience loved it, and it was a nice break from our usual sounding classic jazz pieces. Buddy told me he was Mugsy Spanier's stepson, and when he was young, he sang on one of Mugsy's recordings. He said he sounded like a girl, grinning one of his big, mischievous smiles.

And, though I shouldn't have, I had also accepted a show at a PAC in Cedarburg, WI. I lined up a 6 piece band and a couple of weeks later, the gal in charge called and asked me to reschedule so she could put another show in and move me. I said, ok. I had to recall and replace the players who couldn't take the second date. Another week went by, and the girl called again, asking me to change again. Again, in embarrassment, I called the musicians to see if they could switch the date. Now only two of the original players could go. I obliged the agent when I shouldn't have. I should have held her accountable. Once again, I did what was best for someone else and not for me. I wound up doing a half assed concert and was mad at myself for letting someone push me around. And I was too tired to deal with it.

The two unsuccessful gigs helped bring my moral down. I was depressed.

My kids came home to help me pack; the mess was getting to Jim. I was getting no help from his family. I asked for some kind of reprieve a year before, and got yelled at, accusing me of 'jumping ship'. One of his sisters hissed that I would be nothing if it weren't for Jim.

But, all I needed was a break; a rest. Someone to say, "hey, Judi, take a break, I will help with Jim." They didn't even know it was *my* home, my responsibility to not only pay my mortgage, but the utilities, take care of Jim and his business. I had been running his errands, supplying him his office and necessities, cooking for him and his kids when they came over, and buying the groceries. I was tapped; emotionally and financially. Where did his family think the money was coming from? I had refinanced my townhouse twice already, helping Jim buy a car, and about get myself a badly needed one. Mine had broken down going to my Mom's funeral.

I don't think Jim was very close to his siblings until his later years. When he moved in with me, I felt he didn't have any family life, I felt sorry about that and tried to change his circumstances. He said (his third wife) wouldn't get along with his children from his first wife so his older kids weren't allowed to visit at his third wife's house, I was told. I thought I could change that. I tried to get the younger ones over to my place so Jim could have quality time with them. I got each of them their own personalized toothbrush and toothpaste and utility boxes, pillows and blankets so they would feel they could leave their personal stuff behind for the next visit. I played table games with them, I made popcorn and root beer floats. Ryan adapted right away, enjoying the moment. Christie cried and admonished me that her mother said if I put makeup on her that she would 'kill' me. Where that came from, I don't know. I hardly wore makeup anywhere. Even on stage. In high school, the nuns wouldn't let us wear even mascara. Christie was only about 9 years old. After the move, I didn't see her for another twelve or thirteen years or so, and that was at her Dad's funeral. By then she was a Bear's cheerleader, wearing a bare midriff and clear Lucite platform 'mules' on her bare feet. To a funeral. You can't blame the singer for that one. Actually, I made every effort to get Jim and his younger kids together. They really had 12 whole years to get to know him better before he died.

There were other places I tried to help. Jim told me he had a younger brother and he hadn't spoken to him in years. I said to give him a call. Jim didn't know what he would say. I told him to ask about his brother's family and what his brother was doing. He finally called Tom and that started a better communication within his family. It continued to the end of Jim's life and I was glad for that. I felt it was an accomplishment. One of Tom's kids even came over to visit us in Northbrook. I like Tom. He has very nice kids and he is understanding and realistic as far as I could tell. His son stopped by to visit us, too. It was a good feeling. I think Jim marched to the tune of a different drummer all through his life! But I think his disease and his music led him down some unchartered means to a goal.

Young Ryan enjoyed coming over. He looked so much like Jim's pictures did at his age. I don't know where Ryan is now, but he was a special little boy. He was mischievous. He was nosey, and rambunctious. He would take my rubber stamps off my desk and stamp the ink on my walls downstairs. (I didn't really consider that cute.) Ryan would look in every drawer I owned, picking things out and moving them. When I brought that to Jim's attention, he laughed. I was raised to be fussy. I raised my own kids to not touch anything what wasn't theirs, so for Ryan I had to conjure up some new found patience. There was nothing I wouldn't do for Jim's comfort. And I know there are no other kids like mine. The thought of trying to 'straighten' someone else's out was something I didn't really want.

Often Jim would try to set up a meeting with his ex-wife, to meet at a central point, so he could get the kids. The long drive to his ex wife's house was getting too hard for him. It was hard even for me to go into his ex wife's house. The stench of smoke was overpowering. He depended on me to help get their kids back home to Geneva. It was too hard for him to pack himself up in the car with the oxygen etc. I did that for him. Some days, I would have to bring food to him in bed, just so he could simply have the energy to make it to the kitchen to eat breakfast or lunch or dinner. The stress on his lungs just to breathe used up calories so fast, you could feel heat leaving his body as he ate. He always put on such a strong façade, and he knew how to project his voice, so literally no one knew just how sick he was. His voice never betrayed how weak he really was. Oh, I wished I could have done more to keep him comfortable. Sometimes, before he fell asleep, I could see the fear of suffocation in his eyes. But, he would hold my hand, and eventually drift off. Although I wanted to hug him, a hug was difficult, as any arm wrapping around him, psychologically cut off his air. Most of the time, he would unconsciously leave a button on his shirt open: The one that is the third one down from the neck, in the middle of the chest. The shirt wasn't *really* confining him. Leaving the button open was an unconscious move.

Jim believed in touch healing. I would rest my hand on his back, on the area of his lungs and hope that my energy would transcend to him. Sometimes, after a gig, I would have to 'pound' his back with a cupped hand to loosen any phlegm in his lungs. He was good at touch healing, and I did what he asked. He took his turn when I had an ulcer attack, he would put his hand where my physical pain was, and ask the questions: what color is it, how big is it, how heavy is it, is it moving, etc., etc., until the color and weight of the pain subsided, and kind of moved out of 'sight'. He had a gift for using the right words, the right tension in his voice.

He also had a great radio voice. Projection came naturally and he was articulate. At one time, I took him downtown Chicago to do a radio show with Studs Terkel. I still have that tape/disc of that show. Jim's voice on it is clearly a professional's.

As far as his older kids went, I did my best. When we went to a wedding at one time, his son and grandson rode with us. The grandson had no suit, and his only shirt was wrinkled, so I asked my cousin if one of her kids had something for him to wear. Luckily, a complete tuxedo that had been her son Jason's was no longer in use at her house, and it fit Jim's grandson, so he inherited it. I pressed his shirt at the motel. The rest of the day went well. I encouraged them to come over to visit. I would take them out to lunch or I would prepare a meal for them when they did come. I bought the groceries. They would thank Jim and leave, not giving me a second glance. Some of Jim's friends did that too. Not all the musicians. Many of the musicians were somewhat aware of what I was doing. They knew Jim better than his family did. Others had the notion that Jim was taking care of me, not the other way around. Somehow my house became Jim's and in the end his kids thought my things were his. More than once I came home from work to find that he had sold my stereo or speakers, then told me that it was so that he could buy better ones. Most of the time, he would pay the initial $100 and then I would have to finish off the payments. Somehow, I justified that.

I had to overlook a lot of it and, as I saw it, I would never have wanted to be in his shoes, health wise or any way. What's it all about anyway? I had someone to love and who loved me. As he got older and sicker, I could tell he was more and more in tune with what I had been doing for him. After a month or two at the assisted living apartment in Sparta, he said, "look, Judi was doing the work of nine people," citing his sisters, and the staff and nurses, who were cleaning and taking care of his laundry and shopping and feeding him. Finally, I had some sanction. I am sure none of his other wives would have had the loyalty I did. When he died, some of the things his family was deciding discarding were mine; a lot of it was 'ours'. When Jim had finally gotten his own computer while we were in my Northbrook townhouse, it was my son who came up from Texas to help put it together and show him things he didn't know. Bill would load both our computers with programs and then make sure that Jim's car would get an oil change and he would have it washed and cleaned up…using his own money. But, Jim's older sons, who lived nearby in comparison, never bothered to offer, much less do it without asking, but they would criticize me about how we lived, where we lived and what I had.

After I moved to Onalaska, and while my furniture was still packed in the garage of where I had just moved, my son surprised me by sending my grandson up from Texas to help me. It was so great to see Zachary, who was about to enter high school, and yet this wasn't to be a fun time for him. He worked hard helping me unpack; he slept on the couch while I slept on a mattress amid the boxes. I placed the mattress under the skylight so I could see the moon in the sky. He and I made a table and two seats out of the still packed boxes. After a few days, we took a day off to go to the Dells. It turned out to be a wonderful day, riding the ducks and learning some Wisconsin area history. We went to the 'magnetic' house where we marveled at the difficulty of walking across the floor against the pull of the magnetic fields. On another day, we drove to Westby, a Norwegian community with some great eating places, and we went to see the ski jump. Although the Olympians used the ski jump in Eau Claire for practice, they have competitions and practices in Westby, too. Ski jumps and the Dells were things that Zach hadn't seen before, actually, I hadn't either…at least up close. So with some degree of pride, I was able to supply a couple of new experiences for him. Zach had a round trip ticket from Dallas to The Twin Cities and back, so on the day he left, I drove him to Minneapolis to catch his flight. It was early in the morning. I had to leave him alone to get through the inspection, and I know it was his first time, he was still in grade school, and I hated that I couldn't take him right on to the plane. I left the airport a bit depressed and headed back on the three-hour trip to my new place in Onalaska. I hadn't had a vacation in over 18 years, working every day and evening of every week all of that time. I had never taken a break from the day jobs along with the evening jobs and from taking care of Jim. My body was giving out. I never thought it was heart trouble. My spirit and my brain power were giving out, too, being replaced by fuzzy lightheadedness. I started forgetting lyrics, and even what day it was. I didn't know I had a heart disease then. On the way back from dropping Zach off, I fell sound asleep while driving and my car must have meandered all over the highway because just as it started down a ravine on left side I came to enough to see a semi-truck stopped some distance from me, watching front-on. I looked around and saw a string of cars a good distance behind me, all stopped and quietly waiting for an accident to happen. I flash-responded and swung back up on the highway and found an inlet, barely making it around the turn, still trying to stay awake. No matter how hard I tried, I couldn't help myself from falling fast asleep. Exhaustion can be murder!– Literally. I managed to put on the brakes and turn the car off. I fell back into a deep, deep sleep for the next four hours. I was keeping my guardian angels really busy!

****

CHAPTER 50

Counting Blessings

Music is soothing and therapeutic, especially when I remember the wonderful experiences I had in that field. When I was introduced to music, it seems it was because, somehow, that "Somebody up there" figured it was time for some good times to come back into my life. Guitar was a crack in the door opening...then Jethro, and the light got stronger, then a string of wonderful musicians, Jerry King, Gary Miller, Connie Jones...After meeting Jim, I figured it was at a time when he needed someone like me, and I, him. I was so lucky to have met and worked with Jethro, and learn what I could from him and from the others; like Truck Parham. Truck told me, that as a younger man, he had worked with the Jimmy Lunceford band, as a 'roadie'. He sang somewhat and played bass. His job as roadie gave him the nickname "Truck." Truck also worked with the great Lena Horne and toured with Pearl Bailey and Louis Belson. I loved listening to his stories. He came to the birthday party I threw for Jim's 70th. We started asking ages...he said, " I am a year older than Franz, and don't let him tell you any different. He likes to say he is a year older, but he is not". I had to laugh because by the time you are in your late 80s, what difference could it make? As far as the records I have of their birthdays, Franz actually was born 11 months after Truck. Truck's DOB is January 1911, and Franz's is November of 1912. Other than Franz's birthday, the only thing I can say about 1912 is that it is the year that Alexander's Ragtime Band was published.

CHAPTER 51

Truck's Wild Wedding Gig

One night Truck came to work at Dicks with news of a new gig for me. He was putting a wedding band together for some people he knew. He had Joe Johnson, Franz, Charlie Weeks, George Bean and me. It was a posh wedding on the 95th floor of the Hancock building downtown Chicago. It was black tie, and most of the ladies wore long black gowns. The room was barely big enough for the amount of guests. There was no room for the band which had to be set up in one single line against the huge glass windows overlooking the city. There was no lighting for the band. The only 'sound system' for the band was Franz's amp for his horn and vocals. Previously Truck had promised the couple that we would do the theme from Phantom of the Opera (!). Of course, none of us knew it, but Truck depended on me to get it together and put it in my key and they would simply 'follow me'. I had lead-sheets made for each of them and made the mistake of mailing each of them their sheet in advance. Thank goodness I learned it well enough. That night we were jammed against the wall, and the guys hadn't even previewed the music, much less bring it along. Without lighting, Joe could hardly see the one sheet I brought. The video camera was going; the new couple was about to have their first dance. Luckily, it was a noisy, boisterous crowd. Truck said "OK, Judi, sing it and we'll follow you"! Well, anyone who knows Andrew Lloyd's Weber's music knows you just can't jazz jam on it, the changes are too varied and unexpected. You have to know it. Truck started vamping on his big bass.

Joe got frustrated because he couldn't see the sheet music. All the while the people were drinking and chatting and dancing to the sound of their own noise and the band was trying to do the tune. Franz said, here, I'll do it and grabbed the music off the piano and laid it on his amp. It was so crowded, it didn't matter that he turned his back to the crowd and bent over, mooning the video camera, and no one really noticed, he was just focused on getting the song done. He started the tune, I sang it through, and we finished. Thank God for Franz's abilities. That tune, a cappella, would have been totally lost and boring. At least this way, we could say we did the song we were told to do. This was a boisterous, unusual wedding. They might as well have had jeans on. Before *the* dance, the crowd was milling around, shoulder to shoulder drinking while talking as I said, all at once. The lights flickered as a sign for them to move to their tables for dinner. No one paid any attention. They flickered again. It was getting to George. He had had enough. He went to the center of the room (not an easy task)...and yelled "Soup's on!" The talking stopped as though someone had flipped a switch. And, just as fast, the din of voices started to crescendo again, as though it hadn't halted. Again, George yelled "Soup's On", and the same thing happened. George finally went into a corner, far away, sat down and played whatever he wanted. He was going to earn his keep. Joe Johnson, our most controlled and gentle piano player finally yelled at George to get back to the bandstand and play what we were playing. I was pleasantly surprised that I wasn't the only one who got frustrated at times. The rest of the gig went on and I ducked out without waiting for my check. The next night, Truck came bounding in to Dicks with my check. He was his usual bubbly self. He said, "They loved you, Judi, they loved you"...Truck could have been a politician. He certainly would have amassed a lot of votes!

There were nights at Dick's Last Resort when our gentle piano-man Joe Johnson would do something really outside the box. One night a Corona Beer convention was in town. The party was bustling throughout Dick's Last Resort's cavernous room, and everyone was wearing Mexican hats... the big colorful straw ones. Someone put one on the stage, and Joe picked it up, put it on his head stood up at the piano and started playing and singing "Old Black Joe." It was so out of character that we all cracked up. After all, that quiet, gentle Joe was from Connecticut, where he was brought up as a total classic gentleman. Well educated, he had perfect English diction with a deep, calm voice. He said that in Connecticut, he had always lived in a 'white' neighborhood and "he didn't even know he was black until he moved to Chicago!" I remember that grin when he said that. He once said his favorite candy was those little peppermint chocolates; so whenever I got groceries, I would get a box and put it on the piano for him. He would pop one in his mouth now and then during the gig.

The next corner I turned was good. An hour or so later, I was to meet Bob Ringwald, the father of the actress Molly. Bob is a complete gentleman, and he visited with me; it was a friendly relief. I felt some sort of camaraderie with him, as some of his daughter's movies were made in and around Northbrook, using Glenbrook North high school for the movies. My kids were graduates of Glenbrook North, as was John Hughes, the movie director (Glenbrook South). Talking with Bob was easy. Molly seemed so down to earth, and obviously is a very special daughter. Bob and I went to get a drink and visited some more. Bob is physically blind, and when he ordered our drinks at the bar and paid, I wondered how he did that. He explained to me that he folded his bills in ways that separated the values. When I asked how he knew if he was getting the correct change, his answer was simply, "Most people are trustworthy". We stopped in the hotel restaurant and got some coffee. Soon, in came Barrett, and sat at the next table, the backs of the chairs close enough to bump into each other. Barrett Deems sat alone, the back of his chair against the back of mine. He was listening to us.

After a few minutes, he handed me a French fry from over his shoulder. I ate it. Then he ate one. Then he dipped one in ketchup and handed it to me. I played along and ate it. Neither he nor I said a word. He just kept it up until the French fries were gone. Then he got up and left. I love that kind of humor; it's unpredictable, witty and dry. It was funny to me. Barrett was always kind to me from the first time I met him and until he died. My Jim liked to say that Chicago lost its color when Barrett Deems died *and* when Mike Royko died.

Jim enjoyed writing, too, and besides telling his Margot story, wrote a few other remembrances that showed up in some jazz newsletters that are in the Jazz Institute. Here, I feel I should give you his remembrance of Barrett Deems.

BARRETT DEEMS REMEMBRANCES—BY JIM BEEBE

Judi K and I had just come back from Barrett's funeral when I wrote this letter to a friend.

We have just lost a formidable presence. One of the great drummers and great characters. He was 85 and died in his sleep of pneumonia in the hospital, but he had bladder cancer, pulmonary problems and a host of things wrong. Nothing kept him down for long, though. Major health situations which would lay most of us low he would brush off as though he had a cold.

I've known Barrett since the '60s when we played with Frank Assunto and the Dukes. Then we worked a lot at Jazz Ltd. Don Ingle was on trumpet and can tell you a lot of Barrett stories. Barrett would always be the first with the bad news, "Guess who died today? etc."

He worked with me for several years at the Blackstone Hotel five nights a week. He quit one night and I fired him…all in the same set. One could tell a thousand stories about Barrett and many were flying around last night at his wake. He could be a real contentious s.o.b.

Barrett had impeccable time and swing. Very big ears. He could hear and respond faster than most to anything musically going on. In a room full of people with him on one end and you are on the other end talking about him he would hear it. He was a 24 hour-a-day drummer.

He was on many of Armstrong's greatest recordings and was a contributing factor to their greatness. Trummy Young told me once, "Barrett was the swingingest drummer that I ever played with…a little bit crazy but in a nice way." That nicely sums him up, I think.

Barrett was one of the most colorful characters on the Chicago scene and his wake and funeral reflected this. Many top musicians were there but a lot of peripheral characters as well. Bobby Lewis and George Bean played a mellow jam at the wake and Bobby played 'Over the Rainbow' on his fugal horn at the funeral. Bobby and Barrett were together with Jack Teagarden's band.

Jack's band was driving around the country in several cars and someone asked Bobby how they stood it on these trips with Barrett. Bobby said, "It was easy. We put Barrett in the trunk and the drums in the car."

In 1967 Frank Assunto, Barrett and I left Chicago for Washington D.C. and the great Chicago blizzard struck. 10 hours later we were only 30 miles south of Chicago. I'm driving and Barrett's mouth is going a mile a minute.

I knew that we would be trapped at any minute and I saw three dim lights through the snow.

I said, "Frank, I don't know what is there but we can't go any further and I am going to make a run for those lights." It turned out to be an old motel that had been rented out to some transient 'hillbilly' types. There was one vacant room with a blood stained mattress and a chair. We were there for two or three days. The 'hillbillies' were nice people and fed us, etc. Within 10 minutes Barrett had them waiting on him hand and foot. These people knew that they had a celebrity in their midst but they couldn't fathom who he was.

I drove Barrett and Polly Podewell out to see Buddy Rich once. Buddy was doing an outdoor concert in Oakbrook. It was very touching to see the genuine affection and respect that Buddy held for Barrett. Barrett worshipped Buddy and this meant a lot to him. Buddy introduced him from the bandstand and fawned over him. Backstage the two of them jived each other and carried on in a wonderful fashion.

When we were at the Blackstone Hotel, Barrett started carrying a pistol around. I know that he had never fired it and didn't know how to but he felt secure with it. He always carried a big wad of money and was not shy about showing it off.

Our bass man, Duke Groner, kept telling Barrett to get rid of the gun as he was going to get in big trouble. So one day Barrett is in the coffee shop of the Croydon Hotel where traveling actors and musicians stayed. He is in a booth with the hotel security guy who is also a trumpet player. The security guy is the one who got Barrett the pistol. And Barrett is flapping away about this pistol and making it obvious that it is in his coat pocket.

As it happened the guy in the next booth was an FBI agent. The FBI agent overhears all of this and calls the Chicago Police who come screaming up in two police cars. They run into the coffee shop and take Barrett out in handcuffs. At the police station, Barrett is trying to get one of the officers to get him a cup of coffee. Finally, a cop says, "We don't get coffee for prisoners." Barrett replies, "Oh, yeah? I'll tell you what. I am never, ever playing the Policeman's Ball again." True story. It cost Barrett almost a thousand bucks to get out of that.

In his declining years, Barrett came roaring out of the corner with a swinging contemporary big band. He corralled some of Chicago's best young turks to make this a formidable swinging aggregation. He held forth with this group once a week for several years and just last year put out a great CD on the Delmark label., They recorded another one earlier this year—not out yet.

An important factor in Barrett's life was his wife, Jane Johnson. I remember their wedding about 20 years ago. In the ceremony, "Lawful wedded wife" came out "awful, bedded wife" from Barrett. Jane, about 40 years younger, is a striking woman and a fine musician herself who helped Barrett run the big band. She straightened out a lot of his life, smoothed out some rough edges and added greatly to Barrett's life. I would like to say...thanks, Jane.

Barrett loved and cared for animals. He had about 10 dogs and cats. I gave him an extra cat that I had and he cared for it and gave me regular reports on its wellbeing.

I don't believe that Barrett Deems ever got the full artistic recognition that he deserved. Paul Wertico, a noted contemporary drummer said in the Chicago Tribune yesterday, "You just never thought that he would ever die...he was like the Buckingham Fountain, just a fixture here. His playing had irony and humor—it was an extension of who he was."

I should add that underneath a lot of contrariness, Barrett Deems had a heart of gold. He would be the first to help anyone in need.— *Jim Beebe*

CHAPTER 52

Dick's Last Resort

Dick's Last Resort in Chicago evoked the wildest of Mardis Gras. Since Tuesdays were our nights there along with Thursdays and Sundays, we did each of the Fat Tuesdays Mardis Gras throughout the nearly 5 years we were there. The restaurant would give a prize of $1 per pound of whatever the contestant who won weighed. No holds barred. Outlandish costumes, and uninhibited patrons— one skinny guy came in as a 'Chip 'n Dale' dancer…wearing only a collar and cuffs…. and a tiny black cover over his privates– he was barefooted– and it was cold outside! Had he won, Dick's would have had to pay out a smaller sum of money due to his slight build. One year, the winner was an immense guy who had the build of a sumo wrestler, and was costumed as a ballerina, with a pink fluffy tutu and leotards…I can't imagine where he found those…huge hi-top tennis shoes that were painted like ballet slippers with bright pink laces. Behind us on the stage was a very big scale to authenticate the winner. He stood on the scale and tipped it at nearly 400 pounds. His good sportsmanship paid off. He accepted his $400 prize, and the crowd went wild.

The New Orleans style parades were as wild as Dick's would allow, and that was pretty loose! We were happy that we were up on stage because you would have to be pretty desperate to get down into the tightly woven crowd.

With the type of restaurant Dicks was, we were able to make acquaintances from all over the world. Sometimes the same group would show up twice a year, and they always remembered us. One of those groups was Kikkoman. They hired us to go to Lake Geneva for another convention and we had Franz Jackson on reeds, Joe Johnson on Piano,

Truck Parham on Bass, Dave Kovnat on Drums, Connie Jones on Cornet, Jim and I. That was one of my dream bands; and Dave Kovnat was with us because our regular drummer couldn't go along.

Dave Kovnat, who was Bobby Rydel's ongoing musical director, was also on the festival where I first performed in Decatur. Don Stille was on piano at that gig, and the combination of the two of them gave just the perfect flavor to my "Unchained Melody." Dave and Don were of the age group that had the feel of the 1950s pop, with the do wop triplets that set the group apart from our Dixieland licks. Don's powerful playing melded with Dave and I, while Jim and the rest of the group strengthened the fill. I could feel the power of the song building along with my voice, and we were all in sync both emotionally and musically.

My eyes were closed as I brought the song to the last measure. When I opened them, I saw the crowded room already on their feet and clapping. We hadn't even gotten to the last note! It was euphoric. It was a feeling that came around only once in a while. No matter how great a band works together, the perfect combination of chemistry and mental togetherness doesn't always come together as well. But when it does...nothing can compare. Like golfing, you keep striving to get your best shot...and then there's that rare hole-in-one! Another time like that was at the Bristol, when a bebop sax man named Jimmie Wright came in and sat in. We all did Georgia On My Mind, and whatever that man was doing with the band opened an unfamiliar but comfortable door for me and I belted out a bluesy wail that sparked a hot review from the president of the United Jazz Society of America. I used part of that review on my website home page.

****

After a decade long year run at the Bristol/Braxton, one of my gigs was to sing at a small jazz room called the Sunnyday Tap. It was a perfect, tiny room and a singer really didn't need a microphone, the acoustics were so nice. I had 10 wonderful weeks with the accompaniment of Joe Vito. Joe was the long-time piano man for the great jazz violinist Johnny Frigo. Joe was one of those entertainers who not only could play the piano in great style, but at the drop of a hat had funny additions to whatever a singer was doing.

One night, a couple of my regulars entered the room and I saw the look of recognition on Joe's face. Joe's musical audiences and the jazz people I circled with were somewhat separate. In the middle of the tune, Joe jumped up from the piano and walked through the crowd toward 'my regulars', Frank and Caryl LoPiccolo.

In unison, the two of them held out their right hands as though to shake 'good to see you', and walked past each other, side-swiping their held out hands without joining them. I burst in to laughter and so did the others who were watching. Like old vaudevillians they had it down pat. Then they hugged. I found out later that Frank and Joe were old friends and Joe stood up for Frank and Caryl's wedding many years before. Small world.

Every night that I was at the Sunnyday Tap, Barrett Deems would come in and sit to the side of me and listen the entire evening. He would pretend to be reading the paper never turning a page, and every once in a while, would look up and nod his head as if to approve. A couple of times, when Joe Vito couldn't make it, the great jazz pianist Tom Hope would come in for me. I was comfortable with either player; Joe's fresh whimsy was comic for me, and more on the performing style of Jethro Burns, and Tom was ardently a jazzman who could accompany every style of music brilliantly.

One year, in the Decatur Fest, I was part of the dinner show. Maggie Parker Brown always had a Saturday night dinner show which featured various players and singers who were in the Festival. People dressed up for this event and had dinner reservations for it. Festival patrons were automatically included. Her theme that year was Jazz from New Orleans, St. Louis, Chicago and New York. My section was, of course, Chicago. I dressed as a gangster, complete with fedora and white tie on a black sequined pantsuit, I did a medley of the theme from the movie Chicago, along with the actual song "Chicago". It went over like 'gangbusters' and then I was to introduce Johnny Frigo, as he was from Chicago. I had a song that I had done with Jethro, called "I Love A Mandolin". It was a call and response type, and to introduce Johnny, I sang "I Love a Violin", and behind me, he did the response melody on his violin. It was quite perfect, even though totally unrehearsed, and I was honored to have the experience. Later, I got a note from the head of the Illiana Jazz Society that read: "You were the star of the show". He said he had put that statement in the newsletter, too. Eddie Banjura was a jazz warrior.

Working with so many different players in Jim's band over the years, gave me the experience to handle a lot of different styles. I liked each player for different reasons. The really hot ones made me work hard and forced me to concentrate. No 'unconscious' singing with any of those guys! My life had become a learning factory and I was intent. I still am.

Barrett Deems was always very good to me. Somewhere, during this musical relationship, he gave me one of his famous duck calls.... He actually used them on other singers at times...just to irritate, but he knew I got a kick out it when he would blow it, and he gave me one of those black plastic ones with the floppy rubber end. I still have it. It doesn't have a strong sound like some other duck calls, and when I said that to him, Barrett responded with...it's a girl duck call.

During a visit from Campbell Burnap, Jim and I took him to visit Barrett Deems for an interview. Campbell was in the United States to complete his radio biography series of Louis Armstrong. Campbell was a noted jazz historian who had his own radio show in London. He also had his own band and was a fine singer and trombone player. He was traveling around to all the places that Armstrong had lived and played. He was staying at my townhouse while he did his research in the Chicago area. Since Barrett had been Armstrong's drummer for many years, Campbell wanted to interview him. We got to Barrett's house on Cleveland in Chicago, where Barrett was waiting. We sat around in his small kitchen chatting and then Campbell prepared the machines to record Barrett's answers. I have a raw copy of that interview, unedited. I had heard that Barrett liked mischief and caused plenty of it on the road. I laughed hard when I heard the story of Joe Glaser, Armstrong's manager giving Barrett a 'talking-to'. "What is WRONG with you"? Glaser said sternly. Barrett replied, "Nothing! I feel fine!"— in his distinctly raspy voice. Barrett's lovely wife Jane arrived from her job at Lawry's. She told us of Barrett's drum collection– dozens of drum sets packed away in the basement and upstairs. Most of them were one of a kind and gifts from the companies that made them. Since Barrett's death, I understand Janie has generously donated many of them to worthy causes and museums.
Wisconsin Memories"– the song

In the last few years in the music business, a song writer came into our lives. Pete Maiken, a retired editor for the Chicago Tribune. He was writing for the Beloit College alumnus magazine and decided to interview Jim. Jim was an alumnus of Beloit College. He came out to the Braxton and spent one evening with us, and the resulting story was so detailed, so picturesque and romantic that you would have thought he had been there often.

Later, he sent me some songs he had written. Jim nixed every one of them even when I liked them, and I tended to follow his lead, except for one. It is called Wisconsin Memories, and the beautiful memories it evokes overwhelmed me. Jim's jazz eye couldn't see it. The poetry cadence is perfect and melodic, and it reminds me of the great Dorothy Fields lyrics and how well her words fit the notes. I fell so for the song that Pete asked me to record it. He picked and paid for a band, and we made a recording of it. The song had won a 'best new composer' award, and 'best new song' award in a California music competition, I was told.

After using this band, which has all great players, I wasn't quite satisfied with it, as I felt the music was too heavy for the words to be absorbed. The words are beautiful. So, I called on Dave Baney, a fine guitarist, and the two of us re-recorded it. I asked Dave if he would like to recite a couple of the verses. He did, and he was excited to try something new. I put my own money into the project, paying Dave and the studio, and the artists that were used for the back cover and the print, I paid CD Baby for the pressing, packaging, and finished artwork. It turned out to be a lovely souvenir CD that honors the beautiful state of Wisconsin...or any state that fits the description. Pete was so flattered, he emailed me the rights to the song, and said (to) do whatever you want with this, and I am very proud to have his email.

When Starbucks came to Chicago from Seattle, they opened one of their newest places in Northbrook. I was hired to perform for the opening. During the many weeks Dave (Baney) worked with Jim's Band, we had this 'unspoken' agreement: whenever an espresso coffee machine made it's noise, no matter where we were, we would break into the "Coffee Song" automatically. Needless to say, when we performed at Starbucks or at the Braxton, we sang it often! The idea basically came from working together at the Braxton. Dave made a joke from the fact that every time he started a solo the cappuccino machine would start buzzing. It was somewhat true, too. Murphy's Law. So, I started singing the Coffee Song. He joined right in and we were harmonizing, working it into our 'big ending'. One busy night we were jumping into the song several times; not going through it completely, but just enough to get a laugh from the audience. The audiences loved our nonsense. And I loved our audiences.

Leslie Johnson, Editor, Mississippi Rag

This January 17, 2009, my editor died from Cancer. Leslie Johnson was a real 'Jazz Warrior'. She championed our country's musical history of traditional and classic jazz, supporting everyone from the performers to the people behind the scenes including the many people who keep the jazz societies afloat and interesting. "Jazz Warriors" I called them. They are the ones who create the venues for those of us who are lucky enough to perform in jazz festivals and concerts. Leslie found out that I was lonesome and bored here without my friends and Chicago's action. She gave me my own series called "Jazz Warriors" for her monthly jazz periodical, the 'Mississippi Rag'. I happily contributed features for over a year. She was truly a wonderful woman in Jazz and who will be heartily missed by her readers all over the world.

I have come to grips with my age, but not my limits. If can finally come to grips with my limits, maybe I'll stop tripping and breaking my spirit. I know that I am the only one who can realize happiness for myself. I am darn lucky to have had what I did. How do you put a price on a healthy childhood, extraordinarily wonderful kids, enviable grandchildren, a place in great music and so many treasured memories? You take what the good lord gives you and do the best you can with it.

This book is dedicated to Brian Dale.
My thanks to so many wonderful people
Art Shay
Harry Mark Petrakis
Shelley Finke
Mary Lou Hightower
Jethro Burns
Scott Yanow,
Jerry King, Gary Miller, Franz Jackson,
Jim Beebe, Truck Parham, Sonny Turner,
David Royko, Leslie Johnson, Brian Dale
and to Jim McMerty, CEO of Mintahoe Catering for
letting me use their computer…and then keep it.

Printed in the USA
CPSIA information can be obtained
at www.ICGtesting.com
LVHW011241210224
772413LV00064B/1774